Kingdom Kids

The story of Scotland's children in Revival

Harry Sprange

Christian Focus Publications

Harry Sprange has been a Baptist minister in Scotland since 1974. Since 1987 he has been Director of Kingdom Kids (Scotland), a network of children and young people praying for revival, which is part of the Prayer For Revival Network (Scotland). He runs prayer conferences for children, and is concerned to see them playing their full part in the life of the local church. He is also a keen amateur historian and lectures occasionally in Church History. He is a graduate of London Bible College with BD Hons (Lond).

© 1994 Harry Sprange
ISBN 1-85792-096-1

Published by
Christian Focus Publications Ltd
Geanies House, Fearn, Ross-shire,
IV20 1TW, Scotland, Great Britain.

Cover design by Donna Macleod

Contents

We will not keep them from our children; We will tell the next generation about the Lord's power and his great deeds and the wonderful things he has done... He instructed our ancestors to teach his laws to their children, so that the next generation might learn them and in turn should tell their children. In this way also they would put their trust in God and not forget what he has done, but always obey his commandments.

(Psalm 78:4-7, GNB)

This book is written in honour of the children of Scotland, past, present and future, who set themselves to: 'be concerned above everything else with the Kingdom of God and with what he requires of you.'

(Matthew 6:33, GNB)

Children praying!
Children praying everywhere.
Children praying in classrooms.
Children praying in dormitories.
Children praying in school-yards.
Children praying in factory yards.
Children praying in fields.
Children praying on the hillside.
Children praying by the riverside.
Children praying behind hedges.
Children praying in woods.
Children praying on Glasgow Green.
Children praying on the beach.
Children praying under upturned boats.
Children praying in the snow.
Children praying in homes.
Children praying in attics.
Children praying in half-built houses.
Children praying in churches.
Children building their own huts to pray in.
Children praying in their hundreds.
This is the untold story of Scotland's praying children!

Foreword

When exciting things happen amongst children, in a spiritual context, questions are asked like, 'Is this real?', 'How long will it last?' and comments like, 'Well, you know what children are like!'

In this sort of way we often devalue children's work and, whilst being delighted with large Sunday Schools, full Summer camps and Christian Unions (Scripture Unions?) in schools, we often don't give it its rightful place in church life,

What has been needed for a long time is a book that deals, in a serious way, with the subject of God at work in children's lives - a book that shows how children have been part of the action when the Holy Spirit is moving powerfully.

Here is such a book. Harry Sprange has produced a work of quality which educates, informs and stimulates. His research has been most thorough (a glance at the Bibliography will show you that) and no stone has been left unturned in the search for the evidence of history.

Starting in the 1740's the records in the book quickly show children and young people in Scotland, particularly at times of revival, not only coming to faith in Christ, but also knowing the power of the Holy Spirit in their lives. One of the most remarkable things is to see, time and time again, how these youngsters would be fervent participators at, and even initiators of, prayer meetings and how they would be used of God to speak His word.

We owe a debt of thanks to Harry Sprange to bringing this material to our notice. Who better than him for doing so, seeing as he has given so much of his life to working amongst children?

Read this book and you will have strong seeds of faith planted in you to believe that what God has done many times before, He can surely do again.

Rob and Marion White

Introduction and Notes on Sources

In recent years there has been much serious study and discussion on the place of children in the Christian Church, but little in the way of historical research, and probably none in the specific area of looking at the part children have played in religious revival movements. It is gratifying to discover that Brian Edwards in his recent book *Revival*[1] has devoted a ten page section to children and youth, and from Scotland he includes references to the Kilsyth and Cambuslang revivals of 1742, Dundee in 1839, and Charlotte Chapel, Edinburgh in 1905. Only two books have come into my hands specifically on the place of children in Revival, one written for the children of Ulster, the other for those in Wales.[2] To my knowledge, no-one has attempted to collate the historical material available on Scotland.

This book started as a study of children in the history of the Church, with an emphasis on revival world-wide, but this has had to be narrowed down to a study limited to Scotland, simply because of the sheer volume of material available. One of the first problems I encountered is that most of these sources are anecdotal, and often the precise context and even location is left vague. Many of the magazine and newspaper reports are borrowed from others, or from 'correspondents' which are undated, and may be several weeks after the events described have transpired. This does not make it easy to pin-point precise dates, nor therefore to trace other references. We are still remarkably well served with information, however. James Robe published the events of 1741-2 soon after they happened in the Glasgow Weekly History of 1742, and in his Monthly History, collated and published in 1744. The revival of 1859 ff. was even better covered by the Christian newspapers of the day like the *Freeman* (produced by the Baptists in London) and the *Scottish Guardian* of Glasgow which from 30th October 1859 ran a regular column entitled 'Revival Intelligence'. Other publications were magazine / newsletters like *The Revival* (London, founded mid 1859, after a decade continuing as *The Christian*) and more especially the *Wynd Journal* published in Glasgow from 1st October 1859 until 13th Sep-

1. 'Revival' by Brian H. Edwards, Evangelical Press, 1990.
2. 'The Children in '59' by Rev. Henry Montgomery, reprinted by order of Belfast Presbytery, 1936, and circulated by the Sabbath School Society for Ireland, and 'Something Wonderful Happened' by Mabel Bickersteth, Committee of the 1904-5 Memorial Fund, 1954.

tember 1862, described by the *Freeman* of 26th October 1859 as 'a weekly publication of revival and home mission news'.

The second difficulty has been to define what age group is meant by the term 'children'. There are many instances where a story is recorded about a 'little girl' who it transpires later in the account is fifteen or sixteen years of age - an insufferable insult to any modern teenager! Partly because of the lack of precision in many of the accounts, I have utilised every reference to children that occurs. Where ages are specified I have normally stopped at sixteen, but have included a few additional quotations about older teenagers, 'youths', and 'young men and women' when they seem to be of particular interest. We do need to bear in mind, however, that most of these narratives took place before the Act that made education compulsory in Scotland in 1872, when child labour was common. For example, William Quarrier, later philanthropist of Glasgow, and founder of the Bridge of Weir Children's Homes, was born in 1829 and at the age of six worked a twelve hour day in a Glasgow pin factory for a wage of one shilling a week, and was apprenticed to a shoemaker before his eighth birthday.[3] Even where education was available at an elementary level, it would only cover the age groups of the modern primary school, so that when we read references to the top class, we need to recollect that these would be pupils of no more than twelve or thirteen years of age at the most. Similarly, one entered into domestic service young, and girls at least normally left on marriage.

A quick definition is required as to what is here understood as 'Revival' or 'Religious Awakening'. Although some American churches use the term to refer to any special season of evangelism, we shall restrict its use to the narrower concept of an unusual and spontaneous awareness of the Presence of God, sometimes although not always preceded by preaching and prayer, but which resulted in mass convictions of sin and subsequent conversions. There is also a specialist vocabulary employed: constantly we will find references to persons being 'impressed' or 'awakened', which may only be a first step towards full 'conviction of sin', and 'conversion' or 'assurance' is only entered many days subsequently.[4] Today, the modern evangelist tends

---

3. 'William Quarrier and his homes' by E.M. Sawyer, P & I, Glasgow 1962.
4. For example, William Burns writing in 1840 (Scottish Christian Herald, April Supplement) describes as 'altogether inevitable...a great falling away of those merely alarmed, or but partially awakened, and never savingly converted.'

to lump all these together to claim results, but in most of the accounts which follow, the writers are very cautious indeed of claiming 'conversions', usually adding the rider 'hopefully' to avoid the sin of presumption in Calvinist Scotland!

Finally, all writers face the dilemma of deciding what to include and what to omit. Does one aim at a popular account that is easy to read but lacking in depth, or does one record all available data with the knowledge that some readers will find the results tedious and cumbersome? I have chosen the latter course, in order to make as much of the original source material as possible available to a wider readership. Wherever possible I have quoted the original accounts, leaving the reader free to interpret them, and if necessary to retell them to others in simpler language. Inevitably, this must make my own style clumsy in places rather than polished. By doing so, I hope I can save others the need to plough through the original records, to find some obscure anecdote which a popular writer has used, but with no reference as to source and context. To this end I have endeavoured to write at an academic level with the inclusion of full footnotes and bibliography, but to make the style easier for the non academic reader to follow I have avoided the use of Latin abbreviations (such as 'op. cit.', 'ibid.', 'passim') which can be most daunting for those unacquainted with their usage, except for the universally understood 'e.g.' and 'etc.'. I have also relegated some of the longer quotations to the 'Appendices' section for ease of flow in the main text. In short, I have intended to produce a useful resource document rather than a literary masterpiece! However, while I would not dare to claim that this study is exhaustive, I have tried to include all the references I can find to children being touched in revival, children used in revival, revival touching schools, and the existence of children's prayer meetings. I could not include every reference to childhood conversion, or children's evangelism, or children in church life. It is the part played by the prayer meetings of children in Scottish Church history that has motivated me particularly to probe further and unearth this story, until I have concluded, along with D. A. Currie, that the occurrence of prayer meetings among children 'may have been a distinctively Scottish phenomenon'.[5]

---

5. D.A. Currie, 'The Growth of Evangelicals in the years 1793-1843' PhD Thesis, St. Andrews, 1990, p.358.

List of Abbreviations

Abbreviation	Reference	Located in
AH	The Argyllshire Herald	National Newspaper Library, Colindale
BJ	The Banffshire Journal	Elgin Public Library
CW	The Campaign Weekly	Mitchell Library, Glasgow
EC	Elgin Courant	Elgin Public Library
EMC	The Elgin and Morayshire Courier	Elgin Public Library
GRT	Glasgow Revival Tracts	Mitchell Library, Glasgow
GSS	Gaelic School Society, Annual Reports	New College Library, Edinburgh
GWH	Glasgow Weekly History	Mitchell Library, Glasgow
IA	The Inverness Advertiser	National Newspaper Library, Colindale
RM	The Religious Monitor	New College Library, Edinburgh
SG	The Scottish Guardian	Mitchell Library, Glasgow
TB	Times of Blessing	New College Library, Edinburgh
TC	The Christian	Nat. Library of Scotland (incomplete)
TF	The Freeman	National Newspaper Library, Colindale
TR	The Revival	Nat. Library of Scotland (incomplete)
WHJ	The West Highland Journal	National Newspaper Library, Colindale
WJ	The Wynd Journal	Mitchell Library, Glasgow

1. Scotland in the 1740's

(a) Whitefield visits Scotland

George Whitefield landed at Leith on 30th July 1741. In January 1738 he had set sail for Georgia intending to set up schools in the colony, but had been so impressed by the need for orphan houses that he decided to establish them along the lines of Franke in Halle, and had returned to London to raise money and to obtain a charter. On his second visit at the end of 1739, he rented the largest house in Savannah and soon had more than twenty orphans under his care. His plan was that they should have five hours schooling per day and be taught skills so that they could become self-supporting. He returned to England in March 1741 again with the object of raising funds and the orphans much on his mind. It is not surprising therefore to learn that he spent the six days voyage from London to Edinburgh writing letters to some of these orphans, preserved in his Collected Works as letters 316-8, 327-9 and 331-3.

As the original invitation had come from the Erskines, founders of the Associate Presbyteries which later became the Secession Church, Whitefield first preached for them in Dunfermline, but he returned to Edinburgh to commence three weeks of open air meetings. On the first Sunday evening he attracted a crowd of 15,000 in the 'Orphan House Park'.[1] Not surprisingly on his second Sunday in the city he 'visited and preached to the orphans here',[2] and in another letter describing the crowds notes that 'little children are also much wrought upon. God much blesses my letters from the little orphans; He loves to work by the most contemptible means'.[3]

From Edinburgh Whitefield undertook three tours: the first took him to Falkirk and Stirling, Perth and Crieff, Cupar and Dundee; the second to Glasgow, Galashiels and the borders; and the third by way of Cupar and Dundee again to Aberdeen. Soon after he reached Dundee on 4th

---

1. Whitefield 'Works' letter no 340 to T.G., London, dated 8.8.1741.
2. Letter no 346, 13.8.1741 to Howell Harris.
3. G.W.H. No. 4 [These orphan letters from the hospital in Georgia to Whitefield are appended in the bound volume of GWH and comprise testimonies of boys and girls aged 10-12 and adult comments on them] Letter no 348 to Howell Harris, 15.8.1741.

September, Rev Willison wrote to him commenting on the effect he had
had on the youth of the town:

> As for Dundee, I desire always to bless God for the many tears I
> saw shed, while you were here preaching, and also since your
> departure, particularly when your labours are spoken of. A good
> many of the young people in this place have joined meetings for
> prayer and repeating sermons. I have myself heard some of these
> young persons pray, and have been delighted with their fervour,
> and with the expressions employed, confessing, as they do, that
> they knew nothing of their state till you came among us.

Rev. Willison adds on 22nd March 1742:

> We now see great numbers of (the young) awakened to seek the
> Lord and cry after Jesus. And still their numbers are increasing,
> and prayer meetings setting up so fast in all places of the town,
> that our difficulty is to get houses to accommodate them... Many,
> very young persons were admitted to the Lord's Table here on the
> first Sabbath of this month.[4]

In another letter he states:

> Likewise I desire to be thankful for the agreeable fruits I perceive
> among several young persons in this place, a good many of them
> have now joined in Society for Prayer, and repeating of the
> Sermons, who I apprehend never prayed before. I have been
> witness to some of them myself, and have been overjoy'd to hear
> their Expressions, in particular to hear them pray with great warm-
> ness for you, that you might be delivered from your Enemies, and
> that you might be ascribed to conquer many of them to Christ; and
> to hear them blessing God for sending you...to call them...[5]

Back in Edinburgh on 24th September Whitefield wrote:

> On Monday morning I visited the children in the three
> hospitals...On Thursday evening I preached to the children of the

4. D. MacFarlan p249-250. 5. GWH 11.

city with a congregation of near 20,000 in the park. It is remarkable that many children are under convictions, and everywhere great power and apparent success attend the word preached.[6]

A week later he observed:

The little children in the hospitals are much wrought upon.[7]

Mrs. Peddie later records that 'Whitefield had held a nightly service at 7:00 p.m. in the open air in the park of the Orphan's Hospital where the North British Railway Station now is'.[8]

Here a word of explanation is required: the term 'hospital' was used of institutions where the pupils ate, slept and lived together. For example, Heriot's Hospital was founded in 1628 to provide for the fatherless sons of Edinburgh burgesses (i.e. craftsmen and artisans) with free maintenance and education, and by this time there were over one hundred boys in care. On his last night in Edinburgh Whitefield wrote to Cennick in London that 'he preached twice at the girl's hospital' and:

It would delight your soul to see the effects of the power of God. Both in the church and park the Lord was with us. The girls in the hospital were exceedingly affected, and so were the standers by. One of the mistresses told me, that she is now awakened in the morning with the voice of prayer and praise. The master of the boys says, that they meet every night to sing and pray, and that when he goes into their rooms to see if all be right, he generally finds some at their devotion. The presence of God at the old people's hospital was really wonderful. The weeping of the people was like that in the valley of Hadad-rimmon. They appear more and more hungry. Every day I hear of some fresh good, wrought by the power of God. I scarcely know how to leave Scotland.[9]

It was in all three of these Edinburgh 'hospitals' that a lasting change was affected, as this correspondence published in the Glasgow Weekly History reveals:

---

6. Letter 353 to T.G. London, dated 24.9.1741.
7. Letter 357 to Mr. H. dated 5.10.1741. 8. Peddie p.89.
9. Letter No. 369 to J. C. London dated 27.10.1741 also quoted in MacFarlan p.257.

In a Letter from Edinburgh 21st November 1741:

Soon after I came to Town I waited on one of my Acquaintances, a master in Heriot's Hospital, who surprised me much with several Things he told me, concerning the remarkable Change in the Behaviour of his Boys; some of them were stiff and untractable formerly, and Ring Leaders to the rest in vices incident to that Age, are now (said he) turn'd easy about their beloved Diversion, spending their Time in reading the Bible, and books of Piety, and exhorting their Fellows to do the like.

It was formerly, and always the custom among them, when they retired, after eight at Night, to their several Appartments, to sing part of a Psalm and pray; But then there was little Decency and Order amongst them; while one rehearsed the Lord's Prayer or Creed, some were laughing, some otherwise employed: all were in confusion. But now, in a calm evening, through every corner of that large house; you may hear little societies worshipping the God and Father of our Lord Jesus Christ, breathing from their souls a warm and holy Devotion, acceptable to God through the merits of their Saviour. Thus employ'd, they continue 'till late at night and thus they begin the next Devoted Day. My friend took me where I overheard a Number of them engaged, as I have just now said. After reading some part of the Scriptures, and singing 'Thee will I love, O Lord my Strength, my Fortress is the Lord'; One of them, a Boy about twelve or Fourteen years of age prayed; But Oh! how did he pray? with what Simplicity and Fervour? How much removed were his Expressions from that Tumour and Pride of Language in which our sublime Gentlemen talk to Heaven! Surely the Spirit of God taught him to pray; and I persuade myself you would think so too, could I fully tell you how humble he was in his Confessions; how thankful to God for Jesus Christ; and how fervently he pleaded for the Divine Blessing, the effusion of the Holy Ghost and Grace to all Mankind. When my comrade and I had heard out with pleasure, we slipped away, afraid of being perceiv'd by them, and afterwards entertained ourselves with some reflections upon that Occasion.

In another letter from Edinburgh to Glasgow:

As to Heriot's Hospital, I hear there is a great Reformation there; That Boys there, who were Ringleaders to all Folly and Frolick are now as exemplary for Piety, and encouragers of the rest to seek God, and they have a Society among them for Prayer, and Conference about the Case of their Souls.

As to the Trader's Hospital, the change there is as remarkable. There is particularly there, one Girl that was so vicious, that they were thinking of putting her out of the House, who is now become remarkable for Piety: There are about sixteen of them who have a Fellowship Meeting every Week; And there are two young ladies of about twelve or thirteen years of age, the daughters of a pious lady in this place, who have joined them. They all at these meetings pray by turns; and the one may hear the dear young things telling what the Lord has done for their souls, and speaking of the Love of Christ manifested to them - their mistresses say, they were never so obedient and dutiful as now, which I think a good Proof of a real Work of God on their souls.

As to the Merchant's Hospital: the Word seems to have left abiding Impressions on a great number of Girls there; So that their Way is quite altered: they are grave, and not given to Frolicks as formerly, and have not that Levity in their Air they used to have; and some of them appear to have a saving Change wrought upon their souls: they speak of their lost state by Nature and that they were running to the Pit, when Mr. Whitefield was sent, as the Lord's Messenger, to warn them of their danger. There are about nine of them meet thrice a week for Prayer; Four of these appeared to be under some Concern before Mr. Whitefield came; yet they speak as much as the rest, of the Good they got by means of his preaching. There are about eleven or twelve more, that meet by four, or three, or two, for prayer, some of them very young; and after Diet, they sing Psalms or Hymns by themselves, four or five of the Children that seem to be wrought upon, were among the most Ignorant and Thoughtless in the House and one of them was given to several Vices, such as stealing and lying.[10]

---

10. G.W.H. 10 (concluded in 11).

We are most fortunate in that a letter of one of the teachers in Heriot's, Edward Anderson, (described in the school records as 'Second Doctor') to Whitefield himself has been preserved:

8th. December. 1741
Reverend and Dear Sir,
It is with great Pleasure that I can now inform you that such hath been the Behaviour of the Boys in this Hospital, ever since they had the happy Opportunity of attending your Sermons, and particularly since that Time you spoke with Them in the Hospital that it is evident to everyone that takes Notice of them, that there is a very considerable Change in their lives. An external Reformation prevails among them all; and I hope God hath wrought effectually upon the Hearts of many of them. It wou'd surely be rude to take up your Time with a particular Narration of the many pleasant circumstances of their Conduct since you left us. But I cannot omit to tell you, that one Night a number of them came to my room, and entertained me with very agreeable Conversation, and gathering from their Talk and Behaviour, that they had something to say concerning their own souls I desired them to lay aside Bashfulness, and speak freely so they began to acquaint me with their Grievances: One said, I am troubled with ill thoughts when I pray such thoughts as I fear God will be angry with; Another said: I think it is an exceeding difficult thing to believe in Jesus Christ; I can believe, said he, that Christ is the Son of God and Saviour of lost sinners; but O 'tis hard to believe that he is my Saviour in particular: the rest said That their cases were much the same. I spoke a little to them as I could, and as God assisted me; and when we parted, they went away into the school-chamber, and spent much of that night in Prayer and reading God's Word, insomuch that I thought myself obliged to call at the Door, and desire them to break up their meeting for that Time, the Night being very cold; and before many Days had passed they favoured me with the agreeable News, that they had in a great measure got above their fears; and to this day they continue frequent and fervent in Prayer to God for themselves and for all Men; and not only those few, but the most Part of all our Boys seem to be in love with their Bibles and to delight in Prayer. I have frequently taken a

course through their Rooms, at ten and eleven o'clock at Night, and found great Numbers in raptures of Devotion; some in company together, and others secretly by themselves; and this is their constant practice everyday. The elder Boys teach the young ones to pray, not only by example, but also by advice and Instruction. It was a common thing for the boys in this House formerly to conceal the greatest faults, but now the case is quite altered; the smallest slip is exposed, and zealously complained of; they abhor Vice, by whosoever it be committed, and dearly love every one who is called a true Christian; The other Hospitals and they live now in great friendship and love, delighting to talk of the Goodness of God to lost sinners; Whereas formerly they were too often falling out. Heriot's Hospital is now no more a Den of vicious boys, but a Bethel, for there God is worshipped. Blessed be God, for sending His servant on this generous Errand, and attending his labours with so great success. All Happiness to the dear instrument of this good Work. Let Saints, and all that wish well to Religion, Pray for the Perseverance, and Increase of good disposition to Heriot's Boys. Sir, a letter, however short, will be very refreshing to the Boys and to me. Meantime, the Boys and I join our earnest Prayers on your behalf; wishing you all Felicity, temporal and spiritual. I am, Reverend Sir,
Your hearty Wellwisher, and humble Servant,
E—A—n.[11]

The following April an Edinburgh minister writes to Whitefield to assure him of the lasting effect of his work, and says that 'praise is perfected out of the mouths of babes and sucklings'.[12] On June 3rd Whitefield arrived for his second visit to a rapturous welcome, and the following morning 'three of the little boys that were converted when I was last here, came to me and wept and begged me to pray for and with them. A minister tells me that scarce one is fallen back who was awakened, either among old or young'.[13] On this visit he 'ministered daily at the three hospitals'[14] and the managers of Heriot's Hospital

---

11. GWH 15.
12. Dr. Webster, 20.4.1742 MacFarlan p.259.
13. Letter 422 to Abbot, London, 4.6.1742.
14. Dallimore, 'George Whitefield' Banner of Truth, 1980, Vol 2, p 124. Source of quotation unknown, not in 'Works' of Whitefield.

erected seats for two thousand in their park for him to preach in the open air, before going over to Cambuslang on June 18th.

The effect of the awakening is again seen in the commencement of prayer meetings. A year later Rev. George Muir wrote:

> The prayer meetings are from twenty-four to thirty in number, and so large that some of them will have to be divided. Among them are several of boys and girls, who, in general, seem to be growing in grace and in sound views of divine truth. The little lambs appear to be unwilling to rest upon duties or anything short of Christ. There are several meetings for young women...Many young men meet for mutual instruction and otherwise serving God.[15]

News of these prayer meetings had spread across the Atlantic to Jonathan Edwards, who said of Edinburgh, in his 'account of the concert of prayer':

> The number of praying societies in that city is very considerable. Mr. Robe of Kilsyth (in a letter to Mr. Prince of Boston, dated Nov. 3rd 1743,) says, there were then above thirty societies of young people there newly erected, some of which consisted of upwards of thirty members.[16]

The Glasgow Weekly History has several letters of young people to Whitefield[17] but one will suffice us here: E.B. 'a little girl' of Edinburgh wrote:

> O may the Lord give you His Holy Spirit continually; and O may the Lord grant you may be a Means in His Hands of converting thousands and tens of thousands and pulling down Satan's kingdom, and building up the Kingdom of Jesus Christ...O wonderful love, that He has passed by so many, and taken Pity on so miserable a Worm as me; O when I think of Christ's love to my soul I can do nothing but wonder; O help me to commend Him. Dear Sir, I must conclude, but my heart is full...
> Your affectionate and unworthy servant, E.B.[18]

---

15. MacFarlan p.261. Also quoted in GRT 1.
16. Jonathan Edwards, Works, p.443 in Black's Edition, London 1817.
17. e.g. No 35, letter from ML via Merchant's Hospital. 18. G.W.H. 29.

Another later assessment of the work is found in a letter dated
October 23rd, 1743:

> While I was in town about that time, I visited several of the
> societies for prayer, consisting of young people, with whom I
> was pleased. They appear to thirst strongly after instruction, and
> to be pliable and teachable to a great degree... By all that I could
> see or hear, I am of the opinion that the success of the gospel, by
> the outpouring of the Holy Spirit at Edinburgh upon many of the
> young, and of the inferior sort, hath been extraordinary.[19]

Whitefield visited Scotland fourteen times from 1741 to 1768, but
references to his effect on children are lacking after the second visit. It
is also probably fair to suggest that although his preaching was well
received, he did not witness what may be reasonably called revival after
the events at Cambuslang.

The same would be true of his compatriot and one-time co-worker,
John Wesley, who made no less than twenty-two trips to Scotland
between 1751 and 1790, but did not encounter revival manifestations
north of the Border. References to children in his Journal are comparatively few.[20]

As Wesley was careful to observe and record the religious experiences of children on other occasions[21], it is likely that this was all he
witnessed within Scotland.

---

19. Gillies 'Historical Collections' p.453 (from Robe's Monthly History No ii, p.54).
20. They occur as follows: 28th May 1764 - Wesley was surprised that even lads of twelve
or fourteen were admitted to the General Assembly! 1st June 1764 - In Brechin he
encounters children suffering from strange compulsive disorders, which he describes as
'preternatural' and probably Satanic in origin. 8th June 1757 - In Dunbar 'At eleven I went
out into the main street, and began speaking to a congregation of two men and two women.
They were soon joined by above twenty little children, and not long after by a large number
of young and old.' 8th June 1782 - he receives reports from the north, including
'Newburgh, a small fishing town fifteen miles from Aberdeen, where the society swiftly
increases and not only men and women, but a considerable number of children are either
rejoicing in God, or panting after Him.'
21. See Journal, 3rd September 1773 and 8th June 1784 for instances of revival among
children in England.

(b) Cambuslang

The background to the famous revival at Cambuslang has been thoroughly researched by Arthur Fawcett[22] and need not concern us in detail here, except to say that he traces two strands. On the physical side he observes that 1739 saw an eclipse of the sun, followed by severe storms early in the year, a wet harvest, and a severe winter in which at least 2,000 people died during 1739-40. This led the Glasgow Presbytery to call a day of Solemn Humiliation, Fasting and Prayer for Thursday 12th June 1740. The second strand is a spiritual one: societies meeting for prayer and scripture reading, which can be traced back to the Lollards in the Fifteenth Century and reinforced by John Knox who in 1558 encouraged small groups to meet to pray and read the scriptures together. By the early Eighteenth Century Fawcett concludes 'although both sexes must have been present in some districts, the custom grew up for men to meet with men, and women with women. Further divisions are made at times between married and single persons, and there is abundant evidence of meetings of children, run by children themselves'.[23] Regrettably he omits the sources of his 'abundant evidence'!

William McCulloch had been minister at Cambuslang since April 1731. He appears to have acquainted his flock during 1741 with news of the Great Awakening under Jonathan Edwards in 1734, in Wales under Daniel Rowland and Howell Harris in 1735, and Whitefield among the Kingswood miners in 1738. Because of the smallness of his Kirk, and its state of disrepair, McCulloch often held services in the open air when weather permitted. At the end of January 1742 he commenced an evening lecture weekly, and held daily prayer meetings from Monday 15th February. On the Thursday, fifty came under conviction of sin, and daily sermons were required. By May over three hundred were awakened out of a parish population of only nine hundred.[24] In fact as early as 28th April he wrote to Whitefield:

In less than three months past, about three hundred souls have been awakened and convinced of their perishing condition without a Saviour, more than two hundred of whom are, I believe,

22. Arthur Fawcett 'The Cambuslang Revival', Banner of Truth Trust, 1971.
23. Fawcett, p.67.
24. MacFarlan, p.48. In 1751 McCulloch estimated it as 400 (see GRT 1).

hopefully converted and brought home to God, and have been at times filled with joy and peace in believing; and the rest are earnestly seeking for Jesus, and following on to know the Lord.

Whitefield replied prophetically:

I heartily rejoice at the awakening at Cambuslang and elsewhere. I believe you will both see and hear of far greater things than these. I trust that not one corner of poor Scotland will be left unwatered by the dew of God's heavenly blessing. The cloud is now only rising as big as a man's hand; yet a little while, and we shall hear a sound of an abundance of gospel rain. Our glorious Emmanuel has given much of his divine presence since my arrival. O that it may accompany me to Cambuslang![25]

Four days earlier he had written to London:

I hear of wonderful things in Scotland. I can only fall down and worship. I have seen greater things than ever in England. I expect to see far greater in Scotland. Our Lord will not let his people be disappointed of their hopes.[26]

Whitefield's 1741 visit to Glasgow had resulted in the conversion of young people, as McCulloch wrote to inform him:

Among those lately converted, there are several young people who were before openly wicked and flagitious, or at best very negligent as to spiritual things and yet they are now in the way of salvation.[27]

Whitefield was present at the Cambuslang Communion on 15th August, at which the crowds present were estimated at between 30,000 and 50,000 with three thousand Communicants according to McCulloch, who in the same letter speaks of:

---

25. Whitefield 'Works', Letter 442, 8.6.1742 to McCulloch.
26. Letter 423 to Rt. Hon Lord R—, 4th June 1742.
27. Jos Belcher, 'Biography of Whitefield', American Tract Society, 1857, p.232.

A youth that has a near view to the ministry, and had been for some time under great temptations that God's presence was no more to be enjoyed either in the Church or among the Seceeders, communicated here, and returned with great joy, full of the love of God.[28]

This would confirm Dr. Gillies' opinion that 'young people in general were much benefitted by his ministry, and particularly young students, who became afterwards serious, evangelical preachers'.[29] On his fifth visit to Scotland, Whitefield wrote to the Countess of Huntingdon:

I heard of seven or eight students awakened about ten years ago, who are likely to turn out excellent preachers.[30]

Although we are not aware of younger children converted at Cambuslang, McCulloch carefully has preserved for us the testimonies of a number of teenagers. For example, when Whitefield preached after Communion on 11th July on the text 'Thy Maker is Thy Husband' sixteen year old Margaret Carson felt that not to be married to Christ was 'to have the Devil for your husband, and you sleep all night in the Devil's arms'![31]

McCulloch himself interviewed many of the converts of the revival, to analyse their religious experience. Alexander Roger, described as 'a youth about fifteen years of age', went to Cambuslang to hear Whitefield in June 1742. Feeling his sins he

saw nothing but the wrath of God awaiting me, and hell ready to receive me...I even felt as if I were sinking to the bottomless pit, and that all around were ready to drag me down to it. My feelings of repentance were deep and sincere, and above all, on account of the dishonour which I had done to God.

Under these awful feelings I at last fainted away and on recovering, I was enabled to return with a comrade to my father's house, which was about five miles distant. After reaching home, I attempted to pray, but I could not; my heart was hard as a stone.

28. James Robe 'Narrative,' (1840 Edition) p.226
29. Quoted by MacFarlan p.216.
30. Edinburgh, 30.7.1751, quoted by D. Butler, 'Wesley and Whitefield in Scotland', Blackwood, Edinburgh 1898, p.49.
31. McCulloch MSS ii p.500.

I had no peace at home, and therefore I returned to Cambuslang, and was in time to hear Mr. McCulloch's first sermon that day ... My convictions of sin were so strong, that I was at last forced to cry, nevertheless that I did all I could do to restrain myself. I continued in this state during all the time of that sermon, during the interval, and also during the second sermon.

When it was over, I went alone to pray, pleading with God for grace to close with him on his own terms; and while so engaged, that saying of scripture was powerfully borne in upon my mind, 'Fear thou not; for I am with thee: be not dismayed for I am thy God: I will strengthen thee; yea, I will help thee; Yea, I will uphold thee with the right hand of my righteousness' (Isa. xli, 10). I was now filled with joy and wonder at what God had done; and thus I was enabled, with all my heart, to believe on Christ - to receive and embrace him as offered in the gospel. And ever since the power of sin and unbelief has been broken.[32]

Were it our purpose to study the spiritual experience of teenagers, there is a mine of information available to us here, but as all we are seeking to establish is the presence of young people in the revival two other illustrations will suffice. The testimony of thirteen year old Catherine Anderson from Little Govan is recorded in depth. She visited Cambuslang at the end of February, came under strong conviction of sin on her third visit and continued 'in darkness and distress' until August, when she came into assurance and took Communion. The following year at Communion she claimed 'that I was sick of love' and 'so very lively was my joy, that I had great difficulty in restraining myself from crying out'. Recalling the change in her by March 1744 she expected Christ to speak to her through preaching at church and delighted in prayer, although fear of presumption kept her from 'absolute assurance'.[33]

The other anecdote is that of a father, forty year old Archibald Smith, a mason from Kilbride, who went to Cambuslang to check that it was of God:

---

32. Quoted by MacFarlan p 140-2 from McC MSS
33. Quoted by MacFarlan p 198-201 from McC MSS.

I came home, but in a day or two after I again went out, taking with me all of my family that could go. This was on Saturday, and I remained, and two of my children with me till the Thursday following. On Sabbath night I tried to get into the manse, but could not for the crowd, and after standing awhile, I went into the garden to pray; and as I returned, I found a son of my own, a boy about thirteen, weeping and crying under deep convictions, and I hastened to carry him away to some house, that something might be done to quiet him. But on the way, a remark which I had heard some days before, on the sin and danger of stifling convictions, sprang up in my mind, so as to overawe me. I came back with my son, and about two in the morning he found some outgate. Another [probably his wife] of my family fell under convictions, at which I was glad; but surprised to think that this person, who had been so much more blameless and attentive to religion than I had been, should be so distressed. This also filled me with indignation at my own stupidity and indifference.

He then relates his own gradual awakening, and its subsequent effects on his life. This story is of particular interest to us, in that it is unique in revealing a parent's decision to take his family to such gatherings, as well as his own observations of the effect on his children.[34]

Couper states that 'Boys are said to have prayed in public at Cambuslang', but does not cite his evidence.[35]

The fruit of the revival was conserved by channelling the converts into small groups, and McCulloch refers to 'the erecting of new societies for prayer, both of old and young, partly within the parish where no less than twelve such societies are newly begun, and partly elsewhere, among persons who have been awakened on this occasion'.[36] How young is 'young' we do not know, but as the revival touched the Kilsyth area it was characterised by the meeting together of children to pray, so it is not unreasonable to suppose this to be true of Cambuslang also. Where there is more evidence it concerns those we could today call

---

34. Quoted by MacFarlan p.207-208 from McC MSS.
35. Couper, p.45.
36. Robe, 'Narrative' p.218.

'teenagers'. In dealing with criticisms of the movement McCulloch admits that 'Young people of sixteen years of age kept late hours, some staying all night at the manse, others until one o'clock in the morning,' but can state 'Yet no breath of scandal touched the revival movement.'[37]

A bigger problem was that 'There were also numbers of idle boys in Glasgow, apprentices and others, who, pretending or seeming to be under some concern about their souls, often came out to Cambuslang to hear and join in prayer in the fields together as they pretended. But these appearances with them generally came to nothing, and they brought much reproach upon the work, by their neglecting so often their master's work, and strolling idly through the fields'.[38] Whitefield encountered a similar problem when a company of young people followed him from Glasgow to Edinburgh, but he sent them back with a letter to their minister stating: 'With this ... you will receive several young ones, who I think have acted wrong in leaving their respective employs under parents and masters to go after me. Be pleased to examine them and send them home'.[39]

However, some who attended from insincere motives were awakened. McCulloch instances two young men who went to mock, but 'were both caught the same day, and for a quarter of a year after they continued under very deep conviction', before joining fellowship meetings.[40]

The work at Cambuslang clearly affected people in neighbouring parishes before spreading more widely throughout Scotland. Thus the Rev. William Hamilton of Bothwell could write:

> There are a good number of my people, mostly young, who have been awakened at Cambuslang...All of them are very serious and concerned about their souls, and very solicitous to have others brought to an acquaintance with Christ and the way of salvation through Him...[41]

From further afield Rev. McKnight of Irvine writes to Whitefield on 21.6.1742:

37. McC MSS ii p 474-9.   38. From letter to Robe, 'Narrative' p.253.
39. Letter 434, Edinburgh, 28.7.1742 to Rev McL—.
40. Robe p.254.   41. Robe p.236 dated 7.5.1742.

Blessed be our glorious God, there are some awakenings among us at Irvine; not only those who have been at Cambuslang, but several others are lately brought into great concern about their eternal state, and among them several children; the news of which I know will rejoice you, and I hope will encourage you to visit us, to help forward this great and glorious work.[42]

(c) Kilsyth

It was however to the north that children's prayer meetings appear in abundance. James Robe had been settled in the parish of Kilsyth in 1713, and 'In the year 1740 I began to preach upon the doctrine of regeneration'. It does not concern us here to trace the two years of faithful sowing that followed, but a serious concern began in that parish on Friday 16th April 1742, when Rev. John Willison preached there on his way back to Dundee from Cambuslang. Societies for prayer were formed, and Robe was 'informed that several young girls in the town of Kilsyth, from ten to sixteen years of age, had been observed meeting together for prayer in an outhouse they had access to'.[43] On Sunday 25th April, 'E.F.' a man of twenty-five saw 'a young girl awakened and fainting in the congregation' and bemoaned that he 'was so little affected'.[44] In Article VI 'On the variety and number of persons influenced', Robe estimates the numbers of children and teens touched by God, and relates the conversion of a six year old:

There have been not a few under twenty years of age awakened, and several of them savingly wrought upon. 'Out of the mouths of babes and little children God hath ordained to himself praise, to still the enemy and the avenger.' One of six years of age was awakened; she was in great distress, and cried out much when she was first awakened. When she was brought to me after sermon, I was greatly surprised with such an instance. I enquired at her wherefore she cried, and what ailed her: She answered, 'Sin.' I asked her how she came to feel that sin ailed her: she answered, 'From the preaching.' I asked her what she had heard in the preaching that so much affected her: she answered, 'She heard me say, that they who got not an interest in

42. MacFarlan p.220.
43. Robe, p.35 also reported in GRT, 2.   44. Robe, p.170

Christ would go to hell.' And she said that she would fain have an interest in him. This was upon the 23rd of June. Upon the 27th of June, being the Lord's Day, she was greatly distressed during the whole time of the sermon. Among other things I asked her at night, what she would give for an interest in Christ: she answered that she would give her life for Christ. July 6, Her distress continuing, she was again with me: she said, that it was sin ailed her; for it deserved God's wrath and curse both in this life and in that life which is to come. She was brought to me from time to time untill winter, and I instructed her as the Lord enabled me. I enquired at her if she know any sins in particular she had done against God: she answered, 'Lying and banning.' She frequently told me, in answer to such questions, that she prayed most of all to get an interest in Christ; and that she wanted to get Christ to save her from her sins; and that she was willing to have him to be her Saviour. Her parents went out of the parish to some distance, and I have not heard of her for some years past. There was another of seven years of age awakened the same summer; she lived near me and came often to me; she attained to a good measure of knowledge; she was a member of one of the meetings of the young ones: and, as I was informed, she prayed far beyond what could have been expected from her age. She is since deceased: she died professing to be sensible of her need of Christ.

There were above seventy from nine to seventeen or eighteen years of age awakened. There were some of these who at length lost the impressions made upon them, and their convictions in time came to nothing. There are above forty of them who, after long instruction, and a profession of their acceptance of the Lord Jesus Christ as their Saviour, and of God in him for their chief good and last end, have been admitted to the Lord's Table frequently; and, by what I know of them, walk as becometh the gospel. Some of these were awakened at ten, eleven, and twelve years of age; they gave hopeful evidences of a saving change, and continue so to do. I could give a particular account of the progress of the work of God upon their souls, from the Journal that I kept, as has been done in the preceding part of this Narrative, but forbear, lest I increase the bulk of this book.[45]

---

45. Robe, p.182-4.

On June 11th 1742 Robe wrote to Rev. McLaurin:

> I had a closet full of little ones yesternight making a pleasant noise
> and outcry for Christ; and two of the youngest, one of them but ten
> years of age, fainting and so distressed they could scarcely go
> home. I cannot write to you the wonders I saw: one of eleven years
> of age crying out that she was sick of sin, and crying out with hands
> uplifted to heaven when I told her that if she were willing to take
> Christ he would heal her, 'I am willing with all my heart and from
> the bottom of my heart to take him.' I bade her wait with patience
> and told her she mindeth the fortieth Psalm: she noted over the
> first twelve lines with great calmness. I hear they were very
> distressed last night and this day, I would fain hope that relief may
> not be far from her. O pray for the poor young babes. — tells me
> now she is come to joy and peace in believing, for which I beg you
> will praise the Lord, and employ others to do it. Poor little — speaks
> to the distressed like herself."

This letter concludes with the modern sounding phrase, 'I wish you
were here'![46]

In a slightly later account he dates the conviction of the six year old
previously reported:

> June 28th. 'There were seven newly awakened yesterday. The
> child of six was in great distress during the most part of the sermon:
> I asked her at night what she would give to get Christ; she answered
> with great composure, "I would part with my life to have him," at
> which I was amazed.'[47]

He continues on July 2nd:

> There hath been brought to me about a dozen in great distress, most
> of them young, some of them awakened at home this day, and some
> at Cumbernauld.[48]

In an article on the physical manifestations, Robe observed:

---

46. Robe, p.132. 47. Robe, p.140. 48. Robe, p.141.

There were about half a dozen of boys, in whom also convulsive
motions appeared to come to a greater height, and to make them
insensible for some time. There were also some few women and
several young girls who were seized with such fits whenever
their thoughts about their sinful lost state, and being without God
and Christ, increased their fears to a great height.

Robe denied that the symptoms were like those of epilepsy.[49]

Writing in March 1743 he reports a renewed sense of the presence of
God in Kilsyth:

From Sabbath the thirteenth to Sabbath the twentieth of February
there were ten awakened either altogether new, or such upon
whom their first awakening had long since come to nothing; since
which there have been about eight with me, most of them under
fourteen. All this besides thirteen young boys who had associated
themselves for prayer, without any desiring them and who are
since taken under such notice as is needful for them... There are at
this time nearly seventy, if not above, from eight to eighteen years
of age or thereby, most of whom meet in societies twice a week,
and spend the time in prayer, singing some part of a Psalm, reading
the Scriptures, and repeating their catechism. They are at least
once a week under the inspection and direction of some elder
Christian who meets with them.

The narrative then includes a long letter from an English gentle-
woman to these young people.[50]

Robe details many reports of the awakening touching neighbouring
parishes. Returning to April 1742:

About this time sixteen children, or thereby, in the town of
Kirkintilloch, were observed to meet together in a barn for prayer;
the occasion of which was, that one of them had said to the rest,
What need is there that we should always play, had we not better
go and pray? Wherewith the rest complied. The Rev. Mr. Burnside,
as soon as he heard of it, carefully enquired after them, and met

---

49. Robe, p.153 50. Robe, p. 165.

frequently with them, for their direction and instruction. And, as I
am informed, they make progress and continue in a hopeful way.
This made much noise in the countryside, and deep impressions
both upon young and old.[51]

We have a detailed account of the revival touching the school at
Baldernock, north-west of Calder, from the teacher as related by Robe:

In the absence of a minister the Lord hath honoured their schoolmaster, James Forsyth, to be greatly instrumental in this good
work among them. I shall give the following extract from a letter
of his, dated Baldernock, July 17th, 1742, concerning the impressions made upon and the awakening of several of the young ones:
He writes, 'Since the first of February last, I endeavoured to
instruct the children under my charge, to the utmost of my power,
in the first principles of religion - that they were born in a state of
sin and misery, and strangers to God by nature. I also pressed
them by all arguments possible, to leave off their sinful ways, and
fly to Jesus Christ by faith and repentance; which, by the blessing
of God, hath not been in vain. Glory to his holy name, that backed
with the power of his Holy Spirit what was spoken in much
weakness. I likewise warned them against the commission of any
known sin, and told them their danger if they persisted in the
same, and that their sins would find them out. These exhortations
frequently repeated, yea almost every day, came at last to have
some impression on their young hearts. And I think the great
concern that was at first among them was a mean in God's hand
to bring the elder sort to a more serious concern, and to more
diligence in religious duties; yea, I heard some say, that they were
ashamed to hear and see these young creatures so much taken up
about their soul's salvation. That is some account of the rise of
this good and happy work. There was one of the schoolboys that
went to Cambuslang in March that was first awakened; he, after
some few days, said to me, in the school, will you let two or three
of us meet together to sing psalms and pray? I said, I was very

---

51. Robe, p.34-5, also GRT, 3.

well pleased to hear that they were inclined to such a good exercise; so they joined themselves together, and it hath had very good fruit. For some few days after there were some of them under concern, and that day fourteen days after they first met there were ten or twelve awakened and under deep convictions, some very young, of eight and nine years of age, some twelve and thirteen. They still inclined more and more to their duty, so that they meet three times a day - in the morning, at night, and at noon. Also they have forsaken all their childish fancies and plays; so those that have been awakened are known by their countenance and conversation, their walk and behaviour. The work among the young ones in the school still increases, and there are still some newly awakened. There were some that by a word of terror in their lesson were very distressed, and would cry out and weep bitterly. There are some of them very sensible of their case, both the sin of their nature and their actual transgressions, and even of the sin of unbelief; for when I would exhort any of them that were distressed, to believe in Christ, because he is both able and willing to save to the uttermost, they replied, that they knew he was both able and willing; but they could not believe themselves, unless God gave them a heart so to do; for, they said, they felt their heart so hard that they could do nothing.' Such is the account he gives of the younger sort.[52]

There are also records of children meeting together for prayer in Gargunnock, Monivaird, Madderty and Muthill; the year is uncertain in some cases but most probably was 1743.

The minister of Gargunnock by a letter to me of the 17th current March, writes 'that even the children's meetings for prayer continue, their outward concern continues even in public.'[53]

Rev. Porteous of Monivaird reports 'a noticeable concern among many young ones, of whom they have two society meetings'.[54]

---

52. Robe, p.42-4.   53. Robe, p.291.   54. Robe, p.292.

In the parish of Madderty, south east of Crieff 'a few boys were found in the fields engaged in prayer. They were allowed the use of a house. Many joined them, both old and young; and they continued, when the information was communicated, to make progress.'[55]

We have more information about the awakening at Muthill, which began at the Communion on the third Sabbath of July, 1742, in two dated letters from Rev. William Halley, the first, to Robe, written on 28th September 1742:

> Though some old people have been awakened, yet this work is most noticeable among the younger sort: and some very young (within twelve years of age) have been observedly wrought upon, and the fruits are very agreeable, amongst others, their delights in prayer and their frequent meeting together for that end. And they who have noticed them have informed me of their speaking in prayer the wonderful things of God.[56]

James Robe writes:

> I received on the 29th of October, a letter from the same worthy brother, giving a further account of the progress of the good work at Muthil:
> 'Our praying societies are in a most flourishing condition, and still more members flocking to them; their meetings are frequent, and the Lord is observedly present with them. The meetings for prayer amongst the young boys and girls give me great satisfaction, one whereof began soon after the sacrament, and is now increased to about the number of twenty. Till of late they met in the town; but several of them fell under such a deep concern that I was sent for to speak with them, where I found some of them in tears. Since that time (that I may have them near me) I give them a room in the manse, where they meet every night. And O how pleasant it is to hear the poor young lambs addressing themselves to God in prayer, with what fervour, with what proper expressions do I hear them pouring out their souls to a prayer-hearing God; so that standing at the back of the door, I

55. MacFarlan, p.248. 56. Robe, p.282.

am often melted into tears to hear them. We have another praying
society of young ones lately erected in another corner of the
parish, where one Mr. Robertson teaches one of the charity
schools. The young ones of late desired his permission to meet in
the school-house for prayer, which he very readily granted to
them, (for it is his pleasure to promote and encourage religion
both in young and old,) and there about twenty of them meet
about twice every week, though many of them have a good way
to travel in the night-time. I may say in general, that such a prayer
disposition as appears amongst this people, both young and old,
was never seen nor heard of before, which gives me ground to
expect more of divine influences to come down amongst us, for
where the Lord prepares the heart he causes his ear to hear.'

The letter continues with Halley's verification of the above report
from Madderty:

As to the parish of Madderty, respecting which you desire to be
informed; soon after the sacrament at Foulis, a neighbouring
parish, some few boys met in the fields for prayer, and when
observed, were brought to a house, to whom many others, both
young and old, resorted since, and are now, according to my
information, in a very flourishing condition. This Presbytery is
resolved to divide themselves into societies for prayer, for the
progress of the blessed work, and to have frequent meetings for
this end.[57]

A third letter of Halley, not dated, reports:

Our praying societies are increasing...I cannot express how much
I am charmed with the young ones. We have now three praying
societies of them. One of them, at about two miles distance from
this, paid me a most agreeable visit upon the first Monday of the
year, a day that young people especially used to be otherwise
employed. We had, I think, upwards of forty of them; they
continued in prayer and other exercises till about ten at night. But

57. Robe p.284-7.

> O, to hear the young lambs crying after the great Shepherd! To hear them pouring out their souls with such fervour, with such beautiful expression, with such copiousness and fulness, did not only strike me with admiration, but melted me down in tears![58]

A fourth letter of Halley written to someone in Edinburgh, dated 29th August 1743, again reports an increase in the children's prayer meetings:

> Before this good work began among us, we had but two praying societies, and now they are increased to eighteen, to which many resort, both men and women. We have six praying meetings of young ones. One of them meets twice in the week in my house. I have frequently wished to have had some of the contradictors and blasphemers of this work standing with me at the back of the door, to hear these dear young lambs (some of them below twelve years of age) pouring out their souls to a prayer-hearing God, with such fervour, with such copiousness and propriety of expression, that I have not only been filled with wonder, but melted down in tears to hear them. With great satisfaction I have admitted about forty of these young ones to the Communion table at our sacrament this summer, which occasion the Lord signally owned.[59]

(d) Easter Ross

At the same period, but seemingly unconnected, an awakening took place in a number of northern parishes. Daniel Beaton became minister at Rosskeen in 1717 and 'from the harvest of 1742, to Martinmas 1743, there was a remarkable revival. About thirty-six men and women fell under deep concern, and were some weeks thereafter received into a fellowship-meeting'.[60] At the same time:

> Some children, boys and girls, in the easter end of the parish, about twelve in number, betwixt nine and fifteen years of age, began last winter to meet in a private house, (the landlady being a godly poor

---

58. Robe, p.289. A slightly different version of this letter is quoted in GRT, 3 as a letter from Halley to Robe and is dated March 1743.
59. Gillies, 'Historical Collections' (Book IV, Chapter 6) p.449 quoting Prince's 'Christian History' No. 75.
60. MacFarlan p.251.

widow) every Lord's day evening, and Monday's night, where they exercise themselves in prayer by turns, singing and conferring about what they hear in public. They keep strict discipline among themselves, and admit none into their society, but such as undertake to pray with them. At first, some of the serious people of the place hearing of it came to overhear them, without their knowledge, who were greatly surprised and affected with their massy, sound expression, and the savour they found with them in prayer. And now one or other of the serious people often join with them. They watch close over the behaviour of each other. They are constant hearers of the Word, and examine one another about it. Their outward deportment is grave and quiet, without any childish levity yet discovered about them. They are illiterate, but fond of learning.[61]

MacRae adds the comment 'some of these boys rose to eminence as Christians in Easter Ross'.[62]

There are a few other examples of the spirituality of quite young children in the north, such as Lachlan Mackenzie, later minister of Lochcarron, born in Kilmuir-Wester, Ross-shire in 1754:

Young Lachlan received his first education in the parish school of Pettie, and at the early age of eight he was brought under the power of the truth. He was known to have been called upon at the age of thirteen to engage in prayer at a prayer meeting held in the district, and it is said the aged men regretted, owing to his modesty, he would not be prevailed upon oftener, to come forward in public.[63]

And Rev. John Kennedy later of Killearnan, born in Kishorn 1772:

From his earliest years, even from infancy, John Kennedy gave evidence of a work of grace. One day, while he was four years of

---

61. Gillies, p.455 quoting Robe's 'Monthly History' of 1744, no IV p.45.
62. MacRae, p.194.
63. D. Beaton, 'Some Noted Ministers of the Northern Highlands', Free Presbyterian, Publications, 1985 p.76.

age, a woman notorious for wickedness, heard his childish voice
lisping his petitions to God. She was arrested by what she heard,
and gave evidence afterwards of one who had passed from death
to life.[64]

Towards the close of the eighteenth century we know of the existence of a children's prayer meeting in northern Sutherland. Adult
communicants and specifically invited people were invited to attend a
noon prayer meeting on Saturday in Strathnaver, and this was the result:

Many of the children and young people were so impressed that
when they saw their seniors repair to the meetings, which they,
according to custom, were not expected to attend, they began to
hold meetings of their own. These young people were not 'playing' at meetings, but were earnestly seeking the Lord.[65]

Although records of child conversions are comparatively rare in the
far north, at the same time the same source tells us of Peter Stewart, later
catechist of Strath Dearn, Caithness, who 'was only eight years of age
when he came under concern of soul, and was much given to prayer'.[66]

---

64. D. Beaton, p.124. Also reported in The Days of the Fathers in Ross-shire. Dr. John
Kennedy, Christian Focus Publications, 1979, p.131.

65. Records of Grace in Sutherlandshire, Rev. Dr. Donald Munro, Free C. of S. Publns.
Com., 1953 p.228.

66. Munro, p.244. Two further examples are found in Kennedy's The Days of the Fathers
on pages 161 and 189 illustrating the religious experiences of children.

2. A Century of Societies

The eighteenth century has often been known as the century of Societies, social, literary, philanthropic and religious. Perhaps this was a predictable reaction to the repressions of the previous century when the Stewart monarchy had lived in fear of 'conventicles'. Whatever the reason, the social climate provided a fertile seed-bed for the development of religious non-conformity, the birth of Methodism, and towards the end of the century the foundations of the world missionary movement and the growth of interest in home mission, all of which were to continue well into the nineteenth century, as well as the instituting of Sunday Schools throughout the land.

If Scotland was to take up these initiatives slowly, it was perhaps due as much to the prevailing 'Moderatism' within the Church as to the underlying Calvinism of its theology. Nevertheless, this period did see the legitimisation of religious dissent, first in the recognition of Episcopal worship in 1712, then the founding of the Secession Church of 1733, the Relief Presbytery in 1761, the Glassite Movement, the Scotch Baptists from 1765 (preceded by the totally independent Baptist Church at Keiss, which was the first church in Scotland to publish a hymn-book!). While it is well known that the Disruption of 1843 took off one third of the members of the Established Church into the Free Church, the strength of dissent prior to that has not been so well understood, yet the 1766 General Assembly were told of the existence of 120 'meeting houses' attended by some 100,000 people, and by 1800 five hundred places of worship were in existence, to be followed immediately by a burst of church planting by the Haldanes in the next decade.

Scottish education, despite Knox's vision at the Reformation of a school in every parish, was in some areas non-existent. In 1715 only one in three men and one in twelve women in Fife could write, and in 1720 few in Galloway could read. On the other hand, Rutherglen could boast compulsory education of all its six to twelve year olds as early as 1675.[1] In the Highlands there was little provision at all. Therefore we start our study by looking at the work of the SSPCK, not because of its direct

---

1. Thomas Johnston, 'The History of the Working Classes in Scotland', (Glasgow, 2nd Edition, 1929) p.108.

contribution to religious revival, but because of its indirect importance in laying the foundation on which so many others later built.[2]

(a) The Society in Scotland for Propagating Christian Knowledge
Arthur Fawcett summarises its origins for us most helpfully:

> The first organised effort to forward missionary activity beyond the seas was undertaken by the Society in Scotland for Propagating Christian Knowledge. Beginning in a small prayer society of lawyers, and inspired by an Episcopalian minister, James Kirkwood, it is an outstanding example of Christian Unity that Presbyterians should agree to work in such close association and harmony with Episcopalians so soon after the exhausting struggle with episcopacy. In 1709 Queen Anne gave the Society Letters Patent and, during the years that followed, excellent work was done in organising schools and supplying teachers and libraries to remote, neglected parts of Scotland.[3]

The 1729 report of the State of the Society gave its purpose as:

> To erect and maintain Schools to teach to read, especially the Holy Scriptures, and other good and pious books, also to teach Writing, and Arithmetick, and such like degrees of Knowledge, in the Highlands, Islands, and remote corners of Scotland, and in popish and infidel Parts of the World, and to take Means for instructing People in the Christian reformed Protestant Religion as may be competent.

They were known as 'Charity Schools'. They included provision for poor

> boys having the Irish tongue, whether of Protestant or Popish Parents, who are so poor that they cannot without help attend the schools...to learn exactly the Principles of the reformed Protestant Religion and the English language...

---

2. That is not to imply that the SSPCK had no part in revivals: according to MacRae p.92 their agent, John Morrison, preached in the open air on Harris in 1830 and drew crowds of 2,000. (Further details in Coupar, p.117).
3. Fawcett, p.213.

In 1716 their stated objective was 'rooting out their Irish language, and this has been the care of the Society as far as they could, for all scholars are taught in English,' and 'until 1767, it remained an offence, punishable with dismissal, for a charity school teacher to help his pupils to read Gaelic'.[4] No doubt this was based on the fear engendered by the Jacobite uprising of 1715 (and suitable reinforced by the '45) as much as the general belief in the Lowlands of the barbarity of the Highlands and therefore of their language.

The most important contribution of the SSPCK to the subsequent religious life of Scotland was their publication in 1767 of the first Gaelic version of the New Testament. However, MacInnes comments 'it is significant of the success of the former policy that this edition, consisting of 10,000 copies, was not exhausted when the revised edition was issued in 1796'.[5]

To return to the 1729 report, we are informed that the previous year the King granted £1,000 sterling to the General Assembly annually 'for maintaining Itinerant Ministers and Catechists in the Highlands and Islands'. We are also provided with a list of 78 schools, starting with St. Kilda boasting 28 pupils, and totalling 2,757 scholars. An estimate is given of a 3,000 total as six newly founded schools had not provided statistics. We know that 109 schoolmasters were employed by 1732. It is beyond our purpose to trace developments in more detail, but it is possibly of interest to note that by 1803 the numbers being taught had risen to 16,000.[6]

An example of the work of the SSPCK in providing itinerary ministry may be seen in their sending of John Macdonald from Urquhart to the island of St. Kilda in September 1822, where he preached nightly for twelve days and took Sunday services, which he records in his journal on Monday, September 23rd:

Many were affected, and at one time almost all were in tears; among others, two young people about ten and twelve.

---

4. MacInnes, p.245.

5. MacInnes, p.247. For a greater description of the work of the SSPCK see Chapter 7 on 'Highland Schools.'

6. Report of SSPCK dated 22nd February 1803, and quoted in 'The Religious Monitor' Vol 3, p.74

He returned the following year, and on Sunday May 22nd preached on
the death of Christ:

> The people heard with great interest and deep concern; many
> were in tears - and not a few among the children. Christ crucified
> is the power of God unto salvation.

He made a third visit in April 1827, then toured Scotland to raise
funds to provide them with a church and manse, and in July 1830
accompanied the new minister out there to induct him. On Sunday July
4th he wrote:

> I was pleased to observe some young people apparently im-
> pressed, and deeply so, under the discourse.[7]

Another appointment of the SSPCK was that of Rev. Robert Findlater
to Lochtayside, based in Ardeonaig from April 1810. In a letter to Dr.
Campbell in Edinburgh, dated 9th April 1813, he speaks of the Sabbath
School started in the previous summer, and attracting up to forty pupils.

> There are two in particular, since the commencement of the
> school, who have been under a deep concern; and I am told they
> meet together for prayer and reading the Scriptures, when they
> can get an opportunity. This is the more striking, as I am afraid
> they do not meet with that encouragement from their parents they
> ought to have. It is pleasant to observe any promising symptoms,
> but it is difficult to pass judgement on them, as they are so young
> (about fourteen or fifteen years of age), and though we would
> wish to hope the best, yet we must join trembling with our mirth.[8]

Evidence of a more general awakening began to appear in August
1816 at the Killin Communion, and 5,000 attended the Ardeonaig
sacrament a month later where Dr. John Macdonald was the special
preacher. In a letter dated 11th December 1816 Findlater says:

---

7. Rev. J. Kennedy, 'The Apostle of the North', (Nelson, London, 1866) pp 123, 148, 183.
8. Memoir of the Rev. Robert Findlater by Rev. Wm. Findlater (Collins, Glasgow, 1840)
p.161.

> When I was at Glenlyon last week, I met with from twenty to
> thirty young people, almost none of whom I saw before.

He makes another reference to 'a number of young people deeply
concerned' at Glenlyon in a letter dated 15th July 1817, and on 15th
August writes:

> Since he (Dr. Macdonald) went away, I met with a group of
> young people inquiring the way to Zion, and of whom we may
> say, that they are in a very hopeful way at present.

In none of these references are there any clues as to the age of those
to whom he refers, but towards the end of this last letter, regarding the
number of 'hopeful converts' he states them to be 'upward of a hundred
persons ... including all ages, from eight years old to the advanced age
of eighty.' This appears to be the only direct reference to the age of
anyone touched in this revival. On March 23rd 1818 he again writes:

> It is a wonderful mercy that the Lord gives countenance to the
> word of His grace among us still, particularly among the young,
> and some of the Sabbath school scholars...

And as late as January 17th 1820 he writes that:

> Almost all of the young people, when able to read the scriptures,
> wish to be in possession of a bible.[9]

(b) The Society for Propagating the Gospel at Home

Robert and James Haldane were landed gentry who had spent their early
life at sea. After their conversion they took a deep interest in the work
of overseas mission, but in 1796 James toured Perthshire with Charles
Simeon and in the following spring he visited the west of Scotland in the
company of John Campbell during which they established a number of
Sunday schools.[10] After an initiation into open air preaching at Gilmerton

---

9. Findlater's Memoirs contains a whole chapter headed 'Narrative of the Revival of
Religion in Breadalbane, Perthshire, 1816-1819.' The extracts quoted are found on pages
201, 204, 211, 212, 217 and 227 respectively.
10. DW Bebbington, 'The Baptists in Scotland' (Baptist Union, Glasgow 1988) p.30.

on 6th May 1797, in July he undertook a longer tour of the north. The needs of the children in Montrose struck him in a particular way: 'We were sorry to learn that many of the children in Montrose were unable to read, in consequence of going to the cotton manufactory at a very early age.'[11] Crowds flocked to the preaching, estimated to reach 4,000 at Thurso and Wick.[12] Returning south, the twin needs of education and gospel preaching pressed on them so that 'On the 20th December, 1797, a meeting was called to digest a plan for spreading the Gospel at Home'. In explaining the rationale for the origins of the SPGH, it is stated:

> One Society in particular [footnote: The Society for Propagating Christian Knowledge] chiefly in the management of the most respectable established ministers, has done much especially in the Highlands; but the demands for schools and catechists are so great, that notwithstanding the ample funds of which they are possessed, they are obliged every year to refuse urgent applications. In the vicinity of Edinburgh, much has been done in establishing Sabbath schools within the last three years with the cordial approbation of many good ministers; and the promising appearances they afforded, induced some individuals to enquire what might be done in more distant parts of the country.[13]

Politics as well as sectarianism was strictly forbidden:

> It is not our design to form or to extend the influence of any sect. Our sole intention is to make known the everlasting Gospel of our Lord Jesus Christ.

They wish 'God-speed' to Relief ministers and Burgher Seceeders, and the reports show them also working with Methodist, Congregational, Episcopal and Baptist churches as well as Established.[14]

The stated purposes of the Society were:

---

11. Alex. Haldane, 'The lives of Robert Haldane and James Haldane' 1852, p.156.
12. MacRae, p.187-8.
13. 'An Account of the Proceedings of the Society for the Propagation of the Gospel at Home', 1798 (presumably by Secretary John Ritchie: hereafter denoted as SPGH) p.5-6.
14. SPGH p.8.

1. To appoint itinerant preachers.
2. 'To encourage schools, especially Sabbath Schools throughout the country.'
3. To promote reading of the Scriptures, and provide tracts and Libraries.[15]

Although Couper[16] maintains that the Haldanes did not see Revival, but prepared the way for it, they did witness an immediate success. For example, James' Journal, reporting his 1799 tour of the north records 'at least thirty young people in Inverness appear to have been brought to the knowledge of the truth by attending the Sabbath School and itinerant preaching in that place'.[17] So alarmed was the Established Church, of which until then they were still members, that the General Assembly of 1799 passed an act against vagrant teachers and Sabbath schools, which was not rescinded until 1842. There was a clear expectation of Revival from the start, as these quotations from the *Particular Instructions to Catechists* on the importance of reaching children illustrate:

> The instruction of children in the principles of Christianity has been justly considered an object of the greatest importance and wherever a revival of religion has taken place, it has generally been observed, that young people formed a considerable proportion of those brought under its influence. It is the wish of the Society, therefore, that you bend your attention particularly to children, endeavouring to instil into their minds the doctrines of salvation through a crucified Redeemer.
>
> Adopt the most simple and affectionate method of communicating instruction. Tell the children that you love them, and ardently desire to promote their happiness, and that in no way can this be done effectually but by leading them to the true knowledge of themselves and of Jesus Christ.
>
> Think not that it is a mean employment to instruct children...(as Jesus blessed little children)
>
> In the course of your itinerary therefore, collect the children

15. SPGH p.11.
16. Couper, p.13-14.
17. Haldane, p.271.

in the first instance, and give them tracts suited for them...Ask them simple questions, and endeavour to make them understand them. Long exhortations are generally lost upon children. By frequent questions, and by asking them to repeat sentences after you, their attention is kept up and their memories stored with divine truth...

In no case will you find it difficult to collect children if you discover any anxiety to get them together...You were not appointed a *preacher* but a *catechist*, and it is necessary that you confine yourself to catechetical exercises alone.[18]

The *Narrative of Proceedings* covers in detail the first year of the Society's work using extracts from diaries and letters. References to children abound indicating a widespread response to the Gospel among young people wherever the evangelists went. Their second appointment was: 'Hugh Ross, as a Gaelic catechist...in Dunkeld and its neighbourhood. On his way north he assembled a number of children at Kinross, catechised and exhorted them, and their parents who attended. He soon established a large Sabbath school at Dunkeld...'. Then proceeded to Killin and Inveraray, where he was ill and returned to Edinburgh.

'On the 5th July, Hugh Ross again left Edinburgh; spoke with some children at the north Ferry...[and]...found that several Sabbath schools were established in this neighbourhood.' Through Clackmannan, preaching and examining children, he recommended a second Sabbath School at Callander, and at Port of Mentieth. 'As the children appeared grossly ignorant he exhorted them to get a Sabbath School.' He found Sabbath Schools in Loch Earn Head and Comrie, but not Crieff. He arrived 7/8 at Dunkeld: 'The children especially shewed great joy. There had been no Sabbath School since he left it before. He continued to speak to young and old every night either at Inver or Dunkeld. On Sabbath...the school was crowded in the evening, the children very attentive.' He now 'teaches the Sabbath School in the evening, and through the week he goes to different places...'[19]

From the diary of Mr. Ballantine, we learn that on April 17th he

18. SPGH p.89. 19. SPGH p.16-19

found 'some young people in tears' in Coupar Angus, so he recommended Sabbath Schools be provided for them. Thereafter:

Sunday April 22nd, Aberdeen
Visited one of the Sabbath Schools which is very flourishing

Wednesday April 25th, Inverury Methodist
The young seemed particularly attentive ... no Sabbath Schools here ... Charged them with culpable neglect.

Wednesday May 2nd, Aldearn
They have a crowded Sabbath School ... There is a Sabbath School at a place called the Park, at some little distance, which was begun by the children themselves, and opened with prayer by one of them. Many of these young ones meet together in the woods for prayer. An account of these things which we heard in Elgin, led us a little out of our way to endeavour to strengthen the hands of the people and children.

Sunday May 6th, after attending Inverness Methodist, then in the open air
Young people here are under serious concern. Preached again at 4 to about 1,500 who were deeply attentive. Many young...There are four Sabbath Schools here which we visited in the evening, and which seem to be doing well.

Monday May 14th,
There are also many young people earnestly seeking the Lord. The Sabbath evening schools are a great means of keeping their souls awake. May Jesus himself keep them and teach them, and carry these lambs in his bosom.

Sunday May 20th, Tain
Visited the Sabbath School which is held in the church in the evening. There were a great number of grown up people present ... This is a very flourishing school.[20]

---

20. SPGH p. 21-28.

Finally, Mr. Ballantine writes from Caithness in November:

> Our schools are going on prosperously, I teach one in our little
> chapel which is always full. The children are doing remarkably
> well, and some of them appear to be serious.[21]

Also from Caithness Mr. Cleghorn writes from Wick on 3rd January,
1799:

> We have a Sabbath evening school taught in the New Chapel,
> consisting of about one hundred children and young people.
> They seem eager to acquire knowledge, and I hope some of them
> are asking this important question, 'What shall I do to be saved?'[22]

Mr. Rate, from England was sent to Fife. On Monday 7th May at
Auchtertool he recorded: 'a number of the young people seem to be
particularly attentive and impressed' out of a crowd of 300. Of the
evening school at Cellardyke: 'In the children are to be seen the most
pleasing evidences of improvement and benefit.' And at West Wemyss,
'The Sabbath after I left this place, they began a Sabbath evening school
which prospers. It is well attended by great numbers both of old and
young. Persons of twenty years old submit to be scholars ...'. There was
also a flourishing Sabbath School at East Wemyss.[23]

The author of another report from the Fife coast dated December 4th
is not clear (possibly Rev. Loader from Hampshire) but states: 'Serious
impressions too were made in the minds of some, especially young
people, which appear to be abiding.'[24]

Another Englishman, Rev. Bennet from Rumsey, was appointed to
itinerate around the Aberdeen area:

> August 29th,
> When entering Arbroath I spoke with a poor girl, who seemed
> about twelve or fourteen years old, and amongst other questions

21. SPGH p. 38.
22. SPGH p. 41.
23. SPGH pp 43, 50, 59.
24. SPGH p. 66.

asked her if she knew who was our Saviour? She answered Adam and Eve. Being surprised at her ignorance, I asked her if she went to the Sabbath school? She said no, for they had not been long set up. I mentioned the ignorance of this girl to the people and exhorted them to exert themselves for the Sabbath evening school.[25]

In Dundee at the Relief Meeting House Mr. Slatterie 'heard very pleasing accounts of Sabbath Schools among them, likewise of some children, who were apparently serious...'[26] On Monday 17th December he discovered children's prayer meetings in that city:

There are some girls, from seven to ten years old who meet for singing, reading the scriptures, and prayer, one evening in the week. Also several boys, the eldest of whom is not more than fifteen, who associate for similar purposes, having one of the older members of the congregation to preside among them. Thus out of the mouth of babes and sucklings the Lord perfects his praise.[27]

The end of the month saw him at Aberdeen, of which he could say 'the Sabbath Schools here are very well attended'.[28]

Thus there is evidence of a widespread awakening among children across Scotland at the turn of the century. What is lacking is a detailed description of the individual experiences of children. Perhaps the closest we can come to that is the account of James Haldane's daughter, Catherine, in her sixth year: she died 'in assurance', but for full details I refer you to his biography.[29]

Couper makes the interesting observation that 'it is notable that the districts where evangelical religion made the greatest advances during the next thirty years were all beyond the Highland line. The Gospel seems to have come to them with all the freshness of a new discovery'.[30] It is a sobering thought that even 250 years after the Scottish Reformation, there were parts of the land that had still never heard the evangelical gospel.

25. SPGH p.62. 26. SPGH p.68.
27. SPGH p.68. 28. SPGH p.70.
29. Haldane, pp 307-10. 30. Couper, p.13.

(c) Dr. Alexander Stewart

There was a localised awakening at the turn of the century in central Perthshire. Rev. Stewart had been settled in the parish of Moulin in 1786 at the age of 22. At that time only thirty seven families dwelt there, and thirty in neighbouring Pitlochry. Stewart himself was not awakened until Charles Simeon from Cambridge passed through in June 1796. His preaching changed, and from August 1797 to January 1798 he preached on fundamental doctrines. Towards the end of 1798, his congregation began to be concerned about their salvation, and 1799 saw weekly conversions 'chiefly among the younger people under twenty-five'.[31] There was no visible expression of emotion other than silent tears, but a general awakening from March 1799 which lasted three years. Stewart writes:

> ...I trust I can reckon truly enlightened with the saving knowledge of Christ, I find their number about seventy. The greater part of these are under thirty years of age...Of children under twelve or fourteen, there are a good many who have a liking to religion, but we find it difficult to form a decided opinion of their case.[32]

These seventy referred to were within his own parish, and so formed an amazing proportion of the local population! Blair and Dunkeld were also affected, and the district of Breadalbane was to become the scene of activity of Haldane's missionaries, who reported 145 conversions in Dunkeld in 1803.[33] Dr. Stewart left the area in 1805; his successor was unsympathetic, and most of the converts became Baptists.[34]

However, John Shaw from Moulin became the first evangelical minister on Skye, being settled at Duirinish in October 1805. He saw the conversion of the neighbouring minister of Kilmuir, and paved the way

---

31. Dr. Alexander Stewart, 'Account of the Late Revival', Third Edition, Edinburgh 1802, p.16. This 'account' was in fact a letter to Rev. David Black, dated: Moulin, 1st September 1800, but first published in 1800. Also republished as GRT, 6.

32. Stewart, p.21 Among the converts Couper lists the parents of missionary Alexander Duff, James Duff and Jean Rattray 'then both under seventeen years of age' (p.86) giving us clear evidence of lasting teenage conversions.

33. MacRae, p.135.

34. Couper, p.86, quoting Wm. McGavin of Glasgow.

for the 1812 revival under John Farquharson and blind fiddler/catechist, Donald Munro.

> Conspicuous results were obtained among young people, and even boys are said to have held separate prayer meetings for themselves. Altogether the movement continued for two and a half years, during which time, several hundreds professed to have turned to the Lord.[35]
>
> The awakening...was principally confined to those not much advanced in life - - of the age of *fifteen*, and under, to *thirty*, both married and unmarried.[36]

(d) The ministry of Rev. W.C. Burns

W. C. Burns was the son of Dr. William Burns, the minister of Kilsyth. Prayer meetings had been held regularly in that parish since 1721. He was awakened himself at the age of sixteen, and the following anecdote gives some interesting background to his evangelistic zeal:

> From early age, Burns had a passion for souls. The story is told that when he was seventeen years of age he was brought by his mother from the quiet surroundings of Kilysth, to the great bustling city of Glasgow. His mother was separated from her son while she was shopping, and when she retracted her steps to find him she discovered him in an alley with great tears streaming down his face. She could see he was suffering great agony. His surprised mother exclaimed, 'Willie, my boy, what ails you? Are you ill?' 'Oh Mither, Mither!' he cried, 'The thud of these Christless feet on the way to hell breaks my heart!' [37]

After his licensing for the ministry he supplied St. Peter's in Dundee, during the absence of Rev. McCheyne in the Holy Land. He returned home to Kilsyth and assisted his father at the Communion on the third Sunday in July 1839. At the final service on the Tuesday morning he described the revival at Shotts, and the Spirit descended.

---

35. Couper p.98. 36. GRT, 10.
37. James Alexander Stewart: 'William Chalmers Burns: A man with a passion'. Revival Literature, Philadelphia, 1964.

Six young girls, from fourteen to sixteen years, two of them orphans came next day bathed in tears and seeking Christ.[38]

He delayed his proposed return to Dundee, and saw a congregation of 4,000 the following Sunday, which he described:

Upon Sabbath, the 28th, the Church was crowded, and with the unusual appearance of not a few females without bonnets, and men and children in weekday and working dresses.

He noted that in the afternoon meeting:

After the blessing was pronounced about a third part either remained or soon returned, of various ages, but especially the young...[39]

There was another Communion in September attended by 10,000, and new communicants were admitted as young as twelve. 'They vary in age from twelve to three score and ten: a good many are from fifteen to eighteen years of age.'[40]

An anonymous Church of Scotland minister wrote A Sketch of a visit to Kilsyth in October 1839:

In answer to a question which I put to Mr. B., regarding the younger part of his people, he told us that about 100 boys and girls, between 10 and 16, meet together every night for prayer and praise. He accompanied us to the village, and directed us to the house of the overseer of a large factory there, he himself being engaged with his session. This man showed us great attention, and gave us some valuable information. He told us, among other things that the boys and girls used at first to meet in the haugh for religious duties, contrary to his views of order and decorum. Having attended one of their meetings, however, he came away quite satisfied that they should not be interfered with, but rather encouraged, everything was conducted so well. This was a very pleasing testimony, from a sober, thinking, and judicious man. Many of the weavers were absent when we paid our visit, but with some of them we had very interesting conversation. The first to

38. GRT, 11. 39. GRT, 11, or Gillies p.557. 40. GRT 11.

whom my attention was directed was a lad of 16, whose advancement in the divine life appeared truly astonishing for his years. He told us he had been three years at a Sabbath school in Glasgow; that while there he used to behave with great outward propriety, but that when he removed to Kilsyth he took up with the worst boys in the place; learning to swear, lie, steal, and do all manner of mischief. Under a sermon, preached by Mr. W.B., he became deeply impressed, and ever since he has continued so. I asked if ever he prayed before that time. He said — 'Oh, I used often to be on my knees, *but never knew what it was to pray!*' His views of prayer, its nature, its objects, &c, pleased me exceedingly. I asked him if he were not afraid of falling away; he said If he trusted in himself he knew he would; but that while he trusted in Christ, and His Spirit, he need not fear. '*I* can't keep *grace*,' said he, 'but *grace* can keep *me*.' And then he quoted the apostle's saying,—'If we have not the Spirit of Christ,' &c. He thought the chief cause of sorrow for sin should be *because it pierced Christ*. His heart overflowed with love to the Saviour. He thought his five brothers and sisters equally impressed with himself.

The author attended a prayer meeting, one of seventy held every night in that parish. Next morning we had a conference with some boys, which greatly satisfied us of their information and sincerity.[41]

William Burns himself describes his young people in a letter to his Presbytery Moderator:

I cannot but refer with delight to the continued flocking of the young people to the house of prayer; and to the various meetings for catechetical instruction. At the evening service, on the Lord's day in particular, they are always present in great numbers, and form not the least attentive and serious part of the audience. Immediately after divine service, there is a class for catechetical instruction, to which unwearied by the previous exercises, they flock with the utmost eagerness; and nothing can be more inter-

41. Scottish Christian Herald, February 1840, p.18, extracted from 'The Orthodox Presbyterian' of Ireland

esting and affecting, than to mark the solemn and intense interest which is kept up to the very conclusion of the exercises, and which seems to regret the necessity of at last quitting the courts of the Lord's house. It may be mentioned, for the benefit of others, that one great means in the hand of the Spirit, of bringing about this result, was a catechetical class for the young, commenced soon after the beginning of the revival, by Mr. J. Burns, now missionary in the parish. It was the means of rallying and keeping together, under a course of suitable instruction, the great majority of the young and ignorant, and they continue together, in undiminished numbers, to the present time. But for some such means as this, it can scarcely be doubted that multitudes of these lambs of the flock, whom the general concern had driven towards the fold of Christ, would soon have again been dispersed...Prayer meetings both among the young and old, still continue numerous, and are in general well attended.[42]

While the age of 'the young' referred to above cannot be clearly ascertained, it seems most likely that these were working teenagers from the references to catechism. In a later letter Burns writes:

I refer also with pleasure to the attendance of the youth on the Sabbath classes to the numerously attended and well-conducted prayer meetings every Monday evening in the West Port, besides many others, similar, on that and on other evenings, as well as on Sabbath mornings, and after public worship, and the meetings for prayer in the factory of Messrs W., and the remarkable change for the better on the whole on that establishment.[43]

One further note deserves to be appended:

The missionary's labours in watching over inquirers, especially the young, have been attended with blessing, so that the very youthful communicants have given no cause to regret their being admitted.[44]

---

42. SCH, Supplement April 1840, p.38.
43. SCH, Monthly Supplement, October 1840, p.102.
44. SCH, Monthly Supplement, October 1840, p.103, note 4.

W.C. Burns went back to Dundee on 8th August 1839 with immediate results. Two days later at the Thursday prayer meeting there were tears, and after that nightly meetings for prayer and preaching. That autumn between six and seven hundred came to the minister for spiritual help. On McCheyne's return, Burns itinerated around Scotland before going to China in 1847 with the English Presbyterian Mission, where he died in January 1868. Within Scotland he continued to have a special appeal to young people, for example we know from a report given to the Aberdeen Presbytery, that when he visited Lawers in 1839:

> There were no children addressed apart from the congregation, yet there were a good number of young persons from the age of thirteen and upwards, of both sexes, deeply impressed under the preaching of Mr. Burns.[45]

He also worked in Perth from December 1839. One of the questions asked by the Aberdonians was: did the preachers 'address children? At what hours? In what special terms? And what might be the age of the youngest of them?', this providing us with detail that might not otherwise have been recorded. In reply, Andrew Gray, of West Church, Perth, stated:

> I never knew of any particular dealings with children. There was a strong impression produced upon many of tender age connected with my own schools, and I am happy to say that the good effect of it is still apparent; but I do not believe that any special or peculiar means were taken for causing a religious excitement among the very young (dated 29th January, 1841).[46]

John Milne of St. Leonards replied similarly:

> There was no address specially to children, though a considerable number attended the meetings, and seemed deeply affected. Some of them, on being questioned, were found to possess correct views of their state as sinners. They had prayer meetings among themselves in several parts of the town; and though these,

45. MacRae, pp 142-3.
46. H. Bonar, 'Life of John Milne', p.49, Nisbet, London 1868.

as was perhaps desirable, were soon relinquished, yet I would hope that some on these occasions received impressions, which God will acknowledge as His own work.[47]

In April 1840 Horace Bonar was assisting his brother Andrew at Collace, and at a midweek meeting:

> While he was pressing on all present the immediate reception of the offer of the living waters, many burst into tears, old and young, and among the rest, several boys of twelve or fourteen years of age. A deep and aweful solemnity spread over the whole meeting, and, after the blessing was pronounced, fifty or sixty people remained in their seats, most of them in tears.

The occasion here was that the local Presbytery had called for a fast for the state of the church. Bonar is honest enough to admit that 'of the young people who were that night very deeply awakened, I know three or four instances in which the impression has completely faded away' when he wrote on 20th October, 1841.[48]

In Dundee, McCheyne immediately recognised the effect of the revival on the children. On the evening of his return in November, 'there was not a seat in the church unoccupied, the passages were completely filled, and the stairs to the pulpit were crowded, on the one side with the aged, on the other with eagerly-listening children'.[49] When he wrote *Evidences on Revivals* for a Committee of the Aberdeen Presbytery on 26th March, 1842, he made several references to the children:

I. *re August, 1839*
At this time, also, many prayer meetings were formed, some of which were strictly private or fellowship meetings, and others conducted by persons of some Christian experience were open to persons under concern about their souls. At the time of my return from the Mission to the Jews I found thirty-nine such meetings held weekly in connection with the congregation and five of them were conducted and attended entirely by little children.

47. H. Bonar, 'Life of John Milne', p.53.
48. H. Bonar, 'Life of John Milne', p.62.
49. 'Life of Robert Murray McCheyne', Andrew Bonar, Banner of Truth, 1960, p.135.

VI.
When I first came here, I found it impossible to establish Sabbath Schools...while, very lately, there were instituted with ease nineteen such schools, that are well taught and well attended.

XV.
The ministers engaged in the work of God in this place, believing that children are lost, and may through grace be saved, have therefore spoken to children as freely as to grown persons; and God has so greatly honoured their labours that many children from ten years old and upwards, have given full evidence of their being born again. I am not aware of any meetings that have been held peculiarly for children with the exception of the Sabbath School, the children's prayer meetings and a sermon to the children on the Monday evening after Communion. It was commonly at the public meetings in the house of God that children were impressed, often also in their own little meetings, when no minister was present.

As early as December 2nd he wrote to Andrew Bonar:

Some little children are evidently saved. All that I have yet seen are related to converts of my own. One, eleven years old, is a singular instance of Divine Grace. When asked if she desired to be made holy, she said 'Indeed, I often wish I was awa', that I might sin nae mair.' A.L. of fifteen, is a fine tender-hearted believer. W.S., ten, is also a happy boy.[50]

And on December 25th, he also wrote to Horace Bonar that he 'visited a school in St. George's parish, and preached to many weeping children'.[51]

McCheyne's diary for that period also recalls some of his dealings with the children:

December 31st, 1839
Young Communicants. Two have made application to be admitted under 11 years of age 4 that are only 14, three who are 15 or 16.

---

50. 'Memoir and Remains of Rev. Robert Murray McCheyne', 1892, p.547, by A. Bonar
51. H. Bonar, 'Life of John Milne', p.33.

January 2nd, 1840
Met with young communicants on Wednesday and Friday. On the latter night especially, very deep feeling, manifested in sobbings. Visits of several. One dear child nine years old. Sick bed.

April 5th, 1840
Sabbath evening - spoke to 24 young persons, one by one: almost all affected about their souls.

April 13th, 1840
Spoke in private to nearly 30 young communicants, all in one room, going round each, and advising for the benefit of all.

Reporting on Communion, January 19th, 1840
One little boy, in retiring said 'This has been another bonnie day.' Many of the little ones seemed deeply attentive.[52]

Bonar gives us this tribute as to his concern for children, and provision for them:

He sought to encourage Sabbath Schools in all the districts of his parish. The hymn 'Oil for the lamp' was written to impress the parable on a class of Sabbath scholars in 1841. Some of his sweet, simple tracts were written for these schools. *Reasons why children should fly to Christ* was the first, written at the new year, 1839 and *The Lambs of the Flock* was another at a later period. His heart felt for the young. One evening, after visiting some of his Sabbath schools, he writes, 'Had considerable joy in teaching the children. O for a real heart-work among them!' He could accommodate himself to their capacities; and he did not reckon it in vain to use his talents to attract their attention; for he regarded the soul of a child as infinitely precious.[53]

Bonar has also preserved for us some of McCheyne's writings for children. *Another Lily Gathered* is the story of James Laing who was born on July 28th 1828, first awakened when he was eleven, came under

52. A. Bonar, Life of R. Murray McCheyne, pp 146-8. 53. A. Bonar, Memoir, p.74.

real conviction in October 1841, praying for hours on his knees until he knew he was converted, and then witnessed to others and prayed for them until his death on June 11th, 1842 at the age of thirteen.[54]

In his *Reasons why Children should fly to Christ without delay*, McCheyne speaks of:

The late Countess of Huntingdon...was about nine years of age when she saw the dead body of a little child her own age carried to the grave. She followed the funeral and it was there that the Holy Spirit first opened up her heart to convince her that she needed a Saviour.

The headings that follow are:

Because life is short.
Because life is uncertain.
Most that are ever saved fly to Christ when young.
Because it is happiest to be in Christ than out of Christ.[55]

This provides interesting evidence of the way children were spoken to in this period, with the frequency of child mortality, and the fear that must have produced.

Writing over three decades later, MacPherson is able to affirm:

Many of the converts of the Burns and McCheyne period are worthy office-bearers in the churches. Of the converts in St. Peter's alone, some sixteen became ministers of the gospel at home and abroad, some of whom are now the spiritual fathers of hundreds.[56]

According to Couper, revival was widespread at that time in Perth, Blairgowrie (which had thirty prayer meetings), in the Borders (100 converted in Kelso, Jedburgh Town Hall taken over) and in the winter of 1841-42, 'Leith was so visited by revival fervour that one said the place seemed to be going mad'.[57] But he does not cite information about children in these places.

---

54. A. Bonar, Memoir, p.552. 55. Bonar, Memoir, p.584.
56. MacPherson, Revival, p.20. 57. Couper, p.129.

Burns invited John Macdonald to assist, and on the night of his arrival in Kilsyth, he preached on John 3:36. He noted, 'All was stillness and deep attention - many in tears - children of eight and ten among the rest.' On the Sunday evening after church 'about one hundred and fifty or two hundred men, women and children stood around me anxiously wishing to hear something more from me. I addressed them for about forty minutes...'. On the evening of Tuesday 10th he preached at Banton where 'numbers were in tears, and children from eight to fourteen years old.' In Dundee on the 23rd he met with twenty-two 'under soul distress ... among whom were two girls about nine and a boy of eleven'.[58]

McCheyne's travelling companion to the Holy Land was Andrew Bonar, then settled as minister of Collace, north-east of Perth. His great-grandfather had ridden from Torphichen to Cambuslang in order to witness the revival there, a journey taking him three days because of his frailty! The entire Bonar family seem to have inherited an interest in revivals. As early as January 24th, 1838, while preparing for the ministry by acting as parochial missionary at St. George's, Edinburgh, Andrew wrote in his diary[59] after visiting his brother, Horace, minister in Kelso:

I heard at Kelso of a work beginning; two or three have already come to Horace in deep anxiety, chiefly people that seemed to know the truth. At Jedburgh heard of some young people who have died in the Lord.

On his return from Palestine, he records on November 24th, 1839: 'Have heard of revival at Blairgowrie and other places; Jedburgh also seems moved,' and on Friday 24th January, 1840 writes: 'Delighted to hear upon Wednesday evening the proposal of some of my young people to form a prayer-meeting before the class meets on Sabbath in the session-room.' On Wednesday 26th February he 'heard of a prayer meeting among the young Sabbath School children' and concludes 'I think God is about to bless us'. On Tuesday 8th September he was 'Much refreshed by a letter from Mr. Milne telling me of a boy

58. Kennedy, 'The Apostle of the North', pp 226-230.
59. Andrew Bonar's diary was edited by his daughter, Marjory, and published in 1893, now reprinted by Banner of Truth Trust, Edinburgh, 1960.

converted by my sermon last Sabbath evening at his Communion' (at St. Leonard's, Perth), but was obviously grieved by the lack of response among his own young people because on Tuesday 17th October he 'Met with some of the young people tonight, and spoke most seriously to them as to the danger of deceiving themselves. I have felt very deep grief from time to time at the complete want of decision in some of them of whom I had better hopes'. Bonar told his Wednesday night meeting on July 20th, 1842 of 'the possibility that God the Holy Ghost might use new plans and new measures': and some one had suggested to him 'the formation of a class of young people in my house'.[60] The concept of young people's house groups is not new! At the autumn Communion on November 13th in the same year he notes 'many children were present all day'.

From then on the events of the Disruption appear to overshadow all else, and the next mention of children in his diary is not until the 2nd January, 1848 when 'This morning saw some scholars in the Sabbath-school very attentive, whom I had not often been able to interest'. In September 1850, as he reviews twelve years in the ministry, he laments on the 21st, 'During last year very little fruit; only one old man and something hopeful among young children' but does not elaborate on this statement. At the conclusion of his ministry in Collace on 19th October 1856, he 'preached to the children upon Rev. xxi. 6,7'; and there are other references to his talking directly to the children, in Edinburgh (recorded 12th April, 1857) and on 5th April 1857 'my first sermon to the children here' as he commenced his new ministry in Finnieston, to which we shall refer in the following chapter.[61]

(e) The Gaelic Schools Society
Following the completion of the translation of the complete Bible into Gaelic and its publication in 1806, the way was opened for this Society, which was founded on 16th January 1811 'for the purpose of gratui-

60. Diary entry on Sunday 24th July, 1842
61. On Saturday 19th March 1887 he regrets the giving up of Fast-Days, as it meant 'no more preaching on Fast evenings to children in Edinburgh', presumably indicating that this had been his regular practice? But he still 'preached my children's sermon in Lady Glenorchy's last Thursday' before the Edinburgh Communion on April 24th.

tously teaching the inhabitants of the Highlands and Islands of Scotland to read the scriptures in their native language'. The concept owed much to the Welsh Circulating Schools which had been founded in 1730, and given a new impulse by Thomas Charles of Bala, and this debt is traced in detail in the GSS reports of 1811 and 1854.[62] The basic concept was that of an itinerant teacher who would set up a school in a village for a couple of years, and teach anyone who was willing to read, before moving on to another village. If classes were divided up it was on the basis of ability to read rather than age. Hence one started with simple gospel stories, then progressed to the 'Testament Class', then to the 'Bible Class'. After a decade a teacher might return to deal with a new generation of children who had grown up meantime. At this period there were 31 Gaelic-speaking parishes in the Western Isles, and 131 on the mainland, covering a total population of 400,000 (of whom 100,000 were on the islands), which had doubled since 1750.[63]

The link between the work of this Society and the religious revivals which occurred in their district is clear, as the Fiftieth Annual Report is quick to point out:

---

62. Mr. Charles was part of an extensive spiritual movement among the children of North Wales as these letters of his (quoted in GRT, 9) reveal:

1791: And here at Bala, we have had a very great, powerful, and glorious outpouring of the Spirit on the people in general...especially on the children and young people. Scores of the wildest and most inconsiderate of young people of both sexes have been awaked.

Re Charity Schools: Little children from six to twelve years of age are affected, astonished and overpowered. Their young minds, day and night, are filled with nothing but soul-concerns.

January 1794: In some of the schools we had general awakenings among all the children.

This accounts for the devotion of a child like Mary Jones, who attended church prayer meetings at the age of 8 and prayed for an opportunity to learn to read so she could study the bible for herself. She started saving up for one at the age of ten and at fifteen and a half in May 1800 walked the 25 miles to Bala in her bare feet to obtain it. This story is often quoted at the origin of the British and Foreign Bible Society, but no-one to my knowledge has made the connection with a children's revival taking place in Wales at this time. (The story of "Mary Jones and her Bible" was first published by BFBS in 1867, and rewritten by Mary Carter for them in 1949.)

63. GSS 1811

The place which God has been pleased to give the work of your teachers in the awakenings and revivals of religion which have occurred in various parts of the Highlands and Islands is such that their antecedents might have led you to expect, and such as ought fill the hearts of all the supporters of the Society with gratitude and thanksgiving.[64]

The same report claimed that 110,360 people had been taught to read through 1,008 schools, and that 82,346 Bibles and Testaments had been provided by them.

The reports contain a mine of information which are worthy of careful analysis. Here all we can do is extrapolate some of the references to the religious experiences of children, and quote the specific passages covering revivals:

1827

Rev. James Russel of Gairloch, writing about the school at Mellon of Gairloch, 8th August, 1826 says: All the scholars of the Bible Class, from the child of five years old upwards, can repeat from 25-30 Psalms; and it was truly delightful to hear with what accuracy and solemnity these babes repeated the songs of Zion. Out of school also these children are instrumental in spreading the knowledge of the scriptures, both by reading them in front of their families and by teaching their parents and grown-up brothers and sisters, who cannot attend school to read them; for it is no uncommon thing in this parish, to see a child sitting upon its mother's knee, and teaching her to read the Bible.

1830

At Castlesween in Arygyllshire: A boy about twelve years of age was in the habit of bringing a brother older than himself and another younger, to a neighbouring wood, every evening, even in the winter nights, there to perform the evening sacrifice, which should have been done by his father in the house. If they had as much light as to enable them to read, they read a chapter of the Bible, then sang a psalm and prayed. The teacher contrived to get

64. GSS 1861

near them one night and heard their singing and prayers. He said he not only shed tears, but actually felt ashamed of himself when he heard the little boy wrestling with God in prayer, and acknowledging sins, both actual and original, and praying that God would make His power known among sinners. He went this year to America.

1837
(P.38) reports the death in 1836 of a crippled boy who had been given a Bible at Braes, Portree, Skye, in 1831. His parents wouldn't let him read it at home, so the children helped him build a stone hut he could crawl into and read chapters of the Bible at a time.

School at Barvas. Requotes a report of Rev. Shaw written on 10th April 1817: The very children are known to retire for the purpose of private prayer and one man told me, in an affecting manner, that his son, who is only nine years of age, would insist on his accompanying him in this exercise; and while the child led the devotions, together they addressed that God who out of the mouths of babes and sucklings, thus perfects praise.

The comment is added: It is one of the promises taken at baptism from the father, that he will pray with and for his child. How interesting to see a child praying with and for his father!

Rev. J. Shaw invited: children who could read to attend at the church of Minginish.....(forty children) read the sacred scriptures as perfectly as ever I heard them read ....

1842
Letter of Rev. Gordon dated 23rd February 1841 from Assynt:
Whilst I would desire to speak cautiously - very cautiously, as to the results, I dare not deny that the Lord the Spirit seems to have been at work amongst us. Many young persons of both sexes were deeply and painfully impressed with an alarming sense of guilt and danger, and, no doubt, much excitement prevailed; that excitement is now much decreased, and yet there is a very general and deep interest evinced in regard to religion, and an increasing desire to hear the gospel.

Appendix XII from Rev. Robert Finlayson, Lochs, Lewis, 9th December 1841: There were some boys about six years of age who read the Bible fluently and had committed to memory all the questions of the Shorter Catechism and fifty psalms.

1843

The superintendent reports ("in another place"): There are two young girls of those who are attending this school at present, very promising, and who appear to be truly changed.

Your teacher here has been instrumental in awakening some in this dark corner; and by the appearance which the children made, I have reason to conclude that his labours among them have not been in vain. When addressing the children in this school, I saw a number both of the children and of the parents deeply impressed and bedewed with tears, and some crying out.

At Unish, Waternish, Skye, in August 1840: Unusual concern among the people *was noted. On Sabbath 15th May 1841, the teacher's last day, came revival which went on all night, with meetings day and night for sixteen days, so he got only two hours sleep a night. Rev. Macleod of Snizort concludes:* There are few families in the whole island of Skye, where there has not been one or more individuals seriously impressed.

1844

In Shieldaig and Applecross, your inspector says he was exceedingly refreshed with the conversations he had with the children. They evinced a lively concern about their spiritual interests...At Lochcarron, the awakening began towards the close of April. Scenes of deep emotion ensued whenever anyone addressed the children. The voice of the speaker would sometimes be drowned in the general sob of anguish and contrition that pervaded the whole meeting. There was evidence that this was not merely the excitement of sympathy working upon the susceptible feelings of youth. The Spirit of God was in the movement. The heart was touched. The Spirit of grace and of supplication was poured out from on high, and many a streaming eye seems to have been directed in faith to a pierced and crucified Redeemer. Some boys built a small hut in a retired spot that they might hold regular meetings for prayer in it. They collected their scanty pence, and expended them in the purchase of candles, to be used when the shades of evening darkened on their little meeting.

With scarcely an exception the fourteen schools of Skye all shared in the outpouring of the Holy Ghost.

Rev. Norman McLeod writes from North Uist, 26th January 1844: Can anything be more gratifying than to see about one hundred and twenty of the youth of that district solemnly engaged in reading the Word of God and in similar religious exercises? Yet such a gratifying exhibition may be seen every Sabbath morning in your school at Malaclite...

In September 1843 in the district of Paible (N. Uist) he: commenced labouring in the populous district just mentioned, and he had scarcely set his hand to the work, when several, especially among the young, became sensibly distressed at his meetings under a conviction of sin, and their lost condition. From this as a centre point, the revival has been since spreading south and north. There is hardly a sermon or prayer meeting but some person is newly affected, and there is every appearance of the work spreading more extensively...In this parish, numbers of children, from eight to fourteen years of age are impressed; and it would be an affecting sight to see their parents, as I have more than once seen them, carrying them out of the meeting house, apparently lifeless with exhaustion from overpowered feelings.

1846

The fifteen grandchildren of a poor man on N. Uist attended the Gaelic School, and the whole fifteen were awakened. The good people there told me that they had every reason to believe that ten of them were savingly enlightened in the knowledge of the Saviour. They would say nothing about the other five, but that they were deeply concerned...

1848

From the Inspector's Journal. In a school in Heiskar, an island west of North Uist, I examined last year a boy of twelve years of age who kept family worship in his mother's house - a widow. Two travellers, who were detained for two nights in the island by contrary winds, and under the same roof with this boy, attended his family worship, morning and evening. In leaving the island the one asked the other what was the most striking thing they had met with in the island, and the reply was 'The prayers of that boy' adding 'surely there must be something in religion to which we were strangers.' The boy had never had the opportunity of hearing a sermon - his only means of instruction being from the Gaelic School teachers.[65]

1850

Inspector's Report, School at Ulva. One girl, seven years of age, reading the New Testament, is in the habit of rising out of bed by night to pray.

1851

At Rabhreak, Creich, Sutherland, there was a girl thirteen years of age who died last winter, giving every evidence of a saving interest in Christ. She apprehended death at the beginning of her illness, and felt quite reconciled to God's will. During her illness she frequently expressed her sympathy with her parents being their only daughter; and in her prayers implored, in their behalf, the grace of God to reconcile them to their bereavement. Shortly before she died, her mother, observing that she felt uncomfortable in her mind, asked how she felt. She replied, 'Satan is trying to have me, but I trust in my Redeemer.'

1852

Letter from Rev. Donald Murray, Knock, Lewis, 5th November 1851. Fancy to yourself one of our extensive parishes in the Highlands, say twenty or thirty miles in length, with one or two schools in it, and you can easily conceive that the most of the parishioners cannot avail themselves of either of these. There, in

---

65. The 1845 report mentions revival on Heiskar, and claims that the last visit of the minister was sixteen years previously! (Heiskar is one of the Monach Islands now uninhabited.)

a certain part of that parish, you have planted one of your schools. On Sabbath evenings the school-house is filled with both parents and children; after prayer and praise, the children read the Word of God and are examined on the portion read. They are then examined on the Shorter Catechism. *He goes on to describe family worship at home.* A few years ago, a little girl at Lochalsh, when on her death bed, was heard praising the Lord, that He sent a Gaelic teacher to that place, whereby she was enabled to read the blessed Word, through which she was led to lay hold on the Lord Jesus as her own God and Saviour.

1860

The teacher at Steinish, Isle of Lewis, had abandoned adult evening classes because the adults were going to the revival prayer meetings: There are several in this small village under deep concern about their souls, but none of the weekday scholars as yet, except one girl in the Bible class.

    Kershader, Lewis: I was giving a lesson to the Testament class, and they were reading the nineteenth chapter of the Gospel according to St. John. When reading about Christ's sufferings, seven of them fell down on the floor, shedding tears and crying out. When I asked them what was the matter with them, they answered that they were crucifying Christ with their lives. Those scholars were from ten to twelve years of age. On Wednesday night after that, I had a meeting at the school-house, and seventeen of my scholars began to shed tears, and to cry, and some of them were not able to go home without the help of others. As far as I can judge, I am thinking that it is the work of the Lord that is going on now in this district, and that Christ will see the travail of His soul among them.

    Lionel, Lewis: There is an extra-ordinary movement especially among the young, here at present.

1861

Rev. John McLeod reports of the school at Marig, Harris: There is also a number of the children and adults who have come under the power of the truth. Some of the children were deeply affected, and impressed with a sense of their sins, whilst reading their lessons.

A teacher writes: I am sure the Society will be glad to hear of the revivals of religion in the Island of Islay. To the praise of God we have a large share of it in this district...For the last two or three weeks we have daily prayer meetings and lectures in the school-house. Many of the scholars are awakened, some as young as eight years of age. Our meetings at the time of conclusion, is a scene indescribable, with weeping, crying, and fainting.

For a more thorough treatment of these various spiritual movements throughout the Highlands, and other agencies involved in them, the reader is referred to MacRae. He does attribute the awakening on Lewis in the 1820's to the work of the Gaelic Schools Society, and relates that at Uig by 1827 there were 600 hundred people attending the schools. Sabbath Schools were organised in every hamlet. In 1834 there were thirteen Sabbath Schools throughout the parish. 9,000 attended the 1828 Communion, and regular conversions occurred over a ten year period.[66] He then narrates the story of Kitty Smith who developed an amazing prayer life before she was called home at the age of eight:

In the small island of Pabay, Loch Roag, there lived a little girl whose name was Catherine Smith. Kitty, as she was commonly called, showed herself to be endowed with a truly devotional spirit from her earliest infancy. The religious atmosphere of her islet home was beautifully reflected in her child-life and spiritual experiences. When only two years old she clasped her hands with reverence at family worship. At three she could repeat the 23rd Psalm with such understanding and spiritual relish as proved her to be indeed one of the Good Shepherd's little lambs, and repeated the Lord's Prayer regularly, and sometimes in the darkness and silence of the night. She cultivated the habit of prayer, for which her brothers and sisters often mocked her. She was so filled with love to Christ, and so enthralled by His

---

66. MacRae, pp 82-3. See also Murdo Macauley 'The Burning Bush in Carloway' pp 11-12 who dates the start of the revival as 1822 which was known as 'the year of the swoonings' (Bliadhna an Aomaidh)).

attractiveness, that she continually spoke of Him to her little
companions. One day she went home greatly downcast saying,
'The children vexed me very much today. I will not go with them,
for they said that Christ was black, and that grieved my spirit. I
told them that Christ is white and glorious in his apparel.' Her
grief that anyone should speak a disparaging word about Jesus
was sufficient proof of her genuine affection for Him.

Her mother, on one occasion, saw her intently gazing into a
roaring fire, and asked what she was looking at. 'I am seeing that
my state would be awful if I were to fall into that fire, even though
I should be immediately taken out,' she replied, 'but, woe is me,
those who are cast into hell fire will never come out thence.' On
another occasion, as she looked over the edge of a precipice, she
exclaimed to her mother, 'How fearful would our state be if we
were to fall down this rock, even though we should be lifted up
again, but they who are cast into the depths of hell will never be
raised therefrom.'

Her parents had heard Dr. MacDonald, Ferintosh, preaching
at Uig, when he pointed out the danger of formality and want of
spirituality in prayer; and that many were content with old,
useless, lifeless forms. As they spoke of it after going home, Kitty
said, 'It is time for me to give up my old form of prayer.' 'Neither
you nor your prayers are old,' chaffed her mother. But she
replied, 'I must give them up, and use the prayers which the Lord
will teach me.' When she looked gloomy and sad her mother tried
to cheer her by jocular remarks, but she answered, 'O mother, you
are vexing my spirit; I would rather hear you praying.' Her
favourite song was Peter Grant's hymn on 'The Blood of Christ.'
When she came to the concluding verse, which says, 'It is not
valued according to its worth,' she would, in touching terms,
lament that His blood was so lightly esteemed.

Between the age of seven and eight she was attacked by some
disease which was the means of removing her into the Kingdom
of Heaven. She knew she was dying. Her father asked her whom
she pitied most of those she was leaving behind her. 'I pity
everyone who is in a Christless state,' was her reply. Towards the
end she used to pray, 'Oh, Holy One of Israel, save me from death.

Oh, redeem me from death.' In her last moments, her father leaning over her, said, 'Kitty, where are you now?' to which she replied, 'I am on the shore,' and immediately her soul was launched into the great ocean of eternity. That was in December 1829.[67]

Other details are added in the version recorded in Glasgow Revival Tract no 8., which tells us that after her parents visit to Uig:

...she withdrew to retired spots for prayer. At one time her younger sister returned without her, and on being asked where she had left Kitty, she said, 'I left her praying.'... From the remoteness of her dwelling, Kitty had never attended any place of public worship...but the Sabbath was her delight - and often she would call her brothers and sisters from the play in which they were thoughtlessly engaged, asking them to join in prayer and other devout exercises, and warning them that if they pro-faned the day and disliked God's worship, they must perish.

Nearby at Knock on Lewis, in 1829 the Rev. Findlay Cook was aware of 'three apprentices who were in the habit of meeting regularly for prayer'. They were illiterate and took it in turns to walk the five miles to attend family worship at the manse in order to relay the teaching back to others.[68]

Although we shall chronologically overlap the period covered in the next chapter it seems sensible to insert here such other information as we have from the Gaelic speaking areas, as we have already touched on the 1859 revival in the later GSS reports.

A correspondent from Stornoway writes to the Guardian:

The movement has appeared in almost every school in the parish of Lochs. The teachers cannot make any comment on a passage of the truth without the children being affected. Speaking to a pious teacher the other day, he said he did not feel teaching to be such a toil this year although he had a great many more scholars.[69]

67. MacRae, pp 85-7. 68. MacRae, p.89.
69. SG Thursday 5th January, 1860 and WJ 14th January, 1860.

This newspaper published a letter from a minister in Lewis a month later:

> The revival movement is general over the whole island. The
> revival was a hundred fold more extensive than that which
> visited the island in 1812. There are none of the excesses of that
> period...the Young attend the prayer meetings in large numbers.[70]

This is confirmed by a correspondent on Harris writing on 4th February of:

> Anxious and earnest inquirers at our Communion in the month of
> November last. At that time it was principally confined to parties
> from Lewis, but, blessed be God, it is so no longer, but is now
> exerting its benign influence over the masses of the youths of this
> island, more especially over those who are destined to be the
> mothers of the next generation.[71]

The following year, the Free Church Assembly heard a report on
Skye given by Rev. Reid:

> The blessing had been chiefly confined to those between the ages
> of sixteen and twenty-five - although there were some aged
> persons converted - and some of their schools had been remark-
> ably visited.[72]

This move among children is confirmed by a most touching account
of the poverty experienced at this time on the islands by the children.
The exact location of this report by Grace A. Craigie is not given beyond
'the west of Skye':

> Just now when there has been a great work of revival in these
> islands, the poor little children will be seen crying because they
> are too naked to go to Church. *One Sabbath evening, when a Skye
> woman* was returning from Church, she heard the voices of little
> children singing behind a hill. She went up to where she heard the
> voices, and found four little children 'keeping church for them-

---

70. SG Saturday 11th February, 1860.
71. I.A. Friday 10th February, 1860.
72. W.J. 8th June, 1861.

selves', singing, reading, and praying, because they were too naked to go to Church.[73]

There were a number of different agencies working in the islands besides the GSS, not all of which had happy origins. In 1847, for example, 'The Ladies Association in support of the Gaelic Schools in connection with the Church of Scotland' issued its first annual report, stating that it had been instituted because the Free Church had excluded 'from the Gaelic School Society every individual belonging to the Established Church'.[74]

A meeting in the Queen Street Hall on 1st December 1859 of the Association for the Religious Improvement of the Remote Highlands and Islands was told:

> Several of the schools of the Association have shared in the work of Revival which has been going on in some parts of the Highlands, and very interesting accounts have been received from the teachers of prayer meetings being established among the young, and of hopeful signs of conviction and deep impresssion.[75]

The Eleventh Annual Report of the Association for the Religious Improvement of the Remote Highlands and Islands records:

> During the last six to eight months there has been a decided work of revival in many parts of the Highlands, and in no other districts of the country have the young more largely shared in the blessing. In some places the young alone have been seriously impressed; in others, the movement began among the children, who were engaged in reading their Bibles and tracts whilst herding on the hills, and met together for prayer in the barns in the evening, till the attention of the older people was awakened, and they also were made partakers of the blessing. So great has been the thirst for hearing the Word, that

73. T.R. 20th July, 1861. This poverty is also described in letters from Rev. John Forbes of Sleat, appealing for clothing to allow the poor to attend church–recorded in the 1861 report of the Ladies Association in Support of the Gaelic Schools.
74. Published by Stark & Co., Edinburgh, 1847.
75. I.A. Tuesday 6th December, 1859.

young women have been known to walk twenty miles on Sabbath, besides standing during the service in the crowded places of meeting; and children of ten or twelve years old have walked regularly for months seven miles to church and prayer-meetings, both on week-days and Sabbaths; sometimes in groups, with one reading aloud by the way, or singing psalms and hymns, one giving out the line, and all joining. During the summer, they remained for evening service, passing the interval in the woods, in little groups, engaged in prayer and singing. In one school, at least forty were known to be awakened, and, so far as man could judge, truly converted, whilst as many more seemed seriously impressed, who had not openly expressed their feelings. The teacher's house was crowded for some weeks with anxious inquirers, both by day and night, and ministers who preached there described the scene as one of the most affecting and delightful they had ever witnessed, even little children of five or six years old eagerly listened to the Word of life, and showing how deeply they felt their need of a Saviour.

Regrettably, no location is given of the above, but it continues:

The Rev. Rod. Macleod, of Snizort, in the Isle of Skye writes: In briefly adverting to the state of some of your schools which I have visited since your last report, I shall restrict myself entirely to their religious condition. To begin with Arnisort. You are already aware that a religious movement, such as, happily of late, is not uncommon in many other quarters, has more or less pervaded Skye in the course of this year. That movement assumed a decided form in connexion with my congregation, if not actually in the school, certainly in the school-house of Arnisort. It had been customary for some time to read to the scholars accounts of the Lord's work in other parts, and two weekly meetings were statedly kept for that purpose, to which any of the neighbours that chose might come. At the ordinary prayer-meeting held at night on Feb. 1, an unusual number of people, as if moved by a sudden impulse, attended, by which the teacher, Mr. Fergusson, was taken somewhat aback, and feeling rather at a loss what to say, took James's *Anxious Inquirer*, read the first part of it, and afterwards the 16th chapter of John.

During the meeting an uncommon solemnity was felt; one young girl broke out in cries for mercy, and two young men could hardly stand at prayer; and thus commenced a movement which for many weeks kept the school-house more like a hospital than anything else, many sleepless nights being passed there, and so many going to and fro that it was a matter of wonder and thankfulness that Mr. and Mrs. Fergusson stood it so well. In school the children were often in deep distress at their Bible lessons and in singing psalms and hymns - the latter kindly furnished by your Association. You will now wish to know what results are observable from all this. Here I beg to be excused if I hesitate to speak decidedly of conversions. I have seen enough of such things to teach me to wait, as 'the husbandman waiteth for the precious fruit of the earth, and hath long patience for it, until he receive the early and latter rain'. Yet it is worth while telling, that *forty-six* of the scholars under sixteen years of age have been more or less impressed during that blessed season; many of whom are walking so as to inspire the best hopes regarding them. The Lord bless them, and lead them in safety 'through the land of deserts and of pits, of drought and of the shadow of death,' to a city of rest! But why should I trespass further on your patience with details of this delightful work? I might tell you much of the children's love of the Bible, which many of them must now learn to read in *Gaelic*, because in that language they can best understand it; and of their love of the preaching of the Word, to hear which they gladly go any distance, if not through fire, certainly through water, thinking little of walking in an evening from Arnisort to Portree, at least twelve miles, and returning the same night, cheering each other as they go with singing some of Zion's songs - an instance of which may interest you. Our friend Mr. McPhail and I were one evening at a meeting at Portree, and on our return hither, while refreshing ourselves with a cup of tea, our attention was suddenly arrested by the sound of vocal music passing the house. Mr. McPhail started to the window and listened till it died away in the distance. It was the Arnisort party, chiefly scholars, returning from the meeting at Portree, and intensely interesting it certainly was to hear a manly voice giving out the line, and then the whole party bursting into full chorus, loud enough to be heard a mile away; at such an hour of night it was even sublime. This may suffice regarding Arnisort; but as it may meet the eye of some who take pleasure in clothing the naked, I beg to add that many of the children were often in deep distress, because their parents would not allow them to come to church in the rags they usually wore.

Your school at Kilmaluag has been visited with a large measure of awakening power. No fewer than ten girls and six boys, one-third of the whole number attending, being seriously impressed, and their conduct hitherto is giving general satisfaction, much to the comfort of your worthy teacher there, notwithstanding the amount of labour to which he has in consequence been subjected.

Of your industrial school at Steinscholl, conducted by Mrs. McDonald, the catechist's wife, I have also a gratifying report to make. The school is attended by twenty-six young women, as interesting a looking batch as I ever saw anywhere. Of that number about one-fourth have been so impressed as to give every hope that the true peace of God is in the hearts of some of them at least. Hitherto in your reports, so far as I know, you could only indulge in expressions of hope regarding the religious condition of your schools; I beg now to congratulate you, and your worthy coadjutors, on the decided proofs which the last season has furnished of the Divine countenance being vouchsafed to your labours of love.[76]

(f) Sunday Schools

Although Robert Raikes' educational efforts in Gloucester in 1780 are generally credited as the foundation of the worldwide Sunday School movement, Bready is correct in pointing out that many previous efforts had been made to instruct needy children on Sundays, and Hannah Ball had commenced Sunday School work in High Wycombe some eleven years earlier with Wesley's encouragement.[77] However, it is at least possible that Scotland was the forerunner of this movement.

Before proceeding further it is important to state that the situation in

76. .T.R. 1st February, 1862.
77. 'England before and after J. Wesley', J.W. Bready, (Hodder & Stoughton, London, 1939) p.268 and p.353.

Scotland was very different. In some areas, but by no means universally, there was better provision of parish education for the poor, and on the religious front there was a stronger tradition of ministers catechising their youth, and of family worship at home.

A specifically Scottish history of the Sunday School movement has yet to be written, and information has therefore to be pieced together from passing references. We cannot even be clear as to when the first recognisable Sunday School commenced, although the official Sunday School Union history states: 'As early as the year 1756 a Presbyterian minister started a Sabbath School in his own house which was attended by thirty or forty children. This school he maintained for a period of not less than fifty years, and it has continued unbroken to the present day.'[78] The location, regrettably, is not cited. Dunbar may also have had a Sunday School prior to 1780.[79] MacInnes, however, traces it to Banchory-Davinick,[80] and the following quotation from the Old Statistical Account, supplied by the Rev. George Morrison, which although beyond our remit, does provide an interesting insight into the background of the era:

BANCHORY-DAVINICK: 'The parochial schoolmaster here is Mr. Robert Cormack. He had his education at Marischal College but never raised his views higher than his present situation. He is a most industrious and successful teacher, labouring in his vocation from Sunday to Sunday, and from morning to night. He has the merit of having established a Sunday School here as far back as 1782. Not fewer than seventy on an average, attend regularly in the course of the day; young men before public worship, and young women after it; and this indefatigable teacher attends them gratis from six o'clock in the morning till late in the evening. How inadequate is this man's salary, although among the highest enjoyed by country school-masters. It is £11.3s.10 2/3d Sterling - the number of daily scholars last year was upwards of sixty; but before

---

78. 'The First Fifty Years', W.H. Watson, (Sunday School Union, London, c.1862) p.52.
79. According to James Miller's History of Dunbar (1859) 'a Sabbath School Society was formed in 1819: but it was about forty years earlier that Sunday Schools were established in the place' p.208.
80. MacInnes. p.257: see also pp 257-61 for background on Highland Education.

the commencement of the present War it was greater.'[81]

A theological Moderate like Carlyle of Inveresk supported the idea,[82] but the greatest initiative probably came from the Haldanes, to whom we have already referred, and it was their work which stirred up the hostility of the General Assembly of 1799 to condemn 'Vagrant teachers and Sunday Schools'.

The Edinburgh Gratis Sabbath School was founded 'to promote the religious instruction of youth, by erecting, supporting and conducting Sabbath evening schools in Edinburgh and its neighbourhood, in which schools the children should be taught the leading and the most important doctrines of the scriptures, and not the peculiarities of any denomination of Christians'. It was agreed that the schools be conducted by gratuitous teachers, and the first school was opened at Portsburgh in March 1797. By 1812 they had 44 schools and 2,200 children in attendance.[83]

In 1798 two English Baptists, Coles and Page, who were students at King's College, Aberdeen, started six Sunday Schools, one of them 'in St. Mary's Hill, below the East Church. I think there were about 1,000 people present'.[84] There were protests by the Established Church, and Mr. Morrison of Millseat was summoned before the Turriff Presbytery to explain himself. He told them 'the neglect of the clergy had rendered them necessary' and expressed his determination to persevere. Similar opposition was encountered in the south where at Lauder in 1797 and in Paisley in 1799 the Sheriff demanded to see the books being used for tuition.[85] In Glasgow the Sunday School movement was probably initiated by the Methodists: in 1783 a Wesleyan, Mr. Main, opened one in the east end of the Gallowgate, and there was another held in the High Street. The following year Dr. Taylor, the minister of the High Church

81. Old Statistical Account, Vol XIV, E.P. Publications, 1982, p.20.
82. 'In 1790, when the establishment of Sabbath Schools was regarded by his party with the greatest suspicion, he exerted himself with success to form such an institution in his parish' (Mathieson's 'Awakening of Scotland' p.210).
83. Watson p.53. The Religious Monitor for 1805 (Vol 3 p.434) says they opened 34 schools in a year.
84. Watson p.54.
85. Watson p.55.

also opened one, and the Glasgow Sabbath School Union was formed in July 1816.[86]

We have dwelt in detail on the background to the development of this work because the Sunday Schools were to provide an important channel for the revivals that followed. As early as 1805 we learn that:

> In some of the schools a few of the children meet together statedly for prayer, reading the Scriptures, and religious conversation.[87]

And two years later the tenth anniversary report of the EGSSS informs us:

> In some of the schools there are a few children who appear to be truly pious; and others, concerning whom they have good hopes, from the progress they have made in the knowledge of the Scriptures, and the attention they discover to spiritual things; some of them at times appear much impressed with what they hear.[88]

A letter of I.A. dated 18th October 1808 informs us that:

> A little before nine o'clock, on a Tuesday evening, March 1805, as I was passing by a shed, erected in a new formed street on the south side of Edinburgh, for the purpose of sawing timber, my attention was attracted by the voice of a person within it, speaking in rather a low tone. Curiosity prompted me to make a nearer approach.

He heard a youth praying inside, followed by another:

> His voice and manner seemed to indicate that he was younger than the other. Fourteen years, perhaps, might be the age of the former, ten or eleven that of the latter. He proceeded with less ease and fluency than his associate. But appeared deeply and seriously impressed ... Having finished a third engaged in prayer. He seemed, so far as I was able to judge from his voice, to be older than the second, but younger than the first, or, about twelve or

---

thirteen years. He had a delightful liberty in duty. He raised his voice higher than the others, though it was still much suppressed. His fervour was great. Several of his petitions pleased me much, being exceedingly appropriate to their condition. 'Oh Lord, whatever other children do, as for us, O may we serve Thee, the Lord! - Lord bless us, and our meetings here from time to time - Bless our teachers, and let not their labours, with respect to us and the other children in the school, be in vain...etc...' He prayed for blessing 'on all Sabbath Schools; and that the children in them might be converted unto God'. He prayed for their parents, for their masters, for the ministers of religion, for the success of the gospel, etc... I now understand, that they were boys connected with some Sabbath School, who had agreed to associate frequently (once a week probably) for mutual prayer and wishing to conceal their pious exercises from the knowledge of parents and masters, met in this retired place without the fear of being seen or heard.[89]

The Revivalist magazine in London comments:

It is delightful to learn that children in Sabbath schools throughout Scotland appear disposed to meet for prayer among themselves, unknown to their teachers.[90]

While D.A. Curnie thinks 'this practice may have been a distinctively Scottish phenomena'[91], there was a long history of small fellowship meetings: Robert Balfour, born as early as 1748, 'when he was only about twelve years of age, at that early period joined a society which met weekly for religious conversation and prayer, and on which he afterwards gave the most regular attendance'.[92] He later became minister of St. Paul's, Glasgow. When nightly meetings were held in Glasgow in 1833 there were 'upwards of seventy' inquirers, who 'are for the most part young persons. Within two months, three meetings for prayer have been spontaneously formed among these youths, each consisting of

89. R.M. Vol 6 p.542.

90. The Revivalist Vol 3 (1834) p.174, Editor, Joseph Belcher.

91. The Growth of Evangelicals in the year 1793-1843, PhD Thesis, St. Andrew's, 1990, p.358.

92. Edinburgh Christian Instructor, Vol 18 (Dec 1819) p.838.

from six to nine females; two of them are held weekly, and the third more frequently'.[93]

Circumstances also compelled ministers to increase the formal provision for their youth. Rev. Alex Macleod, who settled in Uig on Lewis in 1824, and saw his 1828 Communion attended by 9000 people, reports:

> In 1827 upwards of 600 pupils of various ages attended the schools...and in 1834 mention is made of thirteen schools in that one parish.[94]

Despite having had a Sabbath school since 1809, 'In 1823 classes on weekday evenings for the young of both sexes from 14 to 20 years were opened up by myself' writes Burns describing the background to Kilsyth.[95] In fact Couper traces the origin of the second Kilsyth revival to the Methodist Sunday School, where in 1835:

> On the last Sabbath of February, while the teacher was addressing the Sabbath School, it appeared as if an overpowering light broke in upon their minds; an unusual solemnity pervaded the school, and soon there were heard in all directions sighs and sobbings...The business of the school was stopped, and for a considerable time nothing could be heard but mingled lamentations and prayer for mercy. Meantime the hour arrived for the adult congregation to assemble for the public preaching, but the hall was pre-occupied by the young people, who could neither be removed nor restrained from crying aloud to God with groans and tears for the salvation of their souls. The congregation was, therefore, obliged to take their places in the midst of the agitated and agonising youths.[96]

One of the valuable functions of the School Unions was to collect data concerning the needs and opportunities presented by the young people of Scotland, which acted as a spur to further evangelistic efforts. For example the Sabbath School Union for Scotland, set up in January 1816, by its third report claimed 39,183 children attending, but esti-

93. The Revivalist, Vol 2, 1833, p.116.
94. Scottish Christian Herald, 16th July 1836, p.310.
95. Scottish Christian Herald, 26th October 1839.
96. Couper p.119.

mated that 200,000 young persons in Scotland had no religious instruction from home, Church or school.[97]

The magazine of the Glasgow Sabbath School Union published an editorial in May 1851 on the decreasing attendance, and in April 1855 a letter questioning the falling off in Sabbath School attendance. On the positive side, that of February 1855 notes that teachers' prayer meetings are on the increase, and in March claims 4,000 Sabbath Schools in Scotland, with 25,000 teachers and 300,000 scholars.

The first reports of the revival in America are given in June 1858, and in the September 1859 issue the story of the Baldernock revival is recalled. The first evidence of a renewed concern among children appears in November 1858, telling of two poor girls aged 10 and 11 requesting a room to pray in; when questioned these girls also admitted to leading a 'Bible Class for very little girls' themselves. Most of the stories printed were about children who died in the faith and cannot be retold here.

The October 1859 edition carries this report by an unnamed 'Correspondent':

Not the least interesting feature of the work is the interest awakened in the minds of the young regarding their immortal souls. Many young people - boys and girls - have come under deep conviction of sin, and have found peace, we humbly believe, in relying on the finished work of the Saviour. We know of a Sabbath School teacher who had the pleasure, the other evening, of conversing with three boys, scholars of his, who had formerly been the most careless of the class, but who now appear to have had their young hearts turned to the Lord. They spoke freely of their own worthlessness in God's sight, but of the wondrous love of Jesus in giving His life as a ransom for poor sinners, and obeying God's law in their stead. They seemed overwhelmed with the vast meaning conveyed by the word eternity. The awful condition of one eternally lost seemed to fill them with awe; but, on the other hand, the infinite glory of an eternity of heavenly happiness seemed a theme of delightful contemplation.

---

97. R.M. Vol 17, p.466.

We saw a New Testament which a little boy, who had lately been brought under the influence of sovereign grace, continually carried about with him. The corners of the leaves were folded in many cases, and made to point to some of the choicest portions of Scripture...We heard on unquestionably authority of two young lads who were discovered a few days ago reading a chapter together in a quiet corner of the work, during a meal hour; and we believe there are many such instances.

Tales of conversions were obviously coming in by December's issue:

We have heard of some indications of blessing to some of our Sabbath Schools. We recently conversed with a boy of about twelve or thirteen years of age, who had been a trial to the teachers and an annoyance to the school, who has now become as gentle as a lamb. He seemed truly in earnest, learning of Jesus.

In May 1860 the story is told of an eight year old girl, playing with others on a village common. When she tired she pulled out a New Testament and sung a hymn 'surrounded by a number of girls and even big boys ... Some listened, but some of the big boys laughed at the little girl.' Later she visited one 'little boy' who was ill, and he told her that he had been awakened on the common. She explained more to him, and later he died in assurance. There is also a mention of a boy named Thomas who carried a lame boy to his Sabbath School.

Other incidents concerning Sunday School children will be related in Chapter Three, so we will conclude this section with a few additional statistics which may be of some interest. In 1860 the Scottish Guardian ran an article called 'Home Evangelisation':

At a meeting in Queen Street Hall - The Lord Provost presiding - the Rev. A. Miller stated that Edinburgh had a population of 170,000 souls, and that among them it was calculated that nearly 60,000 were non-Church-going persons. There were between ninety and one hundred ministers of the Gospel belonging to the evangelical denominations, or something less that one to every two thousand inhabitants. Among the various agencies which are at work to overtake the spiritual destitution in the city, there are 160 Sabbath Schools, taught by 1,800 teachers, and attended by 18,000 pupils...of whom 3,000 were young men and women, and about 15,000 under fourteen years of age.[98]

The Rev. Dr. Mcleod claimed Scotland had 10,000 elders and 30,000 Sabbath School teachers. However, two years later Rev. J. Inglis told a meeting of the Sunday School convention in London that in Scotland 'now there are 40,000 Sabbath School teachers, and 400,000 scholars, besides about 80,000 young people instructed in minister's classes...In 1820 out of 1,700 teachers only 140 were women...now, at least half the teachers were women'.[99]

According to the Glasgow Sabbath School Magazine, by 1867 in ten years there had been an increase of 17,000 attending their schools, but there remained another 23,000 untouched.[100] The Glasgow Sabbath School Union claimed 60,464 pupils in 1866, of whom 28,474 were male, and 31,990 were female,[101] and in December 1869 there is a description of a 'Visit to a Children's Sabbath Meeting' in the City Halls, Glasgow which gathered 'hundreds of neglected immortal souls' of all ages from 'Wee things ... to fifteen'.

(g) Other Movements

The Island of Arran witnessed an awakening at the beginning of the nineteenth century, which appears to be unrelated to other work across Scotland. Under the evangelical ministry of Rev. Alex McBride of Kilmorie 'in March 1812, an unusual condition appeared among the people, and the meetings of the congregation on Sabbath began to be startled by one and another crying out in the agonies of conviction. There had been cases of this excitement in private meetings for some time before but now it appeared in the congregation and became frequent ... Some very young were among the number ... about three

98. S.G. 6th October 1860.
99. T.R. 11th September 1862.
100. S.S.M. March 1867.
101. S.S.M. June 1867.

hundred persons were brought to Christ, young and old'[102] in six months from all over the parish of Kilmorie and in parts of Kilbride. 'Among the children too, there were prayer meetings, and one who remembers those days tells how these young people might be met with coming from or going to their place of meeting, singing the praises of God by the way.'[103] Rev. Angus McMillan, who became minister of Kilbride just after the event, wrote, 'Persons of almost every description and age, from nine years or under, to that of sixty or upwards, were affected; but the number of old people were small compared with that of the young.'[104]

Another isolated report of revival comes from Mr. Carment of Rosskeen, writing in January 1841:

There has been since 1840 a very remarkable awakening and religious revival in this parish and neighbourhood, especially among the young; and numbers, I have reason to believe, have been savingly converted.[105]

102. 'Thirty years of Spiritual Life in the Island of Arran', A.A. Bonar, MacKinlay, Glasgow, 1889, pp 5-6.
103. Bonar, p.7 and Couper p.91.
104. G.R.T. No5, p.4 MacRae, p.28.
105. Annals of the Disruption, Thomas Brown, 1877, Edinburgh, p.13.

3. A Nation On Fire 1859-63

(a) Up the Clyde

On Friday 10th June, 1859, a school boy in Coleraine, Northern Ireland, was under such deep conviction of sin that he could not concentrate on his work. His teacher suggested that he ought to go home and pray by himself, and allowed another boy, who had only been converted the day before, to accompany him. On their way they passed an empty house and stopped to pray inside it, where the boy came right through into assurance of salvation. Immediately he insisted on returning to school and announcing: 'Oh, Mr.——, I am so happy; I have the Lord Jesus in my heart.' This affected the whole school in turn, and one by one the boys quietly slipped out of the classroom, and were to be seen kneeling by themselves around the walls of the playground praying silently. The teacher then asked the first boy who had been converted if he would go out and pray with them. When he began to pray for their forgiveness they broke into a bitter cry which penetrated the school, so that the boys remaining inside dropped to their knees and began to cry for mercy. The same thing happened in the girl's school which was upstairs. Parents who called in to collect their children were converted on the spot, ministers were sent for to help counsel and the school was not finally cleared until 11 p.m. that night.[1]

This revival had its origins in the New York prayer meeting started by Jeremiah Lamphier in 1857, from which it had spread across North America sweeping an estimated one million converts into the Kingdom of God, then crossing the Atlantic into Ulster early in 1859, and the rest of the British Isles later in the year, also resulting in a million conversions. In some places people touched by the revival in one place seemed to take it with them into another. At other times Christians heard reports of the movement, and set themselves to pray for a similar visitation, until it arrived spontaneously.

The events in Ireland were widely reported in Scotland. For example, the Scottish Guardian of Tuesday 26th July devotes four and a half

---

1. This is recorded in full in John Carson's 'God's River in Spate' pp 35-36 and together with many other anecdotes about children in Henry Montgomery's 'The Children in '59'.

columns of small print to the Ulster revival, about one quarter of its total news coverage! This included the following extracts:

From Belfast: On the same twelfth of July the usual bi-weekly meeting of young people was held in the Berry Street church. After an address from Mr. Hanna, a girl about ten years of age was allowed to speak, which she did with affectionate earnestness, and propriety of expression equally remarkable...The meeting, though designed for children was attended by others, and a woman who kept a house of ill fame cried out under strong conviction of sin just as the exercises were concluded.

In Ballymena, 'a boy had been found lying in a field in a helpless state' under conviction.

The following Tuesday (2nd August 1859) the same paper carried a headline 'Spiritual Awakening in the West of Scotland', detailing prayer meetings in the Religious Institute in Glasgow, and also the first report of revival in Scotland: people had been struck down in Port Glasgow on the previous Friday and:

Young men and young women, and two or three Roman Catholics have been already arrested and turned, and before the meeting separated I found a little Roman Catholic boy sitting with his Bible in his hands, saying that there was no mediator but Christ, and that he would have no other, and ever looking to Christ the Mediator to save him.

The following Tuesday's Guardian (9th August 1859) gives extensive coverage to Port Glasgow, in a one and a half column article, which states that the first 'striking down' took place as early as Monday 17th July, and that a daily prayer meeting had been held in the United Presbyterian Church, averaging 62 until July 30th when attendance suddenly shot to over 100. It also reports revival at Greenock. Port Glasgow continued to be an early centre of the movement. The next event quoted probably took place on Sunday 21st August:

On Sabbath afternoon, a little girl belonging to the Episcopal congregation was at the Free Church, and when the missionary who had been sent for visited her, she was crying to Jesus for mercy. The little girl's own minister came in, tried to soothe her and retired, after giving her a pill. The girl, we are happy to say, is now better, without using the pill, and is rejoicing in Christ.

Another little girl was seized at her work, and broke out into a bitter cry. When visited she was still crying for mercy, but made no answer when spoken to. At last, she asked that someone would pray...[2]

This article goes on to detail how the missionary used Psalm 51 in counselling, and how it eventually transpired that the girl had stolen a hymn book. Three weeks later the same newspaper details a family conversion:

In one family an old woman, a young man from Glasgow, and his little brother were all hopefully converted. The younger brother, a mere boy, now acts as a sort of local missionary among his companions in the rope-works (where he is employed) and elsewhere.[3]

Two boys from twelve to fourteen years of age, having heard of the people asking for blessings from above and receiving them, resolved that they would pray for themselves. They went to a neighbouring wood, and having offered up earnest supplication, they came home rejoicing, and are still holding on in the good path.[4]

In neighbouring Greenock, the Scottish Guardian of 16th September 1859 states: 'We hear that in Mr. Fairrie's schools there is a hopeful movement among the children' but unfortunately gives no further details. However, three other references to Greenock all record the existence of youthful prayer meetings:

There is...another evening meeting of the young. Parents testify to the great change in some of their boys attending this meeting, some conducting family worship, and Godless fathers silently looking

2. S.G. Friday 26th August 1859.
3. S.G. Friday 16th September 1859.
4. S.G. 14th January 1860

on. An employer had observed three of his boys slipping into a corner of the yard. He followed them unobserved thinking they were intending to steal. To his astonishment they all knelt down and engaged in prayer, and this has been the beginning of a meeting attended by nearly three hundred men and boys.[5]

A number of young men are zealously visiting throughout the town, and establishing meetings for prayer. Much good has been done by these young men, and a saving change has apparently come over many individuals.[6]

The work has taken the form of small private prayer meetings. You can go to some parts of the town, especially in the East End, and you will find a prayer meeting of that description in almost every second home. And I may say it is as remarkable among children as among grown up people. There are vast numbers of meetings originated and kept up by the children themselves. One large meeting in particular is kept up by boys, but it attended also by ministers or elders, who see that everything is done decently and in order.[7]

While covering the story of the Lower Clyde, it is worth including the Island of Bute from whence comes both evidence that revival meetings were held at an early stage, and that on occasions persecution followed:

The case of a little girl is also very interesting. She is about fifteen years of age and very intelligent. She has been coming to the meetings at the expense of considerable suffering to herself. She told us that every time she attended she was beaten severely, and when asked why she came when she suffered so much, she replied that the soul was of far greater value than everything else, and with wonderful perception for her years, she added, surely God saw fit to deal with her this way for wise ends, and trusted she yet would be able to say it was good for her to be thus afflicted.[8]

5. S.G. Tuesday 27th December 1859 quoting W.J. 24th December 1859.
6. S.G. 13th March 1860.
7. S.G. Tuesday 24th April 1860 and T.R. 5th May 1860.
8. S.G. Friday 9th September 1859.

This may link in with a later report that tells us that a Bible Class for young women began in July 1858:

And it was while thus engaged in searching the scriptures that the most mighty showers of blessing descended. These precious outpourings of the Holy Spirit continued for many nights. The class increased to nearly two hundred, all of whom were either anxious enquirers or were rejoicing in the ecstasy of their first love. The open air services increased too, till the number exceeded one thousand. *There were prayer meetings of* up to a hundred young women.[9]

On the north side of the River Clyde, both Dumbarton and Helensburgh were affected early. By the 9th October a report was being given at the Wynd Church in Glasgow of a meeting recently held in Dumbarton where 100 out of the 500 attending remained behind 'anxious' afterwards, and:

In a small room connected with the hall where this meeting was held, a boy addressed a number of children with regard to their soul's salvation. After much anxiety they went away and were afterwards found in groups by the roadside praying.[10]

The Freeman of 26th October 1859 carries a letter from 'J.W.' of Glasgow dated October 18th:

In Helensburgh the prayer meetings are crowded: and Mr. Anderson, the Free Church minister, stated the other evening that fifteen or sixteen little boys had spontaneously come to his vestry inquiring the way to Zion.

Further details of this period are supplied by the Rev. John Anderson himself:

Another very striking feature of the work here, as in many other places, is its effect upon the young. I think it was in the month of

9. T.R. 26th January 1861.
10. S.G. 11th November 1859 and T.R. 26th November 1859

October last that sixteen boys called on me, requesting that they might have some place where they could meet two evenings in the week to hold a prayer meeting. Several of them had been under deep conviction of sin. The Session House of the Free Church was very readily granted to them, and I have met with them ever since, to instruct and direct them. A number of the boys take part in this meeting. Their prayers are very touching, and very scriptural and brief. The attendance at this prayer meeting has always been most encouraging. Sometimes as many as sixty have been present, and it is quite refreshing to hear their hearty singing of the psalms and their favourite hymns...There is also a prayer meeting of young females which has likewise been greatly blessed.[11]

The young men of Dumbarton were used to spread the message to Bonhill where:

On Sabbath evening, about fifty out of a large Bible class taught by Mr. Parker, the devoted missionary, were brought under deep conviction of sin. Four young men from Dumbarton, had been labouring in the neighbourhood, and had said a few words to the class. Mr. Parker found groups of his young people weeping on the street, and after much time spent in his house in prayer and conversation, eighteen have professed faith in Jesus.[12]

The one thing clear from this incident is that not everyone who experiences deep conviction is necessarily converted at the end of the day.

(b) Glasgow

The revival appears to have commenced in Glasgow on the last Sunday of July in the Wynd Mission:

Sabbath last was felt to be a day of the gracious power of the Spirit in the Wynd Church...In the Sabbath School, the presence of

---

11. Wm. Reid 'Authentic Records of Revival', pp 398-9. Anderson traces the origin of this movement to the Union Prayer Meeting commenced in Grant Road School on 6th December 1858. From August 1859 it was characterised by 'aweful solemnity' (Reid pp 392-3).
12. W.J. 29th October 1859.

some special influence was also sensibly felt. One of the teachers came to Mr. McColl and said 'I can't get on with my class; they are all in tears.' [13]

The following Sunday saw similar results, when 'deeply serious impression' was made on young men:

Three of these, mere youths, though not yet able to rejoice in the Saviour with all their hearts, have already called together their companions in the workshops where they are employed, and the little band join together in prayer three times a day.[14]

A week later we read at the Wynd Mission:

On Sabbath last there was no Sabbath School, but a prayer meeting of the young, which was followed by a signal blessing. As many as thirty young persons had been awakened, and some of these had found peace in Christ.

A little girl, not belonging to the Wynd Church, but who had attended the meetings, and was deeply impressed at the first of these nightly prayer meetings, was asked the other day, if she had found peace. She said she had, and on being again asked if she was sure it was the right peace, she replied 'Oh, yes, it is *His* peace.' [15]

On Thursday 18th August 'young and old were crying and weeping for mercy' at the North Frederick Street Baptist Chapel.[16]

In the following narrative we are given clear evidence of the link between Ulster and Scotland, where the conversion of a 'little boy' over in Ireland sparked off a significant move of the Holy Spirit in the Maryhill area of Glasgow:

A good work of God appears to have commenced at Maryhill. Some time ago a little boy belonging to the village visited the

13. S.G. Friday 5th August 1859.
14. S.G. Tuesday 9th August 1859: this edition also carries other reports from Glasgow and Rutherglen as well as Greenock, plus a report of the Revival in Knapdale as quoted from the Free Church Assembly of 1845!
15. S.G. Friday 19th August 1859. 16. S.G. Tuesday 23rd August 1859

north of Ireland with his mother, and was there brought under the power of the truth. On his return he spoke to the boys of his acquaintance, and numbers appeared to be impressed. While he was speaking to his companions one day, another boy came up, and taking hold of his hand, earnestly exclaimed - 'What must I do to be saved?'... The movement has made special progress among the young and numbers of lads employed in the print works and other establishments including the very wildest of the juvenile population have been meeting together for prayer, and exhibiting concern about the state of their souls.[17]

Shortly after this another eyewitness testified to what they saw in Maryhill:

Many young people...boys and girls...have come under deep conviction of sin, and have found peace, we humbly believe, in relying on the finished work of the Saviour. We know of a Sabbath School teacher who had the pleasure, the other evening, of conversing with three boys, scholars of his, who had formerly been the most careless in the class, but who now appear to have had their young hearts turned to the Lord. They spoke freely of their own worthlessness in God's sight, but of the wondrous love of Jesus, in giving His life a ransom for poor sinners, and obeying God's laws in their stead. They seemed overwhelmed with the vast meaning conveyed by the word eternity. The awful condition of one eternally lost seemed to fill them with awe; but, on the other hand, the infinite glory of an eternity of heavenly happiness seemed a theme of delightful contemplation.

We saw a New Testament, which a little boy, who had lately been brought under the influence of Sovereign Grace, continually carried about with him. The corners of the leaves were folded in in many cases, and made to point to some of the choicest portions of scripture, such as 'Come unto Me all ye who are heavy laden,' etc...'God so loved the world...everlasting life.'

17. T.R. 3rd September 1859 and S.G. 23rd August 1859. This boy appears again in W.J. of 8th October 1859 visiting Newport on Tay which relates 'he and a few other young men commenced to keep meetings.' Presumably in Maryhill?

We heard on unquestionable authority of two young lads who were discovered a few days ago reading a chapter together, in a quiet corner of the work during a meal hour; and we believe there are many such instances.[18]

Many of the Sunday schools in different parts of the City reported remarkable awakenings within a short space of time, for example in Finnieston Mission Church:

Yesterday evening, after the services in the Sabbath School at Finnieston, over one hundred of the scholars out of three hundred remained for prayer and conversation with their teachers, in anxiety about their souls. One of the Sabbath school teachers was absent from the school because she felt that she wanted Christ for her own soul.[19]

This continued the following Sunday, as Andrew Bonar's Diary records for 4th September:

Very solemn today; evidently much prayer is going up. Prayer meeting in evening, at the close of which a great number of the Sabbath scholars waited behind to speak: six of them in bitter distress.

The seeds however, may have been planted much earlier, because on the Monday evening of 2nd August 1858 he had noted:

While addressing the children, very remarkable stillness as I urged them to receive Christ, now.

A later report headed Finnieston Free Church states that 'Many of the young people in the Sabbath School have been awakened, and some of them have found joy and peace in believing.'[20]

Similar events took place in East Gorballs; as this selection of reports reveal:

---

18. S.G. Friday 13th September 1859.
19. S.G. Tuesday 30th August 1859.
20. S.G. Tuesday 4th October 1859.

East Gorballs Free Church Mission: daily prayer meetings during the last fortnight. There has been a surprising movement too in the Sabbath School. A number of the wildest boys - boys, who, under the mild discipline of the Sabbath School, could scarcely be restrained from injuring the furniture, have been brought under serious impressions. On Sabbath week, the Superintendent, teachers, and a number of young converts engaged in very earnest prayer for a blessing on the children, and while the closing address was being delivered, a few were seen weeping. Thirteen, on invitation being given, remained, anxious about their souls. They wept bitterly because of their sins. On being instructed in the way of salvation, and prayed with, a change came over their appearance, their faces beamed with joy. On being asked the reason, they said, 'Because Jesus has come and taken away all our sins.' Last Sabbath the school was larger than usual, many of these having brought their comrades. About fourteen were brought under conviction, but after being instructed and prayed with, a considerable number seemed to find relief and joy. Of course, time alone will thoroughly test the depth and truth of their conversions and their peace, but in the meantime there is an undoubted change in the outward aspects and bearing of the children, and the hearts of their teachers are greatly rejoiced.[21]

East Gorballs Free Church: There is a movement going on in the territorial school in connection with this Church. A number of boys meet together for prayer amongst themselves.[22]

East Gorballs Free Church Mission: The awakening had been very marked among the boys...The Children's prayer meeting which was held at the close of the ordinary service in an adjoining room. To this apartment upwards of one hundred children retired, accompanied by the missionary and one or two friends...This meeting, which lasted about half an hour, was conducted by three of the boys, from eleven to thirteen years of age. The exercises

---

21. S.G. Tuesday 13th September 1859.
22. S.G. 4th October 1859 and T.R. 15th October 1859

were simply praise and prayer, and more earnest or appropriate
supplication I never heard presented to the throne of grace. They
seemed the very outgushings of the renewed heart, just delivered
from the bondage of sin and rejoicing in Jesus, and the liberty
wherewith he makes free...The missionary informed me, that on
Saturday evening they have no meetings in the school-room, and
as the boys cannot let one night pass without praying together,
they meet in each other's houses, and he believes that numerous
cases of conviction and conversion are the result.[23]

East Gorballs Mission Sabbath School: One Sabbath lately, as
the Superintendent was giving the closing address, many of the
boys, who had hitherto been rude and careless, were observed to
shed tears, and others appeared to be deeply distressed in mind...[24]

*William Hood, the Superintendent of the East Gorballs Free
Church Sabbath School wrote on 26th December 1859:* Last
Sabbath some of the teachers and a few converts met before the
school assembled for prayer. Great solemnity pervaded the large
school especially at the close. The anxious were asked to wait.
The room was crowded. One girl who was happy in Jesus, prayed
earnestly, for those present who were in distress. They were then
addressed by the Superintendent, and were urged to decide for
Christ. After which a young boy poured out the desires of his
heart in language most touching. Several gave testimony to the
love and power of Jesus and His willingness to save. During the
past eight or ten weeks the 'inquirer's room' has been filled every
night.[25]

William Reid furnishes us with this account by the Superintendent:
The East Gorballs Free Church Mission District Sabbath School opened
eighteen months ago. 'For some time very few scholars came forward,
and those who did so were more like the children of barbarous parents

23. S.G. 25th October 1859.
24. S.G. 21st October 1859 and T.R. 5th November 1859 quoting the Sabbath School
Messenger for November.
25. W.J. 31st December 1859 and T.R. 7th January 1860

than anything else. They were very ignorant unruly and ungodly.' The brick floor was torn up and thrown at the teacher. 'Our scholars were given to swearing, lying, quarrelling, and fighting with each other; and we prayed and laboured amongst them for a considerable period without seeing any visible improvement in the conduct of any.' When they moved to the Commercial Road Academy, numbers increased. Mr. Gilchrist, their missionary, visited the Ardrossan revival. They prayed on Sabbath September 11th for half an hour before Sabbath School. 'During the closing address at the class not a few were seen in tears and some were crying out loud. I intimated at the close that those who were anxious about their souls might remain. Many did so, thirteen of whom were in bitter agony of soul, crying in despair. One who was a swearer and Sabbath breaker, said he felt himself on the very brink of hell. Some of those who were awakened that night had hitherto been our most troublesome scholars: now they were exclaiming "Oh! my sins," "Oh, what will I do?" It seemed as if the Holy Spirit had shed a flood of light upon their hearts, and revealed a whole life of sin in the space of a few minutes. Casting themselves wholly upon Christ, many found peace in believing, and went away with hearts overflowing with joy.'

Next Sabbath, September 18th, there was more special prayer and an increase in attendance by half. 'While the closing address was being delivered, many present were deeply impressed, and two or three uttered despairing cries. As there seemed to be a number of anxious inquirers, such were invited to repair to the anxious inquirer's room, and by the time I got over to address them, the place was quite filled. Sixteen persons sat weeping, wringing their hands and crying for mercy.' From then on 'there have been cases of conviction every night,' sometimes up to twenty four at one time.[26]

In Springburn the most marked influences were felt by the girls:

At a meeting lately held, a number of persons were in much trouble of mind about their sins, particularly a number of girls about ten or twelve years of age. One in particular sobbed bitterly, shortly afterwards she found peace of mind. After an illness of three days from Scarlet Fever, this girl died last week.

---

26. Wm. Reid 'Authentic Records of Revival' pp 266ff

During a portion of the time she was insensible. Shortly before she died the delirium left her, and her mother asked if she loved her. She said she did, but also said 'I so love Jesus.' She desired those about her to send for a certain person to pray with her, and tell her about Jesus, she would not listen to anything else. About an hour before her death the delirium again returned, and she continually gave utterance to the word 'Jesus', and died with the word on her lips.[27]

On Monday evening a number of girls between twelve and sixteen years of age who had been in an anxious state for some weeks, were rejoicing in their Saviour.[28]

There are so many other accounts about which we lack further information, for example:

A prayer meeting at Bridgeton, which originated with five boys, is now attended by about fifty, and held three or four times a week.[29]
An elder of East Campbell Street Free Church reports: Not a few girls from nine to twelve years have been deeply convinced, and made sensibly alive to the value of their immortal souls.[30]
Free St. Luke's: The movement has been most perceptible among the young, but the awakening has not been confined to them. From the child of nine...persons are found to be labouring under deep convictions of sin, and earnestly inquiring what they must do to be saved.[31]
Mr. Gardiner's meetings in Murdoch's School, Blackfriar's Street: Saturday evening...a little girl from the country, who had accidentally dropped in to the meeting, was melted down under deep emotions. Upon her knees she pleaded with Jesus to save her soul. Her prayer seemed to be heard, for, ere long, with a glowing countenance, she came forwards rejoicing in God her Saviour who had washed away her sins in His atoning blood.[32]
Letter from J.W., Glasgow, dated 14th March: The attendance at

27. S.G. 29th November 1859.
28. S.G. Thursday 26th January 1860 and T.R. 4th February 1860.
29. T.R. 31st December 1859. 30. S.G. Tuesday 4th October 1859.
31. S.G. Thursday 9th February 1860. 32. S.G. Tuesday 10th January 1860.

the children's meeting held in Brunswick Street has increased so much that it has been removed to a chapel for larger accommodation.[33]

At the prayer meeting held in 198 Stirling's Road (presumably Glasgow): Some children who attended with their parents, requested the place for prayer by themselves. Last Tuesday one little girl secured the attendance of about twenty others.[34]

In the village of Tolcross the Glasgow City missionary has a Bible class attended by about sixty young persons upwards of fourteen years of age, some of whom are rejoicing in the Saviour and hungering and thirsting after great grace.[35]

The Revival of 22nd September 1860 simply states that many children were touched during meetings held on Saturday 8th September in the Free Gaelic Church, Bridgegate.

In Duntocher teenagers are singled out for special mention. On Tuesday 13th December 1859 the Scottish Guardian reports a prayer meeting held the previous Wednesday in a large schoolroom of between four and five hundred people 'the great portion of whom were young men and women from fifteen to thirty years of age' to which The Revival adds 'various young persons are holding prayer meetings in one another's houses, and are not ashamed to make profession of the Lord Jesus.' [36] The Guardian of December 20th follows this story with the news of girls of 15, 13 and 17 under conviction of sin.

The Wynd Church was very much at the centre of revival activities, organising prayer meetings and disseminating information through the Wynd Journal from October 1859.[37] A second wave appears to have touched them the following February:

The Wynd Sabbath Schools: During the last few weeks an unusual interest has been awakened among the children...A number

33. T.F. 21st March 1860.
34. W.J. 25th February 1860. 35. W.J. 21st April 1860.
36. T.R. 24th December 1859.
37. See W.J. editorial in 26th November 1859 for summary of progress at the Wynd. Also in 12th November 1859 the testimony of a 17 year old given to a meeting there of anxious inquirers is given in full.

of boys who had professed to have found peace have also met for prayer by themselves, and the Lord is graciously answering prayer in converting others.[38]

A week later The Freeman of 20th February 1860 carries a letter by 'J.W.' noting an 'unusual interest' in the Wynd Sabbath Schools, leading to the start of a boy's prayer meeting. There is, however, evidence of a continuing and steady work among their young people:

Wynd Mission, Lyceum Room: At the Wynd Church last Tuesday night, thanks were offered for five scholars who were awakened the previous Sabbath and found peace in believing. For several weeks the teachers have had to wait with distressed children. The Spirit is graciously applying their instructions.[39]

The Wynd Journal of 31st March 1860 gives a report of their Sabbath School, claiming 654 pupils enrolled, of whom 197 were above 15 years of age, with an average attendance of about 500:

Those 650 children were not brought under Sabbath School tuition without active and persevering efforts on the part of those who undertook the task of gathering in so many. A large proportion of them were wandering about the streets like wild Arabs over the desert.

The teachers are very thankful for the awakening among the children in August last, and for several successive months, indeed for so long as the teachers continued to wrestle for the blessing; but no sooner was the prayer meeting of teachers (held immediately before the opening of the school) given up than spiritual deadness began to appear among the children.

Surely a warning to us all?

We are particularly fortunate in that the history of the Wynd Church at this period was fully written up and analysed by its minister, obviously intended to be a guide to what today we would call 'urban church planting'. Rev. D. Maccoll was inducted to the Wynd Free Church when

---

38. W.J. 11th February 1860.
39. S.G. 28th February 1860 and W.J. 25th February 1860

it was opened after a complete rebuilding in August 1854. He saw the need for a similar work to be established in the Bridgegate, and pioneered this building project from the Wynd, transferring himself to be the new minister there in June 1860, and being succeeded at the Wynd by Robert Howie. Thus he served in both charges at the height of the revival in Glasgow. It is a fascinating account, but we must confine ourselves to his references to the place of children in the work.

His treasurer David Cunninghame had pointed out that local people were not responding to invitations to the Sunday afternoon service because those attending were too well dressed. Thus they inaugurated a 'Sabbath Evening Service for People in Working Clothes.' [40] One Sunday evening:

> A young lad had walked eight miles from a country village to be with us. He was present at the morning and afternoon services, and, much impressed, waited at a friend's for the evening. He was at the door early, indeed before it was opened; but he had to stand aside till a long array of poor, bare-footed, ragged people were with difficulty passed. 'Here,' he thought, 'are the thieves and the harlots entering the Kingdom before me; and, after I have come so far, I may be left out.' Silent tears and prayers followed, there in the crowd. I found him at the close of the service among others waiting...He came back even after his day's work, many a night, with another youth equally in earnest. At last he found peace, prepared for college, and is now a minister of the gospel. [41]

To us today it seems incredible that any 'young lad', as yet unsaved, should walk 16 miles nightly to attend a prayer meeting, yet such stories are not uncommon. Maccoll continues:

> We had great difficulty in finding room in our small church for these crowds. We became ingenious in packing. Pew and passage became one solid mass. The platform close up to the desk would be filled out with the children, and thus the word fired at these dense masses did the greater execution. [42]

40. Maccoll 'Work in the Wynds', p. 135.
41. Maccoll pp 260-1. 42. Maccoll p. 261.

Commitment from the office-bearers and love within the congregation characterised the work:

> One night I found, at the late meeting, two lads of sixteen years of age already members of the church, sitting in a corner with their open Bibles. One had already been conversing with me. I had noticed the other in an anxious state. Well, Johnny, I said, what are you and George doing here? I am trying to clear up his doubts, said Johnny. What does he doubt? His interest in Christ. Well, what are you doing? I am pointing him to the blood. But is he not looking there already? Perhaps he is, but I am telling him to look till it grows on him![43]

Physical manifestations were rare:

> We had not many 'stricken cases' as they were called. During the nightly meetings that continued for many months, when scores of persons were frequently in distress, not more than perhaps a dozen persons were affected with entire physical prostration. These were all young girls; one or two seemed, from their violent convulsions and outcries, as if possessed; the others, some of whom were well educated, remained for hours calm but unconscious. We attached no value to these physical manifestations. They were evidently connected with great mental emotion. Some of these cases were followed by conversion, and some not.[44]

Maccoll seems to have had a great gift of mobilising his whole church into outreach:

> Halls and school-rooms and kitchens were opened in scores by men, and even by boys. There was not a village within walking distance round Glasgow that was not visited by some of these, preaching and scattering tracts.[45]

The Bridgegate church was built with an outside stone pulpit for use in open-air preaching. It was successfully used in the summer of 1860, despite some threats of trouble, but in 1861 the Lord Provost and

---

43. Maccoll pp 262-3. 44. Maccoll p.293. 45. Maccoll pp 337-8.

Sheriff-Principal obtained an interdict prohibiting its use for fear of riots instigated by the Catholics. For two years the outreach service was transferred to the City Hall, again for people in working clothes.

When we were about to vacate the church every Sabbath afternoon, my friend Mr. Smith proposed to employ it for the children, and here during the two years we occupied the City Hall we carried on a special Service, which was soon attended by about five hundred. This was conducted, not as a sabbath school, but as a children's church, and was wondrously helpful in training the children into church-going habits, and bridging the chasm between the school and the church. This service became very popular. Conductor's of sabbath schools frequently visited it, and in a short time nearly sixty similar though smaller meetings were organised throughout the city. Some of the children, above twelve years of age, were trained as a visitation agency, after the model of our adult method, and thus about thirty of these young visitors would issue after morning service and bring in children from the houses and the streets. This service continues now under the superintendence of another elder, Mr. J.D. Gauld, whose devotion to this and other work is beyond all praise. Various office-bearers and sabbath school teachers take part. They meet still at two o'clock, but in the hall under the church, and we hear the young voices rising in their happy hymns and mingling faintly with our service above. Parents often leave their children there, and get them as they leave.

During the last six years much precious fruit has been gathered from this field. Children of drunken fathers and heart-broken mothers have not only been blessed but made a blessing, carrying home the first real peace and prosperity for ten or twenty years. Others have come regularly, though attacked by their companions and beaten by their parents. One has brought eleven; another seven; several leave the sabbath school to plead with others at home to come with them to the evening service. Their love of mission work is most touching. One girl, now at work, in order to have something to give, lays aside her 'sugar money'. A little fellow came back with his mission card and tenpence he had collected, saying, I have nothing but my rabbit, and a boy in the close has promised me sixpence for it! Another little fellow, losing two fingers at his work, was carried to the Infirmary, but found he could still do something for Jesus. In the bed next him was a little sweep, whose face had been sometimes seen in the meeting. Him he taught to pray, and for another in the same ward he searched passages from a large type Bible, and tried to explain their meaning. These children have not only their regular contributions for Foreign Missions, but for the sick amongst themselves, while a few of the older children give a penny a week to educate six poorer than themselves.[46]

Dr. Roxburgh, the Convener of the Free Church Home Mission Committee told the Glasgow Presbytery:

I have seen much to show that this is a remarkable time in Scotland - a day of gracious visitation.[47]

Outbreaks of revival manifestations continued throughout the city for at least two years. For example, on Sunday evening, 29th July 1860 at some time after 11 p.m. 'A boy of about fifteen years of age cried out bitterly, and a girl was for a time in painful distress' in the Bridgegate Church.[48] Also in Bridgegate Mission, a stranger on the previous Sabbath:

...had become interested in the case of a little ragged boy sitting beside him in the gallery. He had no friends, was fatherless and motherless, ran occasional messages during the day, and slept on stairs at night. The stranger made him promise to attend on the Thursday evening following, and in his note from a distance, requested the minister to look for him. At the night the boy came, clothes were purchased, a friend gave him employment and found a lodging. On Sabbath evening he was received into the school. In the class a scholar beside him asked if he had given his heart to Jesus. The boy was awakened and burst into tears: other two boys

46. Maccoll pp 355-7, extracts quoted in T.R. 24th October 1867.
47. S.G. Tuesday 21st February 1860.
48. S.G. Tuesday 31st July 1860 states this to be at Wynd Church, but on 2nd August 1860 corrects it to Bridgegate!

became distressed. The lesson had to be stopped, and three young believers in succession prayed for the other three. All were removed to a private room, where the young Benjamins and Manassehs, with strong crying and tears interceded for their brethren. Some girls from other classes had also to be removed from the school, much distressed. With thankful hearts their teachers saw these dear lambs joyfully yielding their hearts to the Saviour. A serious impression was made on all the school at the close, on hearing these things. With raised hands, all engaged to pray during the week for a great blessing on the school next Sabbath...At the prayer meeting afterwards in the church among many interesting cases was that of a young girl. The brethren who waited with her were forcibly reminded of the child possessed with a devil, who tore him and cast him to the ground. In convulsions and despair, for three long hours she cried 'I'm lost. I'm lost.' But again did Jesus cast out the devil, and she followed, praising God.[49]

One characteristic of the 1859 revival was the stress played upon prayer meetings. These were held daily in the Religious Institute Rooms in Glasgow, and evidently attended by both children and young people:

Union Prayer Meeting at Religious Institution Rooms. Reginald Radcliffe was present, but took no part in the proceedings, as he was in a weak state of health. At the close, however, the chairman said that, there being a large number of children in the meeting, Mr Radcliffe felt he could not let them depart without saying a few words to them, and he therefore desired them to remain after the grown up people had left. This announcement had more than the desired affect, for the adults remained as well as the children. After delivering an appropriate and affectionate address, Mr Radcliffe invited such of the children as might desire to speak personally to him to remain after the meeting had separated.[50]

Religious Institute Rooms daily Prayer Meeting. 'One feature of the meeting during the past week has been the large attendance of young people with much earnestness.'[51]

---

49. W.J. 22nd September 1860.
50. S.G. Tuesday 13th September 1859. 51. S.G. Tuesday 8th November 1859.

We have already instanced cases of children meeting together to pray spontaneously, but at some time during 1860 organised children's prayer meetings were commenced on a regular basis:

GLASGOW CHILDREN'S PRAYER MEETING. The weekly public children's prayer meeting, usually held in the Religious Institute Rooms, was held on Saturday in Hope Street Free Gaelic Church. The area of the Church was crowded by children and their guardians, and there were also a good many in the galleries. Mr. David Kerr presided, and the meeting was addressed by the chairman, Mr. Gordon Furlong, Mr. Radcliffe, the Rev. G. Flindt, etc. Prayer and praise were frequently engaged in. Towards the close of the services the young people who were anxious about their souls were invited to meet with Mr Radcliffe and Mr. Furlong in the adjoining Session House. So many repaired to these places that ultimately it was found necessary to request them to keep their seats in the church, that they might be conversed with there. It is right to explain that many of the children appeared to accept the invitation to retire merely from curiousity, or because desired to go by their parents or guardians. There is no room, however, to doubt that good was accomplished; and yesterday, at the prayer meeting in the Religious Institute Rooms, there were requests for prayer on behalf of one who had been awakened at the meeting and for thanksgiving on behalf of another who had been awakened and had since found peace.[52]

There are now three children's prayer meetings established in the town. One, we think in Mr Howie's Wynd Church, for the children in the East district. Another, where it has always been held, in Ewing Place Chapel, to suit the convenience of the large numbers in the children of the town, and the third one in the College Hall for the accommodation of the children of the better classes. And by this provision it is hoped that the wants of all classes and localities will be met.[53]

---

52. S.G. Tuesday 11th September 1860.
53. S.G. 9th April 1861.

In February 1861 E.P. Hammond[54] came to Glasgow and addressed meetings specifically for children as well as meetings of children and adults together:

> *Glasgow, 2nd March:* Mr Hammond addressed a large children's meeting in the Free College Church on Saturday at noon. Many of the children appeared to be labouring under deep concern about religion, and Mr. Hammond and other friends were engaged conversing with inquirers till four o'clock.[55]
>
> The church was full; the centre, from the pulpit to the farthest wall, densely packed with children of all ages. Children don't go where they don't get something that interests and suits them. It has been a time of great feasting and gladness for the children since Mr Hammond came. They find out that religion is something come-at-able by them; that they are of importance and have their place. Children are beginning to feel that they are recognised, a new and grateful feeling in the heart of the children of the poor.[56]
>
> *Glasgow:* Among the young also, those who have been converted are in their love eager to tell those of their own age of the Saviour. One little fellow was found praying with another boy who was in distress waiting for Mr. Hammond's return for the blessing. On questioning him, he said he thought that he always loved Christ, but one night in the meeting, when speaking to an anxious boy, he 'took a great shaking' when he found he was not sure of his own salvation. On asking him if he was always witnessing for Jesus, he said the boys in the workshop tried him sorely, but one was now converted, and they were praying for the others.[57]

Specialised meetings for children continued on into 1862. In April Harrison Ord was in Glasgow:

> An interesting meeting for children was held in the Wynd Church on Friday evening. Among the inquirers was a little girl some twelve years old in great distress. She thought she had given her

---

54. See later section on Edinburgh, pages 149-50.
55. S.G. 5th March 1861 and W.J. 9th March 1861.
56. S.G. 26th March 1861. 57. W.J. 4th May 1861.

heart to God twelve months ago. "But I don't love him as I used to. I am a backslider." While telling her that if we confess our sins, He is faithful and just to forgive, she said abruptly, 'Please, Sir, can you tell me how to drive the devil away?' 'Does he tempt you?' 'Oh yes, I have often said, get thee behind me Satan, but it's no use.' 'Try, then, this one thing: show him, the blood of Jesus.' 'I did so, Sir, and he left for a little while, but he soon came back again.' Then show him the blood again and again!'[58]

Hammond returned at the end of the year:

At least two thousand children and adults in Dr. Ormiston's Church. Some twelve churches have joined in the movement. I have just come this morning from an inquiry meeting, appointed especially for the children. Several hundreds were present and very many of them were in tears. I could but feel that the Spirit of God was present convicting of sin. The dear ministers seem most hearty in the work.[59]

Meanwhile the presence of children continues to be noticed in other meetings. For instance at a revival meeting in the Glasgow City Hall:

The chair was occupied by Mr. David Smith, Trongate, who was supported by a number of persons, chiefly youths, while the back seats on the platform were almost entirely filled by boys and girls... The meeting was eloquently addressed by four young men, one of whom follows the occupation of a chimney sweep.[60]

And at the Saturday evening prayer meetings in 'Mr. G.'s house', The Revival describes people sitting on planks and 'an additional row of children set upon the face of the sideboard in front.' [61] There is also a reference to an 'Awakening in a female seminary in Glasgow' [62] which is frustratingly anonymous, but may refer to a move in a Free Church School.

---

58. T.R. 26th April 1862.

59 'Word and Work' (a continuation of the Wynd Journal at the end of 1862), 19th December 1862.

60. S.G. 24th November 1860.

61. T.R. 5th October 1861. 62. W.J. 27th April 1861

Before we finally leave Glasgow let us also visit one last Sunday School as reported by the Glasgow Sabbath School Magazine:

A Teacher writes: Visited this evening a Sabbath-School in Gallowgate. There are 20 girls and 10 boys of an average attendance; 10 of the girls are above 15 years of age. This is one of the most interesting schools I have visited. The teacher's heart is so much in her work that she teaches a class on Sabbath morning as well as the one in the evening. God has been very graciously blessing her labours during the last eighteen-months; no less than eight grown-up girls having been awakened in this school, who are now rejoicing in having found Christ, and giving good evidence of a saving change having taken place. A very interesting boy has been awakened. His mother came to the teacher wondering what was the matter with him. He would get up in the bed during the night, and begin singing hymns, praying, and reading the Bible. She thinks that he, too, has found Christ. One night, shortly after the Lord began the work of his Spirit, a number of the girls were so much affected, that they went to the Green and had a prayer-meeting among the trees, and ever since He has been graciously blessing the work.[63]

A fuller description of a Bridgegate Sabbath School meeting and one of Hammond's children's meetings held at the Wynd Church are given in Appendix C.

(c) Beyond Glasgow

In Kirkintilloch the first references to children reveal them coming under deep conviction of sin. The Scottish Guardian carries the story that on the previous Sabbath 'a young girl was struck down in the Free Church Sabbath School and had to be taken into the vestry.'[64] The following week it tells how an eleven year old girl was carried into the Wesleyan meeting after being struck down in the Free Sabbath School,[65] the latter presumably being her home church? The focus of attention then becomes the Wesleyan Church:

---

63. W.J. 7th September 1861.
64. S.G. Tuesday 11th October 1859. 65. S.G. Tuesday 18th October 1859.

On the evening of the half yearly fair: 'One young person in deep conviction seemed almost convulsed; she lay back as pale as death, but fully absorbed in the interest of her state, for while the hymn was sung, *My God is reconciled His pardoning voice I hear* she started up, and with a countenance now radiant with joy, with upraised arms walked up and down the pew, exclaiming, 'My God is reconciled. My Jesus.' Amid this rapturous deliverance, other penitents laid hold of the hope set before them in the gospel and rejoiced together.'[66]

Children are noted as being in attendance at the church's daily prayer meeting,[67] and a 'correspondent' of the Scottish Guardian later recalls the work in the Sabbath School and its resulting prayer meeting

During the revival not unfrequently the hoary haired and the little child met at the feet of Jesus, and together sought and obtained mercy, but of late, the number of children thus found at the Redeemer's feet have been very considerable, and prayer meetings for the young, and conducted by them, have sprung up in various parts of the town. In the Wesleyan Sabbath school many of the children have been the subjects of this gracious work, evinced in the general aspect of the school —in an increased and regular attendance—in good order and behaviour—in reverence and solemnity during devotion— in attention and earnestness in the lessons of God's Word—and a relish for spiritual things, with love for prayer.

To encourage and strengthen 'the new-born lambs', the teachers set apart one evening of the week for the Sabbath Scholars Prayer Meeting, which has proved a great blessing, and under the watchful care and superintendence of the teachers, is calculated to promote the children's piety, and haste the glorious harvest of the Sabbath school. This interesting meeting is the children's meeting - they engage in prayer to the number of nine or ten during the allotted hour. Their language is astonishing, and no less remarkable their earnest pleading and deep solemnity. They seem to come direct to the throne of God, and with the simplicity of a

66. S.G. Friday 4th November 1859. 67. T.R. 19th November 1859

child, and the sublimity of the language of the sacred writers, make known their wants and supplications by prayer unto God. Great concern is also manifested by the young converts for their friends and companions. Using a New Testament phrase, 'they bring them to Jesus', and at the means of grace, earnestly plead for them. There is much cause of rejoicing and thanksgiving to almighty God for this work among the future and the hope of the church.[68]

One further story remains from the Kirkintilloch area, in a letter from 'D.M.' to the Wynd Journal dated 11th January 1960:

At the Hillhead prayer meeting on Sabbath evening the first instant, a good many anxious souls remained at the close for further prayer and counsel, of whom five professed to find peace before leaving. One of these was a little boy, about eleven years of age, who, when advised to go home on account of the lateness of the hour, replied that he would stay to see what Jesus would do for his soul: he was not disappointed in his wish, for before he left, he was rejoicing in a crucified Saviour...On Sabbath last, a scene of similar description took place at which six professed to find peace. The little boy above mentioned was again present, and appeared very happy. He engaged in prayer, and prayed earnestly for those who were anxious in the meeting, for his father and mother, and for his brothers and sisters. A pleasing circumstance is, that young females, who have themselves lately believed in Jesus, have no hesitation in engaging in prayer for those around under conviction.[69]

Further south, in Hamilton, by the end of October 1859 'many young people are among the converts' and 'A meeting composed exclusively of boys has likewise been held for some time. Upwards of one hundred assemble together for prayer and devotional exercises.'[70] The Hamilton Advertiser reports almost nightly meetings held in various churches and draws attention to 'the large meetings of the young of both sexes.'[71]

68. S.G. 26th April 1860.
69. W.J. 21st January 1860.
70. S.G. Tuesday 25th October 1859 and W.J. 29th October 1859.
71. S.G. Tuesday 15th November 1859.

An anonymous letter reports that at a Wesleyan meeting held in Craigen's Hall:

> One or two boys, apparently about twelve or fourteen years of age, took a prominent part in the devotional exercises which they did in so earnest and forcible a manner that many were much impressed.[72]

At Hamilton Town Mission, Mr. George Dykes:

> Requested a friend to make a few statements to his Sabbath Scholars respecting a Sabbath School that had existed in Ireland some thirty years ago: how the children there had formed a prayer meeting, how the Lord had heard their prayers for themselves, their friends, and for a large district of country around them.
>
> An appeal was made to the children present, Would they go and do likewise? The hint was taken and acted on immediately. One meeting was begun, then another, until they have attained their present number.
>
> On one occasion, an individual went, through mere curiosity, to visit a boy who had been stricken the day before, and putting the question, 'Well, my lad, how old are you?', the boy started to his feet, and raising his hands and his eyes to heaven with the most intense earnestness in prayer, he replied, 'I am but a day old: O Lord thou knowest that I have lived twelve years a hell-deserving sinner. God be merciful to me a sinner, and pardon all my sin, for Christ's sake, Amen.' The aged one bowed the head; the heart was touched by this unexpected answer, and retirement was immediately sought for reflection and prayer.[73]

A letter from 'J.H.' dated Hamilton, 16th January 1860, states:

> On the following Friday evening in the Congregational Chapel, the arm of the Lord was revealed in still greater power. There a young lad who had come to the meeting through idle curiosity,

---

72. W.J. 21st January 1860.
73. W.J. 4th February 1860.

who had seldom prayed before, and who had never prayed in public was stricken. After a severe struggle of half an hour, he burst out in such earnest prayer, in such soul-piercing strains that the hardest hearts melted. This was electric: the Lord himself did give the Word. Cries for mercy were heard in all parts of the house...On these two nights about forty were added to the church.[74]

Further south at Larkhall a teenager's public prayer released the revival at the Religious Institute Rooms last Sabbath:

At the close of the last speaker's remarks, a young lad about sixteen or seventeen years of age burst out into the most eloquent and touching prayer, and by that means with God's Spirit, brought a great many to cry out for mercy. Twenty or thirty were in an anxious or prostrated state.[75]

And at lunch time a prayer meeting is found in the local school:

The more advanced scholars attending the Parochial School prefer, during the interval at midday, to hold religious exercises rather than divert themselves with their wonted plays and amusements. The correct sentiments uttered, and the good common sense evinced, as well as the piety exhibited on these occasions are strikingly astonishing, beyond what might be expected of boys at their age.[76]

At Holytown:

The revival has extended to the young. One night lately a boy, fourteen years of age, who had been under conviction for a fortnight, fell down on his knees, and with a heavy load at his chest, implored the Lord for mercy, which he speedily obtained. On the following evening, at the close of the public prayer meeting, several boys were dealt with in tears. They have since

---

74. W.J. 28th January 1860. The context of this extract is not clear and could refer to events as early as the preceding August.

75. S.G. Tuesday 18th October 1859.

76. S.G. Tuesday 29th November 1859.

been observed holding meetings by themselves for prayer. One or two sudden deaths have made a solemn impression on the community - the hearts of many have been melted and subdued.[77]

On Thursday 22nd November 1860 E.P. Hammond commenced nightly services in Motherwell Free Church and a correspondent of the Scottish Guardian informs us:

On Sabbath and Monday nights there were hundreds of such inquirers - old men and young men, matrons and girls, parents and children together.[78]

Revival usually acts as a stimulus for evangelistic activity, and in August 1861 the Airdrie Advertiser records:

A Sabbath School was to be opened in the hall of the Independent Chapel on the morning of Sabbath last, at ten o' clock, for the ingathering of those children who are running wild and careless about the streets.[79]

There are two other accounts of events in Sabbath Schools, but in neither are we given any idea of the location:

In a village near Glasgow on a Sabbath evening lately, a teacher was reading to her class the case of the conversion of a little boy. It was blessed to the awakening of a boy, about ten years of age, who became very distressed. She took him aside and prayed with him, and had the happiness of seeing him rejoice in the Lord. The next Sabbath the boy was asked to give thanks in the class for his own conversion, and to pray for his fellow scholars, numbering about thirty, from the ages of six to sixteen. While he was praying, seven of the scholars were awakened, and became so distressed that the rest of the class had to be dismissed. The anxious were taken to the teacher's house...*where they professed faith in Jesus.*[80]

---

77. S.G. Saturday 21st January 1860.
78. S.G. Thursday 29th November 1860. 79. S.G. 20th August 1861.
80. W.J. 5th May 1860 and T.F. 23rd May 1860.

In a country Sabbath class...On a recent Sabbath, while the teacher was reading of the revival among the miners, given by the Rev. Mr. Alexander of Duntocher in an early number of the Journal, an arrow reached the heart of a little boy, for whom his teacher was concerned, his life being in daily danger from the choke damp in the mine in which he is employed. Kneeling on a chair, he poured out the burden of his heart, and was at last enabled to sing: 'I love Jesus, yes I do; Jesus smiles and loves me too.'...A tiny little girl became much distressed. She went home with a heart full to breaking. Her parents, hitherto indifferent, were awakened and now made alive to their sin in neglecting the spiritual training of their children, one of whom had thus been cared for by others. They prayed for themselves and their child all night till morning came and the father had to go to his work. A young sister said to the still crying child, 'Come away to the park, we'll have more room to pray there.' The mother was busy preparing breakfast. While doing so she was obliged to desist, and rushing out to a haystack near, she poured out the bitterness of her soul, and the Healer came. They are now a happy family serving the Lord.[81]

(d) South-West Scotland

North Ayrshire witnessed revival scenes among children at a very early date if the following report is accurate in its dating, and may provide evidence of the first children's prayer meeting caused by this awakening within Scotland:

Ardrossan: There were prayer-meetings in the Harbour Store led by Mr. Sillars four weeks ago: here in one part of the store were clusters of girls singing, in another place a whole row of boys kneeling at a form and crying aloud to God for mercy.

After a meeting in the Free Church they tried to persuade the anxious to go home:

Mr Stewart said to one little girl of fourteen - You must go home. She said, Oh let me stay, I am so happy. But we are going to close the door, and you cannot stay here all night in the dark. Oh yes, she said, I am so happy, I will stay here all night with Jesus. She had ultimately to be led to the door with gentle violence and taken home...Within the last fortnight prayer meetings have been got up by children among themselves.[82]

The question is sometimes asked if there is any evidence of the revival touching people of a particular social background. Usually we are not given sufficient details to assess this, but on this occasion the article continues:

The higher classes have generally kept aloof from the movement. Some of them indeed were frightened, and a number actually left the place in terror...the movement is now making headway among the middle classes.

The same newspaper adds that in neighbouring Saltcoats (probably referring to the previous Sunday, 4th September):

The young have been getting a large blessing with us. *A special prayer meeting of forty Sunday school teachers led to this:* Very many were deeply awakened - some crying out, some on their knees in earnest prayer - and it was not till after three hours beyond the usual time the school could be dismissed. In answer to the earnest prayer on the part of the teachers, the Lord seemed to comfort many of the little mourners at length, and it was as difficult to restrain the singing now as it had been to assuage the weeping before. I dare not speak of numbers...

Shortly after this a letter from a Captain Crosby informs us:

Since I wrote to you, I have been labouring in Stevenston, West Kilbride, Dalry and Kilwinning, and the work is going on in these places. The work is going on at Ardrossan. Oh, how wonderful is God's work! He takes the little children to confound the mighty and wise; some little children down by the harbour store met to

---

sing and pray, and the Holy Spirit was so mighty on them that the people became alarmed and sent for me. I was not here and they went for Mr. McColl. These children are now rejoicing in Jesus.[83]

A year later Mr. Radcliffe[84] and Mr. Weaver, a converted miner and prize fighter from Lancashire, visited Saltcoats:

There was a special service for children on Saturday, the principal addresses being those of Messrs Radcliffe and Weaver. Mr Radcliffe was peculiarly telling and happy in addressing the young; and judging from what we saw after the meeting, and again on Sabbath evening, after a very crowded and solemn meeting in the Free Church, the impressions made on some of the young must have been very deep. On Sabbath evening several of them were thrown into deep distress. One child broke forth into a very remarkable prayer for about twenty minutes, full of impassioned earnestness, which arrested many. Several men and women of various ages were powerfully awakened at the Sabbath evening meeting.[85]

Nearby at Irvine there are two anecdotes concerning praying children, the first in a letter from 'R.B.' dated 29th December 1859:

A little boy, about ten years of age, on returning home one evening began to pray. He had evidently been impressed with a prayer offered in the meeting. On the following day he was observed forming the centre of a little circle of companions with uplifted hands, and earnestly asking our Father in Heaven to bless the little hearers. A Roman Catholic was attracted to the spot, listened, wept, and was heard to exclaim 'Surely this is the work of the Lord; and if a little boy like this can thus pray, shame upon those who have grown up to old age in neglect of this duty.' [86]

To which the Scottish Guardian adds:

83. S.G. 16th September 1859 and T.R. 1st October 1859.
84. See later section on Aberdeen (page 161) for an introduction to Reginald Radcliffe.
85. S.G. Tuesday 25th September 1860.
86. W.J. 7th January 1860.

Irvine: We understand that the work of revival has commenced in this place. A prayer meeting has been commenced by a dozen boys of about fourteen years of age, and carried on with much earnestness.[87]

In Kilmarnock the Ayrshire Express reports:

Meetings for engaging in devotional exercises had been prolonged to an unwarrantable hour. ....The attendance at the meetings referred to was in each case very large, the audience consisting in great part of young ladies and girls. At one of these, where the assembly consisted almost entirely of youths and young females of from twelve to eighteen years of age, a lad but recently recovered from physical conversion was put forward to address the meeting. It is cause of rejoicing with many that his efforts were in some measure crowned with success, and that a good many cases resulted from his exertions. Most of those who have been struck down are young people of both sexes, and employed during the day in the factories in that part of the town.[88]

The same newspaper a year later carries a hostile description of a meeting in Dunlop on 22nd October, 1860:

Stewarton: Being anxious to see for ourselves how the revival prayer meetings were conducted in Dunlop, we went over on Monday night - a distance of two miles - and remained there from 7 o'clock till midnight. Entering the parish church at the hour above mentioned, we found it filled in every part with a well dressed, and at that time, well-conducted audience. The services were conducted by Rev. Mr. Gebbie, the parish minister, assisted by the Rev. Mr. McLeish of the Free Church, and were commenced with praise and prayer. There were no cases of prostration for some considerable time; and the first that took place was that of a young man belonging to Stewarton, who was standing near the platform, and was seized instantaneously with the mysterious

---

87. S.G. 10th January 1860.
88. A.E. Saturday 8th October 1859 quoted in S.G. 11th October 1859.

visitation; and while being assisted to the vestry a number of the congregation sung a hymn appropriate to the occasion. And now commences a scene among the 'converts' which almost baffles description. They were most supplied with a hymn-book, compiled by Richard Weaver, the Revivalist; and gathering in circles they sang portions of its contents, with frantic gestures, and in every variety of time and tune. While in one corner of the church a party was singing to the tune of 'Wait for the waggon' another, not far distant, were enlivening the audience with 'Betsy Baker'. To persons unaccustomed to such scenes the spectacle of young men and women, boys and girls, embracing each other in transports of religious delirium - swaying their bodies backwards and forwards - standing on the seats and stamping time with their feet to the tune, and howling forth at the pitch of their voice 'Christ for me', must have been anything but pleasant to their feelings. *The meeting divided, because of the size of the crowd, and some accompanied Mr. McLeish to the Free Church where* matters were conducted with a little more propriety, *but both went on until 3 a.m.* The conduct described above has been repeated every meeting since with little variation.[89]

As if to compensate for reproducing such a negative report the Guardian adds that quieter meetings took place in Stewarton Parish Church on the Tuesday, and in the Free Church on the Wednesday. Two days later it publishes this letter of the Free Church minister of Stewarton to stress that the above occurred in Dunlop, and that:

united prayer meetings here, which are conducted by the ministers of the Established, Free and United Presbyterian Churches are altogether void of extravagant excitement being remarkable only for the deep solemnity and earnest spirit of inquiry which characterises them - James Clugston.[90]

A week later there is an altogether different perspective in a letter from William Pinkerton, Free Church minister of Kilwinning, who

89. A.E. Saturday 27th October 1860 quoted in S.G. Tuesday 30th October 1860.
90. S.G. Thursday 1st November 1860

discounts the previous letter, and reports evidence of genuine conversions, including whole families and the local publican. He described the Communion Monday as 'Brighter and better days they were even than those of Livingston and the Kirk of Shotts.' The meetings were calm and solemn, 'It is the Lord's work'. 'During the past fourteen months - the most remarkable period perhaps in the history of Scotland's Church - I have visited many revival scenes, and taken part in many revival meetings and I feel constrained to say I have not witnessed anything so deep and widespread, and so evidently from above.'[91]

The Wynd Journal picks up on the visit made to Dunlop by Rev. Pinkerton of Kilwinning when he led the meeting in the Parish Church on Tuesday, 30th October:

> The meeting broke up at eleven o'clock...When nearly all had left, there were two interesting little girls seen crying bitterly, and evidently unwilling to depart. On being asked what was the cause of their crying, they said that they had come to find Christ, and had not found him; and when further asked why they wished to find Christ, they said it was to have their sins forgiven and to get a new heart. The Rev. McLeish endeavoured to comfort them by saying that Jesus was also seeking them, and they would be sure to find Him, for He Himself said 'I love them that love Me, and those that seek me early *shall* find me.' They were greatly comforted, and as the poor little things had walked all the way from Stewarton (2 miles) they were glad to get home in a conveyance which was going that way.[92]

An unnamed Professor of Divinity recalls his boyhood in Ayr:

> I was only a schoolboy at the time of the Revival, but I have a vivid recollection of a meeting for boys, which I attended in connection with it, early in the year 1859. The meeting was held in one of the classrooms of Ayr Academy, and was conducted by the then young minister of Ayr, now the venerable Dr. Dykes of that town. In those days hymns were unknown in Presbyterian

91. S.G. Thursday 8th November 1860.
92. W.J. 24th November er 1860. A report of the revival at Dunlop is found in the A.E. of 10th November 1860.

church services; and I recall the deep impressions made on me upon that occasion, not only by the address, but by Miss Charlotte Elliott's hymn 'Just as I am.' I heard it then for the first time, and it came home to me as the gospel in song.[93]

Regrettably, there do not appear to be other records of this series of meetings, or references to young people in the vicinity of Ayr.

Letters from Leswalt by Stranraer dated 20th February 1860 and 12th March 1860 respectively state:

We have meetings every night of the week except Saturday. There is also a meeting held by little boys who unite to implore the descent of the Holy Spirit upon this place. The meetings are largely attended.

I am delighted to see so many children regularly coming to us. It is a hopeful symptom. One of them, a little highland girl was arrested by the Spirit of God on Friday 24th February. We learned shortly afterwards that she had been made the special subject of prayer at a meeting in Gourock on the 22nd.[94]

In Dumfriesshire we hear that 'eight young men and boys'[95] are seeking by December 1859 in Ecclefechan, and in Eaglesfield Free Church 'a very interesting work is going forward among the children of the Sabbath School.'[96] There was widespread revival over the whole of the district following E.P. Hammond's visit to Annan early in 1861, although the foundations of the work preceded his arrival, as this account given by Rev. Machray in Glasgow about his visit to Dumfries reveals:

after attending a meeting of ten or twelve boys, aged perhaps, eleven or twelve years and finding that they had brought to me two boys like themselves, who had been awakened but had not found the Saviour. They had tried to bring their young compan-

93. Reminiscences of the Revival of Fifty Nine and the Sixties, AUP, 1910, p.112.
94. W.J. 3rd March 1860, and 17th March 1860. Rev. Thomas Bell from Leswalt had visited Newtonards - see W.J. 8th October 1859.
95. S.G. 13th December 1859.
96. S.G. 3rd January 1860, from the Dumfries Standard.

ions to a knowledge of the Saviour, but failing this brought them to me; and I believe these dear boys were greatly blessed by God in awakening many of their companions, and leading them to a knowledge of the Saviour. They have carried on their prayer meetings from that time until the present, and have been the means of advancing the work of God among the young in Dumfries. Many young girls were also converted, and they also thought they should have prayer meetings...all this was going on in 1860.[97]

An unnamed minister writes to a friend in Edinburgh, dated 21st January 1861, concerning the work in Annan:

On the Friday evening the Free Church had been filled with children, among whom the Lord is doing, not only the greatest work I have ever seen, but one as great as anything of which I have heard. At noon, on Saturday, there was another meeting of the children; the Free Church was again filled; and, until late in the afternoon, Mr. Hammond, myself, and a number of the Christian friends, were conversing with such as were anxious for the salvation of their souls...Yesterday, Sabbath,...at three o'clock the young met in the Free Church, which was again overcrowded. Addresses, to which they listened with intense earnestness, were delivered by Mr. Hammond, the Rev. Mr. Gailey, and myself, and at the close a very large number waited to have the way of salvation more clearly explained in conversation.[98]

In the village of Penpont (near Thornhill) there had been a Saturday evening prayer meeting since early in 1860, but with a very small attendance until February 1861 when it was suddenly too great for the large school room. According to Rev. Laing:

Much of this was owing to some godly mothers who were in the habit of meeting regularly for prayer. At the close of one of their meetings, it was proposed to send for Robert Cunningham, who

---

97. T.R. 27th April 1861 (quoting Scottish Guardian, but I have not located the original).
98. W.J. 2nd February 1861.

willingly came, and his visit was much blessed in the district. A girls' meeting was also begun at this time, and in the following way:- After hearing a sermon on the Penitent Thief, a little girl going home with a companion, said to her, Oh how much I would like to be converted, that I might be the means of converting others. Her prayer was heard, and she at once sought to carry out her purpose, and a meeting for girls was successfully instituted. Some time after, Mr. Hammond came to the place, and in the evening the church was crowded. An inquiry meeting was held afterwards, and there were many remained in deep concern about their souls, and night after night the people flocked to the meeting, and a glorious work ensued. One evening, he (Mr. L.) found a group of young boys in the meeting; he went up to them thinking they had come from curiosity, and to his great surprise he found that they were all deeply anxious. After the meeting broke up, they retired to a field and there continued in earnest prayer. When Mr. L. came to know of it, he advised them to choose a more suitable time and place, when they told him that they had already arranged for a regular prayer meeting by themselves in a neighbouring village, where a friend had allowed them his house for the purpose. On the night appointed for the meeting, Mr. Laing visited the house where the boys' meeting was thus begun, and found many present. While speaking to the woman of the house in the kitchen, a man came in who was opposed to the work, and who at once began to scoff at it. While thus engaged, a young boy's voice was heard in prayer in the adjoining room, where the boys had met. The scoffer was silenced, he turned pale, and rushed outside to weep. That boy was his own son.[99]

---

99. W.J. 7th September 1861, presumably another version of an account previously given in 4th May 1861?:
Dumfriesshire: In another place, after leaving a meeting in the church, a group of boys retired to a field to arrange for a prayer meeting for themselves. After securing a room they invited the minister to be present to direct them. The minister came. While speaking in the kitchen to a woman, a man came in who was a notorious drunkard. While speaking to this man of the Saviour, a noise was heard in the room. It was the children kneeling in prayer. He paused to listen. The voice of a boy was heard praying with fervour and great

124

In Lockerbie 'lately' in the Free Church:

> After the usual forenoon service, the whole congregation re-
> solved itself into a prayer meeting, and was addressed by two
> laymen as well as by a young lad, a native of the town, recently
> brought to Christ. There were few dry eyes while the youth
> related how, in spite of himself, he had been led to close with
> Christ, *and 120 remained anxious afterwards.*[100]

Finally, at Half-Morton the Eskdale Advertiser informs us:

> Three meetings are kept up weekly for children, varying in
> attendance from fifty to ninety. Some of them have been hope-
> fully converted, and the boys and girls, separately, hold prayer
> meetings among themselves.[101]

(e) Argyll

Last century Argyll may have been closer to the Highlands culturally
and linguistically than it is today, but with regular shipping services to
the Clyde ports and from Campbeltown to Ulster much of it was less cut
off. It is therefore not surprising to hear of early interest in the revival
with prayer meetings attracting 4,000 in a town of only 9,000[102] from the
end of September 1859.

The Rev. Alex. Munro told the Free Church General Assembly that
in October 1859 in Campbeltown Free Church: 'young men and women,
old men and women, and even children, were brought under the influence of this gracious movement.' And '...the increase in our Sabbath
Schools is very great.'[103]

At the end of October a letter from Campbeltown said:

unction. The minister turned to look at the man. He was trembling and agitated. He hurried
outside to pray, weeping bitterly. Who was it amongst these boys who prayed so
touchingly? That ungodly father's youngest son.

100. The Revivalist, London, May 1861.

101. W.J. 11th May 1861.

102. Edwin Orr, The Second Evangelical Awakening, pp 66-7. The A.H. of Friday 4th
November 1859 reported six weeks of nightly prayer meetings averaging an attendance
of 1,500.

103. MacRae pp 40 - 42

In the neighbourhood of this town...we met with two cases of deep conviction, the subjects of which had not yet attained to the peace which passeth knowledge. One of these was a boy of ten or twelve years of age; he had for some days been in this state, at times obtaining comparative peace; but when his sins would come afresh before him, he would weep like one that refused to be comforted. He was calm when we arrived, but after reading of the Scripture and prayer he began to weep bitterly, and when asked the cause of his grief, his artless answer 'that his sins were fashing him' was truly affecting, and would we think, be sufficient to convince the most sceptical that the Holy Spirit was working in the mind of the youth. My friend endeavoured to point him to the Saviour and we left him. May the chief Shepherd take all such lambs under His own guidance.[104]

Likewise, an anonymous lady writer 'witnessed...the strong policeman kneeling in the lobby, when Mr. Colville was at prayer, beside a very little boy, and another very wicked woman - all with broken hearts on account of sin, seeking forgiveness.'[105]

The Argyllshire Herald devoted its editorial to the Campbeltown revival on 18th November, reporting the visit of the Free Church minister from Rothesay:

The evening previous to leaving town Mr. Elder gave a special address to children, many of whom we hope have thus been in their early years, savingly impressed with love for a crucified Saviour; and the intensity of interest and attention shown by the children, manifested the sincerity of their feelings. There were also a number of young men - anxious inquirers...We also understand he witnessed a most interesting scene in the female school, where on one of the days of his visit a great proportion of the children were brought under deep conviction, resulting in many cases of prostration.

Three weeks after this, Messrs. McLean and Stewart conducted a mission in nearby Drumlemble, where 'a strong concern for the soul has

104. A.H. Friday 21st October 1859.
105. John Colville, by his widow, Elliott of Edinburgh, 2nd ed. 1888, p.94.

entered into many families. Servants, brothers, sisters and young ones are alike impressed.'[106]

According to the Argyllshire Herald even on the island of Gigha nightly prayer meetings had been held 'for some time back...Indeed the island has become an Island of Prayer - little boys on their way home from these meetings, though the nights be dark and stormy, remain among the rocks and hills, praying alternately till a late hour...'[107]

In a letter from Kilberry and Tarbert we read:

> We have had an awakening here. During the preaching of a sermon by Rev. Mr. McPherson of Killean, lately, many were in tears, and towards the close of the prayer, a great number were crying out. A young girl of sixteen years of age got such a view of her danger that she sunk back into her seat almost in a state of unconsciousness. She addressed the people who gathered round her in Gaelic regarding their insensibility and hardness of heart, and also prayed. She slept none that night, but she found peace in Christ the following day. You may well believe that this incident made a great impression.[108]

In a later report we are informed that the movement began during the Communion season in the second week of November in the Gaelic speaking Free Church under Rev. Campbell and Rev. McPherson of Killean:

> Ever since the Holy Spirit has been carrying on his gracious work to a considerable extent, so that there are many adults, male and female, and children who have been, apparently, through deep conviction, brought to obtain rest in Jesus.[109]

Children feature prominently in the account of another 'recent visit' by Rev. McPherson of Killean. In a letter from Kilberry:

---

106. A.H. Friday 16th December 1859.

107. S.G. Tuesday 29th November 1859 and W.J. 3rd December 1859 from A.H. of Friday 25th November 1859.

108. S.G. 29th November 1859, W.J.. 3rd December 1859 quoted in A.H. of 2nd December 1859.

109. S.G. Tuesday 3rd January 1860

There were seven or eight individuals - chiefly young people - awakened. There have been meetings every night since. At the close of one of these meetings, a boy, ten or twelve years of age, came forward and invited the others present to engage in prayer. He then offered up a very impressive prayer.[110]

On 4th April 1860 a 'correspondent' from Lochgilphead records:

The writer has just learned that on last Saturday night when there was no public service, two juvenile prayer meetings were held in this village, by little children, when they sang hymns, read a portion of Scripture, and several engaged in prayer, and these prayers were fervent, comprehensive, and correct in doctrine and expression; they confessed the corruption of their nature, prayed that the Holy Spirit would subdue that corruption, asked for a blessing on fathers, mothers, brothers and sisters with thanksgiving that they were not as heathen children, but had Christian mothers to lead them to Jesus.[111]

Within a matter of weeks the West Highland Journal is reporting from Iona:

In this lone isle of Iona there are at present many anxious souls seeking the way to Zion. The movement is making general and unostentatious progress. The work is not confined to one class - the old, as well as the young, are brought under no ordinary seriousness and concern, which in many cases, we trust, will issue in sound conversion to God.[112]

Regrettably we know nothing more of whom 'the young' refer to.

Other reports from the islands at this period have already been given in the previous chapter: see section under 'The Gaelic Schools Society'.

_____

110. S.G. Thursday 8th March 1860.
111. A.H. Friday 6th April 1860.
112. W.H.J. Friday 27th April 1860.

(f) Lothian

In comparison with most other districts of Scotland, West Lothian seems scarcely touched. There were revival meetings held in the Congregational Chapel in Linlithgow early in 1861, for we read: 'on Monday night a large meeting of children was also held at five o' clock in the chapel, and many of them seemed deeply moved by what they heard.'[113]

We know that frequent prayer meetings were held at Newtown, a village 'inhabited exclusively by miners', near Bo'ness, as a result of the work of Mr Tough of the Scottish Coast Mission in the district. A correspondent of the 'Caledonian Mercury' gives us this touching story:

The miners may be divided into two classes - the Romanists and the Orangemen. *There was an Irishman* accustomed to work excessively hard in order to earn high wages, and on receiving his monthly pay *he drank it away for days on end*. He had one child, a girl about six years of age, who, though clothed in the veriest rags, had sharpness and vivacity in her speech, and an indescribable grace in all her movements, astonishing for her age and station. The poor child was totally ignorant of everything save hard work and misery - with these she had been early acquainted. The wife of this person was fortunately a woman of steady habits, and considerable energy and perseverance. She had been among the first to attend the revival meeting, and along with her daughter, continued to do so. On one occasion a number of the children attending the various Sabbath Schools in the neighbourhood were invited by that Christian and kind-hearted lady, Miss Hope of Carriden, to visit her magnificent grounds. The little girl, through the kindness of the missionary, was invited to go along with them; but, alas!, she had neither shoes nor stockings, nor a bonnet to cover her head, and her one poor frock were a mere colourless rag, torn in many places. The child wept bitterly when told by her mother that she could not accompany the rest of the children, but must stay at home, as she had no clothes. Her mother also endeavoured to inform her of the reason, namely, want of

---

money, caused by her father's drunken habits. This the child appeared to comprehend, for that very night, when her sire returned from his work, she crept to his side, and looking up to him with her large, searching eyes, said, 'Father, what gars ye drink my claes?' The man started at the question, and falteringly replied, 'Hoot, wench, you're raving; I dae nae sic thing.' 'Yes, ye dae, though, ' continued the child; 'Mother says if ye were na getting fou, I wad hae braw claes, an' gang wi' the rest o' the bairns to the woods o' Carriden, an' rin amang the green grass, an' no hae Jock the farmer chasing us wi' his whup, like when I gang into ane o' his parks; but I've nae claes, an' a' the bairns 'ill be there but me.' This simple but touching appeal, coming from so young a child had apparently an effect upon the hitherto callous heart of the drunkard, and he sat thoughtful and silent. When his wife and Katie were about to depart for the meeting, instead of going to bed, as was his custom, he said 'Wife, I don't mind though I go with you to the meeting tonight.' He went, and from that night, so far as his drinking propensities were concerned, he became an altered man. Next payday, the little girl was envied by all the miners' children in the Newtown, so altered did she look in her new clothes. She has since visited the green glades of Carriden; and her laugh was as merry and her smile as bright as the happiest there. Her rags and wretchedness are now forgotten.

From the above hurried and imperfect sketch, it is demonstrable that great good has resulted from the revival movement in a very umpromising district, even when unattended with those peculiar physical manifestations which are so well calculated to arouse mere idle curiousity and excitement.[114]

Apart from these two isolated reports, Edinburgh is the only real centre of activity in Lothian, as there is a similar dearth of material in respect of both Mid and East Lothian.[115]

One of the most remarkable stories of 1859 comes from the Pilrig School, Edinburgh, situated in James Street, off Leith Walk. William

---

114. Quoted by S.G. 25th October 1860.

115. Wm. Reid does include a chapter on Dunbar, North Berwick and Cockenzie in his 'Authentic Records' but does not specifically refer to either children or youth.

Robertson of Alexandria had been assistant teacher in East Gorballs Territorial School, and a teacher in East Gorballs Free Church Sabbath School. At the end of June he had been present at an awakening under Rev D. Maccoll in the Wynd Church in Glasgow, but moved to Edinburgh at the beginning of September to commence work as Headmaster at Pilrig on September 4th. He attended Finney's mission at the Evangelical Union Church in Brighton Street, but did not come into assurance of his own salvation until 10th November after Finney had left. Earlier than this, former pupils and teachers from East Gorballs had written to him, telling him of the awakening in that school, and of prayer meetings being held by the children in the middle of the day. Many of the children had professed conversion, sent testimonies, and asked them to be read to the Edinburgh school. As a result his own pupils requested the use of a classroom for prayer-meetings, which he agreed to after consultation with Rev. W.G. Blaikie of Pilrig Free Church.

After his own conversion Robertson led his assistant into assurance the next day, and a week later, before school on Friday 18th November they prayed together specifically for the conversion of the six oldest children in the school: 5 girls and a boy monitor. Robertson himself recorded:

The work of that morning went on in much the usual way with this exception. During the Bible lesson, one girl, usually very thoughtless, was rather trifling, talking continuously to her neighbour. She was removed to another seat and went quite readily. After some time she began to cry. I did not think anything of this, but after the lesson was finished, and when all the other children had gone to the playground for a few minutes, she continued in her seat still crying. When I asked her what was the matter, she answered that it was for her sins.

This girl was not one of those we had prayed for...During the rest of the forenoon she sat in her class evidently quite unable to take any part in the work. She sat with her hands clasped, from time to time heaving a deep sigh, but speaking to no one. *She requested that at the prayer meeting they should sing Psalm 16:1-4, which they did.* At one o'clock the school work was resumed for the afternoon. The highest class had a writing lesson.

Copybooks and pens had been distributed, and work was beginning when I noticed a girl crying. She was seated at the end of one of the seats. On my asking what was wrong she answered that it was her sins. Just then the teacher came up to me and told me that a great number more were crying: he wished to know what he should do with them. I told him to show them into the classroom. Those girls for whom we had been praying that morning came in one by one, crying most bitterly. Oh, the solemnity and the awfulness of that moment, I never shall forget. God was manifestly in our midst in awakening power, answering prayer. The lad prayed for was also awakened that day... After these five girls had entered the room, there was a pause, as if the Lord would have us notice how He had heard our cry and was answering our morning prayer. Shortly after, other eight boys and girls came in and took their seats beside their companions. *They sang a hymn, and he spoke briefly to them.*

There was an intelligent girl, Katie B- sitting at the end of a seat, and as she was nearest to me I said to her, 'Katie, could you not trust Jesus?' quoting some of our Saviour's own most gracious words. She looked up into my face, her large bright eyes filling with tears, and answered, 'Yes, sir, I could trust Jesus,' and then starting to her feet she began to speak to her companions, naming them, 'Oh Hannah, could you not trust Jesus?' 'Jemima, could you not trust Jesus?' quoting some of our Lord's words.

Her companions looked up in astonishment at her, and as she went on telling them of Jesus and His power to save, I saw that the Lord was Himself guiding and teaching this dear girl. I thus left her with her companions and returned to the school-room. Here I found all the children in tears, everyone without exception, and the assistant doing his best among them, telling them of Jesus. I did not imagine they were all anxious; some of the younger children were crying, no doubt, out of sympathy with their elder brothers and sisters. I went to the youngest class, saying that this would never do, or words to that effect. Some of them took out their books to begin work, but others looked into my face and burst out afresh into weeping. It was quite evident that all work was impossible for that afternoon. Accordingly we brought all the children together into the larger schoolroom, locating them in a gallery gradually rising from the floor. There would be about ninety altogether in this department. They were all together in this gallery, and all of them either crying or with faces showing traces of tears. I should have said that earlier in the afternoon, when the feeling was greatest, I had sent a boy to call Mr. Blaikie. He had returned from the manse with the message that Mr Blaikie was not at home, but that as soon as he had come home he would come along to the school.

Just as we had gathered the children into the gallery, the former Superintendent of the Sabbath School paid us a visit. It was long since he had promised us this visit, and it so happened that at this moment he arrived. He was naturally very much astonished at what he saw, and on his inquiring as to what was the matter, I invited him to apply to the children themselves. Our visitor did so, and on applying to a boy near him he got for answer that his sins were the cause of trouble. With reference to this boy spoken to, the teacher afterwards told me that shortly before, when he had seen his cousin, a girl of thirteen, crying, he had made fun of her, calling her a baby and so forth. He had asked her what was wrong, and in reply she had exclaimed, 'Oh, Frankie, it's my sins.' In a few minutes he sat down beside her and seemed as much distressed as any.

After having spoken to this boy, our visitor asked if they were all in the same state of mind. I replied that they all said so when asked. Later on I remarked that surely the Lord had sent him in to visit at that moment, and invited him to say a few words to the children. He did so, but was too much overcome to say much. Thereupon I shortly addressed them, and after the singing of a hymn they were dismissed to their homes. Before they left, however, I asked if they would like to come back next afternoon and have a meeting, when in all likelihood the minister would be with us. They all expressed a desire to do so, and accordingly a meeting was arranged for three o'clock the next afternoon.

When the children had left, I went and called for Mr. Blaikie, but meeting him on the road I explained what had happened. He was greatly impressed with what he heard, and readily promised to be at the meeting next day.

We had our meeting on the Saturday afternoon as arranged, the older children being present in good numbers. Mr. Blaikie and a friend of mine from Glasgow gave two short addresses. Of the service nothing special is remembered except that the children were very attentive.

On the following Monday morning we had no special prayer for anyone, as we thought there might be a repetition of the experiences of the Friday, and all work stopped. We feared that some of the parents might complain. On this account we did nothing. At the close of the day, however, we both felt that we had done wrong in not praying. We might safely have left the answer to prayer in the Lord's hands. We had, however, some very blessed little talks with the children, especially with those belonging to the highest class, all of whom, some eighteen in number, made a profession of having come to Jesus.

On the Tuesday morning we resolved to pray for the children of the second class, leaving the result in the Lord's hands. He again answered prayer, not as we expected, but in a different way, by the children coming in groups during their intervals desiring to be pointed to Jesus. The work of this day was again deeply interesting. There was deep anxiety, although not the great movement of the Friday.

The mother of Jeannie, the first girl awakened came to Mr. Robertson to ask what he had done to her daughter, who usually lost her temper if her dinner wasn't ready when she got home, but just sat quietly by the fire sighing. Jeannie's sister and Mr. Robertson prayed together after school one day for the mother's conversion, and later this woman, a drunkard, was converted.

As I was leaving Free St Luke's Church one day, the father of two girls in Pilrig School accosted me, anxious to speak about them. He had been much annoyed, he said, by his girls singing hymns at home, and at length after some time he had forbidden them to do so, at least while he was in the house. The girls had been greatly disturbed about this, as was also their mother, but, concluding that their father only wished not to hear them singing, they continued the singing after they had gone to bed, covering their heads with the blankets. He heard them singing, however, and an arrow of conviction entered his heart. It was in great distress of soul that he had come to me saying, 'My girls will be on the right side of the throne and I will be on the left. I never taught them to pray. Is there any hope for a sinner like me?'

It was a great joy to point this awakened father to the Lord Jesus as his Saviour, and to show him that there was certainly forgiveness for him. We can only imagine the joy of these two dear girls, when they learned that their father also was trusting in their precious Saviour.

Whilst the Saturday morning meetings were in progress, one girl, Jeannie, was on her way to the meeting, when she met a companion, Lizzie, whom she invited to come with her. 'Gae wa' wi' yer meetin's; gaun tae a meetin' on a Saturday mornin'! No, I'm gaun tae nane o' yer meetin's,' was the response, and she then commenced to call her names - hypocrite, Methodist, and such like.

Jeannie went quietly on to the meeting, not answering a word. On the following Saturday morning, on her way to the meeting, she saw the same girl coming down the lane. There was no escape, and she wondered what she should do. Having lifted up her heart to the Lord, praying to be helped, Jeannie went straight up to her friend and greeted her with these words, 'Oh, Lizzie, will ye no come tae the meetin' this mornin'?'

Lizzie burst into tears and said, 'Yes, Jeannie, I'll gang tae the meetin'. Oh Jeannie, if ye only kent what a week I've had. I laughed at ye, and ca'ed ye names, when ye wanted me tae gang tae the meetin' last Saturday mornin', and ye never said a word. Oh, I've been sae wicked. I wanted tae meet ye and I hoped ye wad ask me. I'll gang tae the meetin'.'

They were both present that morning, but I knew nothing of the proceeding till Lizzie and another girl came to my lodging in great distress of soul. They both wished to give their hearts to Jesus. The last accounts we have heard about Jeannie are from America, where she is working in the Salvation Army.

One Friday evening, Mr. Robertson had addressed a children's meeting in the hall of Pilrig Free Church at short notice:

The power of God was felt in a remarkable way in that service; many of the little ones were undoubtedly in an anxious state. At the close of the meeting I invited only those who were anxious about their souls to return, and about forty or fifty did so. These I dealt with as in a class. After a brief address I finally said I would not ask any one particularly if he or she would trust Jesus, but that I would be very glad to hear afterwards from any of them who had been enabled to do so. I knew that they would be pleased to come and tell me.

Following this one mother was converted on hearing her son's testimony, and on the way home two girls, Aggie and Jeannie, stopped Robertson, and said 'Please Sir, can you tell us how we may fight for Jesus?' Aggie in fact died shortly after:

The other girl, Jeannie, about the same time was laid down with scarlet fever. For a long time she lay in a very critical condition. The doctor had given up all hope. She had relapsed three times. I called one evening to inquire for the girl, when she had been in a state of unconsciousness for several days. Her mother, an earnest Christian woman told me the following remarkable story.

On hearing that there was no hope of recovery, the mother became very anxious just to have a few minutes' conversation with her dear lassie before she died. 'I went into that little room there,' she said, 'and prayed if the Lord would be pleased to restore my Jeannie to consciousness once more before she died, that I might ask her, if all was well for eternity? When I came back into the kitchen,' she continued, 'Jeannie was lying with her eyes open, and immediately began to say something about her little sister, who was playing on the floor. Oh, Mr Robertson,' she said, 'I just ran over to the bedside, saying: "Oh, Jeannie, have you found Jesus?" "No mother," was the reply, "but Jesus has found me."

'What more could I want?' exclaimed the mother, as she spoke to me, 'I was willing to let my Jeannie go now.' The invalid girl, however, had had more to say, and so the mother went on, 'but,' continued she, 'Jeannie said to me, "Mother, I'm not going to die. I'm to get back to school to 'fight for Jesus' ".'

The mother feared that her daughter was now wandering in her mind, but the girl's words came true. She was raised up; she did get back to school, and still lives. She is a teacher in London, and is seeking to win others to that Saviour, Who found her, as she said, when she was a child.

After this wonderful awakening in school there was much interest in Bible study. It was not an unusual sight to have groups of children in the playground with their Bibles in hand, engaged in some search in connection with the word of truth, or it might be one child who had discovered some precious promise showing it to others.

One day I noticed a group of older girls talking together and looking somewhat sad. I stepped over to them and asked them if Satan had been tempting them to think that they had made a mistake and that they had never been truly converted. They all looked at each other in surprise, wondering how I had come to know. They had just been speaking about this very thing, and were startled that I should have put just such a question. Continuing in conversation with them, I asked if they ever expected that Satan would be anxious to put them right if they were wrong. They replied at once, 'Oh no !' and immediately their faces brightened. It was a great pleasure to remind those girls that in their trouble about such things it was always wiser to ask Jesus to put them right where they were wrong. Satan wished to hinder their prayers, and if he could lead them into darkness and doubt he would interfere most successfully with their praying in faith.

The one boy, the monitor, for whom we prayed on that memorable Friday morning, and who was amongst those awakened, did not come to a decision for some time. Long did he labour under conviction of sin, but when spoken to about religious things, he could scarce be induced to utter one word in reply. Later he told me that he had often followed me from my house to Carrubber's Close, anxious for some conversation, but yet too timid to speak.

After his conversion his influence as a Christian worker was much blessed of God, especially in connection with a class of lads whom no one else could manage. In the early days of the awakening in Pilrig School an effort had been made to reach some young lads, who were in the habit of frequenting some stables in the neighbourhood of the school. A class had been formed of these lads on Sabbath evenings. Their conduct during prayer was at first so irreverent, that the teacher who then had them in hand was obliged to give up the practice of prayer in public in the class. For some time he struggled on with the class, but with no success. In time the monitor, of whom we have just spoken, took the class in hand. He was not much older than the lads in question, but his influence among them was most marked and his work was greatly blessed of God.

One Friday the Headmaster asked the prayer meeting to pray for him as he was going to address a meeting at Bonnyrigg that evening. 'The meeting that evening was a very remarkable one; there was a great breaking down on the part of both old and young.' He was convinced 'there must have been special prayer somewhere for that meeting'.

When I returned home on Saturday morning, I received notes by post from two girls telling of a prayer meeting they had had. One of these girls was the daughter of the drunken woman already referred to, and the other was the daughter of a Roman Catholic father. After doing some household work in their own homes, these two girls had met to go for a short walk. They went down Pilrig Street, and in the course of their walk turned into a nursery through a gap in a hedge, and there behind the hedge they had their prayer meeting. In their letters to me they said they were so sure that there was to be a great blessing, that they could not wait till Monday morning when they would see me at school, but they felt they must write and tell me about it. They were so conscious of the Lord's presence with them in their meeting behind the hedge.

We close this section with one final anecdote from Mr. Robertson:

> In the school there was one little lad, who was a very sweet singer.
> Sometimes in the course of our singing I would stop to listen to
> his clear, sweet voice. This lad frequently paid a visit to a printing
> establishment in Leith Walk, and when there it was his great
> delight to get seated beside a case in which many papers of
> different kinds were all kept together. One day in this case he
> found a sheet on which was printed the hymn 'Just as I am'. In
> childish innocence he began to sing, and his singing at once
> arrested the attention of all in the workshop, or at least in the
> room. One of the workmen told me afterwards how he had run
> forward to the lad, spreading out his arms around him lest any
> harm might come to him. But there was no need. Indeed, it was
> quite the reverse. Many of the workmen were sceptically in-
> clined, but there they were seen standing around the little lad
> drinking in the precious words of the hymn with tears in their
> eyes.

Writing this up some thirty years later, he is able to note that he is still
discovering former pupils who are continuing steadfastly, and others
being restored after backsliding. He himself was later involved in
Moody's 1874 visit to Edinburgh, and in 1884 became Superintendent
of the Carrubber's Close Mission. The full story is told in 'William
Robertson of the Carrubber's Close Mission' edited by his son, Rev. R.
M. Robertson (Oliphant, Anderson and Ferrier, Edinburgh 1914). All
the above extracts are from Part 1 which is autobiographical.

Carrubbers Close quickly became the focal point of the revival
movement within the Edinburgh area. In April 1856 James Gall had
been commissioned by the Edinburgh Sabbath School Teachers' Union
to discover how many children in the city had no religious influence,
and he estimated there were 8000. On May 30th 1858 he knelt with three
other men in the empty hall known as Whitefield Chapel, of which they
had taken a five year lease after the ejection of its previous occupants,
the Atheist Club, who could not afford the rent. They consecrated
themselves and the building to start a Sunday school for children
unreached in any other way.

The four men after prayer, went out into the Close and High Street, and by dint of coaxing and importunity, succeeded in bringing down to the Chapel a few children whom they found playing about. Inviting the same children to return, and to bring with them as many companions as they could, we met again in the evening in larger numbers, and thus inaugurated our Sabbath School system...Our numbers were at first small, both of children and teachers, but our doors were open wide to all, and the numbers soon increased.[116]

On 30th September 1859 the Scottish Guardian, in the first appearance of its column entitled 'Revival Intelligence', reported the first manifestations of revival in Edinburgh:

In a large public work near Fountain Bridge, where there are hundreds of young men and women employed, a young woman was recently struck down, and her cries were so vehement as to be heard all through the building. This young woman now gathers all the others - about two or three hundred I should say - every day at the dinner hour, and holds a prayer meeting for a short time.[117]

From then on things happened very quickly. The Mission had started a nightly meeting from Sunday 28th August and:

From the 14th October when the first anxious enquirer remained behind, there was for many months no meeting at which there were not some conversions. Night after night the careless became earnest, the earnest became convicted, and the convicted at length found peace in the blood of Jesus. A second meeting became an established arrangement, and as the interest deepened

---

116. 'These Fifty Years: The Story of Carrubbers Close Mission, Edinburgh', The Tract and Colportage Society of Scotland, Edinburgh, 1909.
117. The Wynd Journal of 8th October 1859 reports this incident and adds that 'nightly prayer meetings are held in connection with Fountainbridge Church, and several hopeful cases of awakening have occurred among the young'.

there was often considerable difficulty in clearing the chapel before eleven o clock.[118]

On Sunday evenings they could not accommodate the crowds, and when hundreds had to be turned away, they moved for three months into the Theatre Royal, and then into the Free Assembly Hall. By December they were planning children's prayer meetings:

> In addition to meetings for young men and young women already in operation, a separate prayer meeting for children is about to be formed. While the usual meeting is going on within the chapel, about twenty lads meet in the hall below to ask a blessing.[119]

By October 1859 the 'Bible Class for young females numbered above forty' and 'these young people have kept a prayer meeting among themselves for the last eighteen months.'[120]

Two months later we are supplied with a description of the class run by Mr. Gardiner for older boys. This is his report dated 7th November. Apart from one lad being described as 'twelve or thirteen' we are not informed of the ages of the others, although at least some of them are obviously at work.

> On Monday, the 24th of October, in the second meeting, I again met with the young lads I had had previously. I felt that I had more that night than I could deal with. I would rather be confined to one or two inquirers at one time than a number. When there are many, I cannot deal so personally with them; too much inclined to be general. However, trusting to the Holy Spirit, I endeavoured to be as personal in my remarks to them as I could. They were soon all in tears, except one. I said to him, 'William, you seem to be anxious, but there is something awanting. What is it?' He said, 'I want to feel my sins, for I cannot come to Christ till I realise that I am a sinner.' He knew that he was a sinner in the sight of God, for he had been taught that from his youth. But now

118. 'These Fifty Years: The Story of Carrubbers Close Mission, Edinburgh' The Tract and Colportage Society of Scotland, Edinburgh, 1909.
119. S.G. 16th December 1859.
120. W.J. 22nd October 1859

he wanted to know practically, and feel himself lost and ruined. We prayed together that God might open his eyes, that he might behold himself as God sees him. Each had prayed that night for forgiveness. I pointed them to the Saviour, and read to them part of the 11th chapter of Luke, 5th to 14th verses. I said to each that they must be importunate in prayer, giving God no rest ; and if they were so, Christ had given them the promise that he that asketh receiveth, he that seeketh findeth, and to him that knocketh it shall be opened. They went away that night without having found Christ, but with the determination to seek Him until they found Him. They all came back the next night, still without Christ. Having conversed with each, I found that it was decision that they wanted.

I spoke of the necessity of deciding at once. They were all deeply affected. I said to them, in the words of Joshua, 'Choose ye this *night* whom ye will serve;' and asked all those who would decide upon following Christ, and who would now give themselves to following him, to come to a separate form. At first none came; they all sat still, with their faces covered with their hands, as if in prayer. Having sat for some time in this manner, William came forward to the seat, and then followed William C., John N., and James Y. We then knelt down, and one by one came by my side and gave themselves to Christ. Each prayed; and I prayed with and for each. When these four had all prayed, Peter W. burst out in earnest payer, and gave himself to Christ also. This solemn scene so impressed me with the power of the Holy Spirit, that I felt myself humbled to the dust.

On rising from our knees, I said, 'Can you put your trust in Jesus?' and the answer of every one was 'I can trust Him now.' That night, when they left the meeting, their faces were lit up with a holy joy, and I was melted into tears as each came forward before leaving the hall and grasped my hand with both theirs, and smiles upon those faces, which were scarcely dry after the tears of repentance they had been shedding that night. That night, when I left the hall, there were two of their number waiting for me. One said, 'Can we have one of the rooms below tomorrow night, as we are to have a prayer meeting among ourselves?' I found that the rooms were disengaged. I told them that they could have it. Next night I went about the close of their meeting. When I entered, I found them all there with their Bibles in their hands, one reading the parable of the prodigal son. I prayed with them, and they all came up to the hall, and went up to the printing room, where they have had a regular prayer meeting every night since, several of themselves engaging nightly. The first thing each set himself to do after he had found Christ, was to bring others of his companions, and to tell them what He had done for their souls. These five young lads have now increased to thirteen, all of whom, I am satisfied, have been born again.

I spoke to one of the number, a boy about 12 or 13 years of age. One night I asked him if he was still trusting in Jesus? 'Oh yes,' he said; 'but when I am praying at home my brothers and sisters laugh at me and mock at me, but I pray on never minding them. Jesus is upon my side, and I'm not feared for them.'

This lengthy account then instances several examples of some of the problems the lads encountered specially at work and the advice they were given. It then continues:

On last Saturday night, when I went up to the printing room I was surprised to find only three there. On making inquiry, I found that the rest had met with their companions and others to hold a prayer meeting in Chalmers' Close. There were eighteen present at that meeting.

Gardiner concludes his article by exhorting Sunday School teachers to have personal dealings with each of their pupils and pray more earnestly for them, then:

These children would be the means of converting parents, and brothers and sisters, who perhaps would never enter a church door or prayer meeting.[121]

The area of influence began to spread:

---

121. W.J. 10th December 1859

In the Grassmarket a very wonderful work has commenced. Mr. D—, a medical student, had long attended a school there to instruct poor boys. Lately, they had become so unruly that order was despaired of. One night last week they had to give up working, and Mr. D— commenced to pray. Suddenly one after another of these wild ragged boys cried out for mercy and in a few minutes they had all begun to pray for themselves...While those boys were praying two prostitutes passed by the door. They listened and passed on. The Spirit forced them back and they began to cry for mercy.[122]

On 20th February 1860 James Gall Jnr. wrote to the Wynd Journal observing:

At first the conversions among us took place chiefly among the young women; after that we noticed that the movement was particularly marked among the men. At present it is pre-eminently an outpouring of the Spirit upon the children.[123]

From the start, the work at Carrubbers was a layman's work, encouraging everyone associated with it to play their full part in its outreach. Thus when Mr. Alex Jenkinson brought his class of 150 young women into the Mission and became Superintendent of the morning Sabbath School, 'he found the most important employment for the young women of his evening class by setting them to teach the little children, while they themselves also received lessons in teaching. In this manner the morning school has become the normal school for the training of young teachers, who as soon as they are admitted to the fellowship of the church, are also admitted to the membership of the Mission.'[124] Children and young people were thus allowed to take their part in the proceedings:

On Saturday night last the meeting in the Whitefield Chapel presented a very striking aspect. A great many people remained after the first meeting apparently in great anxiety about their souls. They were scattered in groups over the floor - in one corner

122. S.G. 30th December 1859 also T.R. and W.J. 7th January 1860.
123. W.J. 3rd March 1860. 124. 'These Fifty Years'.

a group of half a dozen boys listening very attentively to one of their companions with New Testament in hand, explaining some passages to them; opposite were four or five boys kneeling and praying with great earnestness - one of them entreating God to have mercy on a little fellow by his side, who appeared to be in great distress of mind. In the gallery a boy was lying on the floor praying earnestly and distinctly for all who were present, for all their fathers and mothers, brothers and sisters; whilst deep wailing was heard proceeding from an adjoining room. They continued in this state till a late hour.[125]

We read the following comment on the children's prayer meeting:

The prayer meeting for children in the city now numbers several hundreds. The great desire of these young persons is for prayer, and to unite themselves to the Lord. There is no difficulty in getting them to attend the meeting - the difficulty is in getting them to leave it. Their prayers were enough to put older people to the blush. They contained many striking expressions.[126]

The Mission had established prayer meetings in many different areas around the City, including Blackhall, Newhaven, Slateford, Portobello and Musselburgh. In Blackhall:

It was stated a great work is also going on at this place, particularly amongst the young. A number of the young people had erected a small house, formed of sticks gathered in the wood, and covered with straw, in which a number of them are in the habit of meeting for prayer when they come from school.[127]

Regrettably the location is not given of this incident:

Carrubber's Close branch meeting 'in a very ungodly district':
20 lads came in for 'fun', some twelve or fourteen stayed behind for conversation at our second meeting, evidently impressed ...After addressing and praying with them, I felt somewhat at a

---

125. S.G. Tuesday 28th February 1860 and T.F. 21st March 1860.
126. S.G. 15th March 1860 and T.R. 24th March 1860.
127. S.G. Tuesday 28th February 1860.

loss how to proceed, because, while their attention and interest
seemed to be greatly increased, I was myself very much exhausted. When about to rise from prayer, I observed five or six of
our boys from Carrubbers Close kneeling behind me, and knowing that under their teacher Mr. Gardiner they had become
accustomed to engage in social prayer, I asked them one by one
to pray for the conversion of the souls of these young boys by
whom we were surrounded. They did so, shortly, but with much
simplicity and earnestness: and I could not but notice the stolen
glances of solemn wonder which these kneeling inquirers cast at
the boys as if to make sure that their ears were not deceiving them.
After we rose from our knees, I said 'Now boys, go in among
them, and tell them about Jesus.' In a moment they proceeded to
distribute themselves among the group; and as I went around
among the other classes, I could observe from a distance the
proceedings of these young missionaries, some with their arm
drawn round the shoulder of their companions, and others in
groups upon their knees in prayer.[128]

Neither do we know which boarding school had a nightly prayer
meeting to which nearly all the girls came, following the conversion of
one of them during the Christmas holidays at a Carrubbers Close
meeting.[129] Even before that someone had reported from Carrubbers
that in 'some of the schools, prayer meetings have, with the full concur-
rence of the teachers, been commenced by the pupils at play hour.'[130]

In other parts of the city too meetings were crowded. The 'Correspondent' of the Whitefield Chapel reported that 'the attendance at the
children's meeting held in Brunswick Street has increased so much that
it has been removed to a chapel for larger accommodation.'[131] The
fishing community of Newhaven seemed to be particularly responsive:

On Saturday night last, at the close of the meeting, there was
extraordinary excitement. The room was crowded with fisher-

128. W.J. 11th February 1860.
129. W.J. 31st March 1860.
130. T.R. 26th November 1859.
131. S.G. Tuesday 28th February 1860.

men and others, and about one hundred ragged wild-looking boys. All behaved with the greatest decorum; and at the close of the meeting there was a universal wail for mercy, the prevailing cry being, 'God, be merciful to me a sinner.' A little boy, a convert from this chapel, had come from Edinburgh to be present, and was very busy telling the boys the wonderful story of redeeming love.[132]

On 11th March 1860 'W.J.I.' reported to the Whitefield Chapel a meeting which may have taken place as early as Monday 27th February 1860:

At the commencement of our conversational meeting the crush was so great in the hall, and so many persons standing outside, that it was proposed amongst ourselves to try and get the boys and girls from the gallery, and so make room for those of maturer years. A special meeting for the young was promised for the next evening. Still they were sorry to depart; and, as one of us was trying to coax them away with this promise, a fine boy of about fourteen years of age with tears in his eyes, looked up, and with tremulous voice, said, 'Sir, I might be dead before tomorrow night.' This was unanswerable. It was a rebuke which we ought never forget. We did not at the time take into consideration that the same Holy Spirit was busy with the young, as well as the old, and that their souls were also very precious in God's sight.[133]

Also at the Currubbers branch meeting in Newhaven on Tuesday February 14th, James Gall Jnr. noted 'a deep stillness ... Even the children seemed rivetted on occasion', and two weeks later the Free Church was 'densely packed by what appeared to be the whole village assembled, men, women and children'.[134] Reminiscing in later years Richard Hill recalls:

Newhaven was one of the first towns visited, and soon it was in a blaze. The schoolhouse could not hold all the people that came, but the ministers opened their churches, and they also were filled.

---

132. S.G. 28th February 1860 and W.J. 3rd March 1860.
133. S.G. Thursday 15th March 1860.
134. W.J. 10th March 1860, letter dated 1st March 1860.

Things of eternity seemed to press the community, so that nothing short of salvation would satisfy the people. The children turned up the boats to have their own prayer-meetings.[135]

In July, 1860, Rev George Fisch of the Evangelical Church in Paris attended some of the meetings in Newhaven, and wrote: 'Some young lads stopped me in the passage, saying that they wished me to carry a message to the boys in Paris - "Say to them that we are very happy now that we have among us a prayer meeting, and that we shall think of them".' [136] His own assessment of the work in Scotland is interesting: 'The revival in Scotland is as extensive as that of America and of Ireland; it is perhaps more solid and more profound.'[137]

Before we leave the story of Carrubbers, there is one other reminiscence of the prayer meetings worth quoting, from Sir Alex Simpson, MD:

Even children had their place in the movement. A little girl, accompanying her mother, put in a request that her brother might be led to read the Bible. When she arose to leave the meeting, immediately after prayer had been offered, her mother wished her to stay, but let the child go when she said, 'I want to go home and see him reading it.' [138]

In the October of 1860 Messrs Radcliffe and Weaver came to Edinburgh and conducted six weeks of continuous meetings, which obviously included those specifically for children, because we are informed:

It is stated that Mr. Weaver's services in the Free Assembly Hall have been brought to a close by the Assembly Hall Committee. On Saturday night Mr. Weaver, while addressing 1500 children in the hall, said, 'I can't meet with you again. Your little feet are spoiling their fine carpets. But never mind. You will not be thought unworthy to tread the golden streets.' [139]

135. 'These Fifty Years' p.71. 136. S.G. 17th July 1860.

137. S.G. 26th June 1860 quoting 'Archives du Christianisme' of the previous week.

138. 'These Fifty Years' pp 77-8.

139. S.G. Thursday 8th November 1860 from a report to The Mercury.

While in Edinburgh the two men and their helpers twice visited the Calton Gaol, where they were allowed to speak in the Chapel and talk to individuals.

Young Lady G— spoke to the boys, one poor fellow told us he was going to hang himself yesterday; and showed us the iron rail which he intended to use, outside his window. He was in an agony of mind, though only about fifteen years old. We told him that we hoped today he had got something better to hang upon. Jesus had hung on the cross for him. I believe he rested his weary young soul on Jesus that day.

It was a touching picture to see young Lady G—, with her arms around two of those boys at the same time, entreating them to come to Jesus for pardon.[140]

A summary of the situation in Edinburgh is given in the annual report of the Committee of the Edinburgh Sabbath School Teachers Union. It is a matter of great regret that the location of these events is not given, but it does underline for us how widespread the work was:

In many districts of the country, 1859 will long be remembered as truly a Pentecostal time - a year of prayer and of the outpouring of the Spirit. Gratefully do we acknowledge that the Spirit of grace has blessed us also. One Superintendent writes: 'An interesting religious movement in the school; and at the request of the scholars a prayer meeting is held. Every one of the scholars attends.' Another says: 'There have been a good number of very interesting cases of conversion in one of the senior classes, all of whom continue to give good evidences of a decided change in life.' ... Respecting another school, meeting in a destitute locality, it is reported: 'Some of the boys (along with others not at this school) commenced a prayer meeting, which is still continued, in the house of the parents of one of the scholars.' 'We are not without evidence that the Lord is blessing us,' says another Superintendent, 'For several weeks past, we have been meeting every night with a class of twenty anxious inquirers.'... 'A hith-

140. Recollections of Reginald Radcliffe, p.97.

erto unprecedented awakening has taken place, chiefly among the senior scholars; about fifty of them have been, as far as men can judge, hopefully converted to God.'[141]

How Couper can adduce that Edinburgh had 'stood aloof in a somewhat marked way from revival work', and that 'The revival of 1859-60 was scarcely felt'.[142] I cannot understand. Presumably, he was unacquainted with the obvious response to the Gospel among the youth at least of the city?

In 1859 a student of the New York Theological Seminary came to Edinburgh to study at the Free Church College. On the recommendation of Rev. Dr. Lindsay Alexander, the President of the Congregational Union, in 1860 he was invited to Musselburgh to assist in pulpit supply. Edward Payson Hammond had intended on being a missionary to Bulgaria, but he had been involved in the American revival of 1858, and found multitudes of both adults and children responding to the Gospel in Musselburgh. Edwin Orr states that 'his greatest contribution to the religious life of Great Britain was his great emphasis upon child conversion'.[143]

Dr. Alexander feared that the work might not be genuine, and came to see for himself. He was led to realise that the work was of God and was influential in Hammond remaining in Britain for two and a half years, and concentrating on work as an evangelist. There are several accounts of Dr. Alexander's visit to Musselburgh, and the longest one, delivered at the annual meeting of the Congregational Union in Glasgow in May 1860 may be found in Appendix B. He also described events in Musselburgh to a 'conversazione' held in the City Hall (presumably Glasgow?) on Wednesday 4th April. Dr Alexander was impressed by:

The number of children that seemed interested in the work that was going on in the meetings. On entering one of the meetings, he looked in at the vestry, which was full of children with Mr. Hammond in the midst of them. He was further struck at seeing a number of ragged-like collier and fisher lads - that class of young men which had seemed almost beyond the reach of

---

141. S.G. 24th March 1860. 142. Couper p.143.
143. Edwin Orr, 'The Second Evangelical Awakening' p.212.

evangelistic efforts - apparently a hopeless class. There they were in a room listening with the greatest attention. They were engaged in singing.[144]

E.P. Hammond was introduced to that meeting, and at a breakfast meeting the next day, was commended for 'the wonderful manner in which he stings into intense activity everyone in his church - the children to distribute tracts ...'. In January 1861 he went to Annan and the Dumfries area and was powerfully used among both adults and children. But his influence was to spread far beyond that. Orr suggests:

> Hammond used what were then considered novel methods to interest juveniles, and set T.B. Bishop and Josiah Spiers afire with the idea of *child evangelism*, and the result of their application of his principles to their problems was the foundation of the Children's Special Service Mission (CSSM.)[145] *(Later to become Scripture Union.)*

Later, Hammond wrote his own book called 'The Conversion of Children'[146] to argue the case for belief in the genuine conversion of children, which he illustrates with examples and testimonies from his ministry in Scotland and England as well as subsequently in America.

While Dr. Alexander was in Musselburgh his attention was drawn to a boy from Prestonpans who he felt should have been in bed (see Appendix B.) 'The Doctor sometime afterwards inquired whether the boy still attended the meeting, and he was told that the revival movement had commenced at Cockenzie, and that he attended the meetings at that place, which was in his own neighbourhood.'[147] Towards the end of that year the Revival provides us with a sequel indicating that that prayer meeting still continued: 'Boys and girls, young and old, began to pray aloud for mercy' at a Friday evening prayer meeting. 'Upwards of a dozen boys and girls confessed...that they had been brought to God.'[148]

---

144. S.G. Saturday 7th April 1860.
145. Edwin Orr, 'The Second Evangelical Awakening' p.212.
146. 'The conversion of children' by Rev. E. Payson Hammond, D.D., Revell, Chicago, 1901.
147. S.G. 7th April 1860 & W.J. 14th April 1860.
148. T.R. 17th November 1860.

(g) The Borders

Before the end of 1859 the revival had spread right across Scotland to the eastern Borders, causing the Rev. John Turnbull, Free Church minister at Eyemouth, to write 'I have been told that the very children are praying at the shore and the rocks.' [149] The Wynd Journal instances a most remarkable story of a three year old being the instrument of leading her mother into assurance, and of a family conversion:

> At Eyemouth, to test the work, a minister had visited a number of families and was convinced that, out of sixteen families, fifteen had had one or more conversions among them. One woman was weeping bitterly over her lost condition. 'Mother,' said her little child, three years old, 'why are ye crying? Didn't Mr. Turnbull say that the blood of Christ cleanseth from all sin?' That word was her deliverance. One family, whose members all professed to be converted save the father, proposed to begin family worship. 'I have no objection,' said the father, 'but you won't have it in my home. Ye may go where you please.' They went to a neighbour's house to have it there, and to pray for their father. He sat down alone by the fire, and a strange trembling seized him. He rushed out to the garden and fell on his knees a convicted sinner. He was enabled to lay hold of Christ, and ere his children had ceased their prayers, he stood among them praising God. [150]

Later, John Turnbull provides us with his own account of youthful prayer meetings:

> In the dark and stormy nights of December our boys held prayer meetings in the boats which were laid up at the end of the town: in unoccupied houses where they had neither fire nor light. They now meet, sometimes to the number of thirty in the house of a Christian friend. Our young girls have a meeting in a place which has been provided for them in the town. It was only a few weeks ago that the existence of a servant girl's prayer meeting came to my knowledge, from the circumstance that one of my Bible class told me that she had found peace at that meeting. And on one occasion I was surprised to

---

149. S.G. 20th December 1859 and T.R. 31st December 1859. 150. W.J. 3rd March 1860.

hear that a little girl, not more than twelve years old, at family worship had opened her mouth and poured forth prayer for her father and mother, brothers and sisters, filling them with wonder and making tears of joy flow from their eyes as they rose from their knees.[151]

At the United Presbyterian Church in Berwick Upon Tweed:

> About 50 of the children came into the vestry afterwards of whom 40 were deeply affected and wept sore. The Rev. — gave notice of another meeting on the following evening. About three times the number came into the vestry. Many professed to have found peace on the previous evening.[152]

Subsequently the children met for prayer in homes. Further into England 'thousands of senior scholars' had been converted on Tyneside.[153]

Despite two and a half years of evidence of children's conversions and their participation in prayer meetings, one of the saddest tales of this period must be that of girls being turned away from a prayer meeting because they were too young, as related by Rev. Paterson, described as 'an agent of Carrubber's Close Mission' writing from Peebles:

> At Eddleston, a neighbouring village, we had excellent meetings...several young men have begun a prayer meeting. They are not ashamed to own their master. The young women have done the same. A little incident occurred the first night they met: a few young girls were present of about ten or twelve years of age whom we thought rather young for such a meeting. I told them so, and when going out wished them to accompany me and to leave the young women alone. The poor girls wept as they left. Next day they came to the manse to consult with the ladies about a meeting for themselves, and wishing some of them to take the oversight. Mrs. D— said that they should not, and that such meetings were intended for those who gave their hearts to Jesus. They answered: 'But we have given our hearts to Jesus.'[154]

---

151. Wm Reid 'Authentic Records of Revival' p.334.

152. T.R. 21st June 1861.

153. Edwin Orr, 'The Second Evangelical Awakening', p.212. Accounts of prayer meetings in T.R. 1st July 1861.

154. T.R. 15th March 1862 quoting W.J.

Also in 1862, William Aimers tells, in the Carrubber's Close Mission Journal, of the effective testimony of a teenage boy in Highton, two miles from Kelso:

A little boy, of about fourteen or sixteen years of age was brought to Jesus at an early stage of the revival meetings. He lived with his father, mother and sister. Night after night he went home grieved that there should be no family worship at home. One night he could bear it no longer; he spoke to his father about it, and entreated him to take down the family Bible, and commence the reading of God's word. His father put him aside gently at first, but the boy still persisted, and asked his father to reach him down the Bible, 'for,' said he, 'if ye'll no begin, I must do it myself.' This so exasperated the man that he raised his hand and struck his son for what he thought his presumption, and when the boy ran out of the house, peace and quietness were apparently restored. A long silence ensued, till the father became somewhat alarmed at his boy's long absence. The night was dark and he was ill at ease, till going out to see if he could find him, he heard a voice as if proceeding from an outhouse, and on stealthily approaching, he overheard the boy praying for his poor father, who would neither read the Bible or pray. He returned in agony to his house. 'O wife,' said he, 'there's something awfu' gaun to happen, he's oot there praying for his prayerless father. Oh, it's terrible, for its true.' The arrow was directed by a never-failing Hand - the Spirit had commenced a work of grace in that careless man's heart, and he and his wife and daughter were eventually brought to the Saviour through the instrumentality of that little boy. The last time I saw them they were indeed a happy family, rejoicing in the Lord Jesus.

The same boy was met by a careless young woman one day, who began taunting him and saying 'And so you're converted?' 'Yes,' he replied, 'are you no?' 'No,' was the reply. 'Then if ye're no converted, ye maun be condemned.' The word 'condemned' stuck to her. She couldn't get rid of it: it was directed by the Holy Spirit. She did what all must do who wish peace: she came to Jesus as a poor penitent sinner sueing for mercy, and she found it in Him, where all fullness dwells.[155]

---

155. W.J. 16th August 1862

In Ancrum, Roxburghshire, Rev. John McEwen traced the awakening to prayer which began towards the end of September, 1859.

It was cheering to see several of the young of both sexes, brought to feel their need of Christ, and to seek after Him for hidden treasure ... It is pleasing now to see these young persons walking in the fear of God, and in the comfort of the Holy Ghost; and to know that they meet frequently together for prayer, and to encourage each other in the good way of the Lord.[156]

There is no clue in this text as to whether he is speaking of young adults, or those today we would call 'youth'.

(h) Spreading North: Fife, Central and Tayside

It is difficult to document the development of the Revival movement consecutively when we only have snippets of information. For example, from Kirkcaldy we hear that the 'Boy's prayer meeting continues to increase'[157] but we have no record of its commencement. In Cellardyke sixty adults are converted and 'as many children'.[158] Two slightly longer reports tell us of the response to the Gospel among younger people in Fife. 'JCB' of Anstruther wrote on 2nd April 1860:

Some twenty to thirty of those wild boys ... who have left school but are yet in no regular employment, and run about full of mischief. They were weeping, every one of them, some crying aloud - the Holy Spirit had convinced them of sin.

A number of little girls of ten or twelve years of age had been meeting together for prayer for some weeks. They now meet every night, and the cries of these children before the throne of mercy would have melted the heart of a rock ... 'Oh Lord, we have hard, hard, HARD hearts.' 'Though young in years we are old in sin.' 'We give our whole hearts to Thee.' Many, if not most, of these girls have found Christ and their smiling countenances tell how they are rejoicing in Him.[159]

---

156. Wm Reid, pp 273-6. 157. T.R. 4th February 1860.

158. T.R. 14th April 1860. The Cellardyke Revival is described by Rev. Alex. Gregory to Wm. Reid but adds no detail as to children. In fact he specifically excludes children from his computation of '300 persons (not including children)' who 'have evinced more or less concern about their souls...' (Reid, p.477).

159. T.F. 4th April 1860 & T.R. 14th April 1860

William Paterson wrote from Newburgh on 6th January 1862 (quoted from Carrubbers Close Mission report):

> On Sabbath evening our meeting was in the first United Presbyterian Church, Newburgh. There was a large attendance. Great solemnity was apparent among the people. After the benediction was pronounced about two hundred remained for a second meeting. I spoke for about an hour longer, and pronounced the blessing again. Even after that, fifty at least remained; there were many young people of about twelve or fifteen years of age...[160]

In the late summer of 1861 five weeks of meetings were held in Kinross:

> At one of these meetings the case of a little girl was particularly interesting. She had been very anxious, and a lady from Glasgow was conversing with her, and pointing to the already finished work of Jesus. After much prayer, the little girl was able to rest on the words 'it is finished'. On the way home she met an old woman who had also been anxious, and running up to her, exclaimed that she had found Jesus, repeating the words which to her were of such blessed import.[161]

In Auchterarder there is early evidence of a schoolboys' prayer meeting, this report being dated 21st April 1860:

> A week since, a few of the boys attending the Free Church school have waited on their teacher, Mr. Ferguson, and asked him to be so kind as to leave the key of the school-room with them, during the interval hour, viz., from 1-2 p.m. as they were anxious to hold a prayer meeting. The meeting was attended the first day by fourteen boys from between the age of eight and fourteen years. The number is now increased to thirty-five. The girls belonging to the same school have, since then, also begun a meeting. The number as yet is twenty-five, but as both meetings are only in their infancy, the numbers, it is hoped, will soon increase. These meetings are to be hailed with much joy.[162]

---

160. W.J. 1st February 1862.
161. S.G. 14th September 1861 & W.J. 21st September 1861.
162. W.J. 28th April 1860.

And from the same district this account of a twelve year old boy reaching assurance:

> One of the Sabbaths we spent here was a precious Communion Season. In returning home in the evening, we were accompanied by a young lad of about twelve years. We were led to ask him, if he was to be left outside when so many were coming to Christ. Sitting down beneath a tree, we read together of the glorious finished work of Christ. He seemed struck with the idea that the work was 'finished'. We then went into the house, where all the family individually engaged in prayer and thanksgiving for the Lord's goodness during the day, each remembering by name the young son who was now anxious about his salvation. After all had engaged, the poor lad burst out into earnest crying to the Lord, 'O, Lord, have mercy on me, a sinner, I am on the outside! Lord, have mercy on me.' Prayer was continued by all in turn, each time the young lad getting more strength to wrestle for the blessing. It was felt to be a delightful time, and though thus engaged for three hours, it seemed to have been only for a few minutes. In his last prayer, he said, 'O Lord, I have tried often to come to Thee before, but I have come really thi' nicht. It was my sin, Lord Jesus, that nailed Thee to the cross,' and so forth. We then rose from our knees, and after a light was procured, he was referred to several passages of scripture, John 3:14ff and to Isaiah 53. He paused and repeated the words 'With His stripes we are healed'. He was then asked what he thought of Christ. 'But I am not saved,' he quickly replied. 'But could you praise Jesus for what he has done?' 'I think I could.' He then joined heartily in the praise of the Lord. He continues to profess faith in Jesus ...[163]

'Many young people were quickened'[164] in Alloa through the ministry of John Colville in the spring of 1863.

A letter from Comrie reports 'a prayer meeting for the young at which between twenty and thirty attend'.[165] This may have been daily but the context is not clear. In Crieff 'a good deal of anxious enquiry has

163. W.J. 6th September 1862. 164. 'John Colville' by his widow, p.129.
165. S.G. 7th February 1860.

prevailed among the children, especially in one of the schools'.[166] The Newcastle Daily Express seems an unlikely source of information, yet carries a letter from the wife of the Free Church minister of Strathfillan to her sister in Newcastle, including this extract:

Tell your children one little girl at a meeting was overheard praying 'Come Jesus, come to me this very night; come to me and my three sisters' ... A girl under great concern being beckoned by him to come near, just made a great rush over, so great was her anxiety.[167]

In August 1860 when open air meetings were being planned in Perth for Tuesday 21st and Wednesday 22nd, 'arrangements have been made for spiritual addresses to the young'.[168] This was probably the visit of Messrs. Radcliffe and Weaver, where they were both touched by the way the children they were staying with joined in praying for the meetings as Radcliffe's wife recalled:

No sooner were we seated in the cab, to take us from Springland to the City Hall, Perth, than one of the party began to pray for a blessing. Mrs. George Barbour of Edinburgh, pleaded with God; and little Maggy, though only seven years old, prayed sweetly...On the 2nd of September 1860, nearly all the guests remained at Springland praying for the evening service. The children present also prayed aloud; and Richard Weaver told me he had never had such a blessing to his own soul since he was converted.[169]

When Richard Weaver preached in Crieff 'a large number of young girls sobbed aloud' according to The Scotsman.[170]

A letter from nearby Bridge of Earn dated 3rd July 1860 informs us:

About twenty boys and girls are deeply moved. Grief for sin and love to Jesus appear blended into one tender emotion in their souls. Some of the younger members of the congregation have thrown themselves especially into the work of dealing with them. It is affecting to see them lingering about the church door, as if loathe to go away though the hour is late.[171]

In Dundee young people seem to have been particularly responsive to the Gospel. 180 people attended a meeting on Sunday 30th October 1859 when 'at the close fifteen young people remained in great distress of mind'.[172] The Scottish Guardian traces a move among the mill girls of Dundee starting with two in November, until one hundred now attend a lunch-time prayer meeting, and 'fifty or sixty of the girls have given evidence of having undergone a saving change'.[173] Also from Dundee, Rev. W.B. Borwick records the existence of several children's prayer meetings:

From the first, the awakening has pre-eminently been among the young. No special efforts have been made, by way of sermons, exclusively preached to the young, except very occasionally. They have been impressed or drawn to the Saviour at the ordinary services, at their schools or at their little prayer meetings. Whether thought right or wrong, little children, when their hearts are touched, will pray and pray together. Little children of even eight and ten and twelve years of age have prayer meetings and 'take heed that you offend not one of these little ones that believe in me,' says Christ; and these meetings are still more common among the more advanced. I had occasion to leave my Bible class two weeks ago, and to see what they would suggest, I said I did not like to dismiss the class or get a substitute, as he might not know the usual way of going through the exercises. Immediately they whispered one to another and it was at once suggested to me that they would hold a prayer meeting among themselves. Two prayer meetings were the result - the one for the boys, and the other for the girls; and it has since been their request that both meetings be kept in connection with the Bible class.[174]

He then goes on to instance cases of child conversion.

171. W.J. 14th July 1860.
172. S.G. 1st November 1859.
173. S.G. 3rd March 1860.
174. Wm. Reid, 'Authentic Records of Revival', Nisbet, London, 1860, p.179.

An anonymous account, regrettably undated, describes the visit of William Paterson of Aberdeen, to Dundee, where he 'specially addressed the young'. There were nightly meetings for anxious enquirers which increased to several hundreds, and 'The awakening, though not wholly was chiefly among the young...In connection with those meetings of anxious enquirers, a number of small prayer meetings have sprung up, both among young men and boys - young women and girls, who conduct them themselves with great propriety.'[175]

Moving north there is evidence of the Revival reaching the Montrose area before the end of 1859, and of young people being touched by it, as this letter to the Scottish Guardian reveals:

I am sure you will be delighted to hear of a few more cases of conversion in connection with the revival at Montrose. The first of the cases I am about to mention was that of a servant girl. This girl was a poor, ignorant and unfortunate creature, and had lately been engaged in the family of an elder in one of the churches in Montrose. When the revival had been going on for two or three weeks, she became very alarmed, and was in a dreadful state of mind. Her master talked and prayed with her, but she became worse; so sinful did she see herself in the sight of a holy God. Seeing that he could do her no good himself he went for his minister to come and pray with and for her.

When they reached the house they found her on her knees in an awful state of despair. 'Come, come!' said her master, 'Kitty, that will never do.' And both he and the minister kneeled down beside her. At length she found peace and joy in her precious Saviour. There was a little boy in the family, about ten years of age, who was deeply interested in what he had seen and heard, and was deeply impressed. What made it all the more remarkable in his case was that he was a very mischievous boy. He kept close by the servant girl, and attended the meetings for prayer. At this time an uncle of the boy came to Montrose from some distance to do some business. The servant saw him to be a careless, if not a godless man, and watched and tried every opportunity she could get to direct his attention to the great work of the Lord that was going on; but she could not get him to listen to her, but always answered her by saying 'Gae awa, woman, I winna hear a word about them, nor I winna believe in these things ava.' One evening he was sitting at the parlour fire with the father, when the little boy, who had been at the prayer meeting, came in. He first threw his arms around his mother's neck and kissed her, crying, 'Oh!, mother, I've got Jesus.' He did the same to his father, who said, 'Oh George, I am afraid you are only excited, and will soon forget all.' 'No, father,' he cried, 'I've found Jesus and I know He will never leave me.' He next embraced his uncle - who was a witness to this scene - and said, 'Will you come to Jesus, Uncle?' His father, thinking the boy was perhaps giving offence, said to him, 'sit down George, like a man, on your seat'. However, let me say, the work was done in that soul; the arrow of the Almighty had pierced him by that little boy. There was deep silence in that room, and the father observed the lips of the strong man quiver, and to the astonishment of all, he said, 'Man, I think there must be something in these revivals after all.' This then opened the mouths of both his sister and her husband (who are both godly people), and while they were speaking to him of the manifestations of the Spirit on a great many, the seat could no longer hold him - he began to shake violently. He rose and went to a large table in the middle of the room, and made it shake so, that they thought it would go to pieces. He continued in this state for several hours, till, wet with perspiration he sunk quite exhausted. He was put to bed, and the next day being Sabbath, he rose and got ready for Church. He was very cheerful up till this, but whenever he heard the sermon he fell into the same state, and had to return home; and before he left Montrose he was rejoicing in Jesus.[176]

The effect on families was also noticed in Ferryden, the fishing community opposite Montrose, as Rev. Nixon describes in his 'The Work of God at Ferryden':

---

176. S.G. 7th January 1860

The children are treated reasonably, affectionately, quietly, Christianly, and they are not like the same creatures. They notice the change in their parents, they hear it, they see it, they feel it, and they are themselves changed. They are wonderfully tractable and obedient. And even among them, there are not wanting evidence of a spreading concern about their personal salvation.[177]

He also testified of 'one youth, who was a noted swearer, said to my brother, Mr. Lister, lately that he did not think he could swear now though he tried.'

Later, in a report to the Free Church General Assembly given on Tuesday 22nd May he concludes:

From what he had seen in Ferryden, he could not help saying that a sound religious education for the young in church and Sabbath school seemed to him to form the best basis for a satisfactory revival. In Ferryden those who were known to have been well educated in their childhood were much more satisfactory cases than those whose education had been wholly or partly neglected.[178]

Andrew Bonar had visited Ferryden in December 1859 and found the Lord 'working wonderfully' on Sunday 18th. The following day he 'came home from church accompanied by a band of children who sang hymn after hymn.'[179]

(i) Aberdeen

The move of the Holy Spirit in Aberdeen pre-dates the work in Clydeside. Prayer meetings had been established as early as 1857 when the first news came through of a spiritual movement in America. When reports of the American Revival were read at the Free Church Teachers' Association prayer meeting, the young men there began prayer meetings in the Free Bon-Accord Church, which led on to the formation of the Aberdeen YMCA, and also drew together a team of workers. According to Mrs. Gordon: 'At the same time Mr. Reginald Radcliffe, who had been much engaged in evangelistic work in England, was

177. S.G. 17th March 1860. 178. S.G. 23rd May 1860.
179. Diary, 19th December 1859.

praying earnestly in his Liverpool home that the Lord would give him some fresh work to do.'[180] Radcliffe was the son of the Town Clerk of Liverpool, and was brought up in the Church of England, had qualified as a lawyer in 1850, and was already well known for his philanthropic and evangelistic work. He had begun ragged schools in Liverpool, preached in the open air, and provided tracts for the crowds that gathered at race-courses, executions and fairs across England, Scotland and Ireland. He was invited to Aberdeen by William Martin, the Professor of Moral Philosophy at Marischal College, and arrived on a ten day visit, on the afternoon of 27th November 1858. He stayed four months until his health broke down. The next day, a Sunday, he began work among young people at a small Congregational Mission hall in Albion Street in the east end of the city. 'The Lord gave His blessing, and many of those dear children were converted. The change of heart and life at home, in the nursery, and at school, was so evident, that the parents began to attend the meetings also, and were likewise touched by God's Spirit.'[181]

Within a fortnight larger and more central buildings were required, such as Greyfriars Parish, Free North and Free Bon-Accord, with support from Revs. James Smith, Charles Ross and George Campbell respectively. At the same time Brownlow North was conducting a mission in Aberdeen, and in early February they were joined by the Morayshire Laird, Hay Macdowall Grant of Arndilly. The local Presbytery of the Established Church banned them from preaching as laymen on February 22nd, but this only increased the crowds, and the General Assembly finally overturned that decision on 10th May. One of the early converts, Mrs. Gibbon, wrote later:

> It is difficult with our present familiarity with such an occurrence to conceive the novelty it then was to see a layman occupying a Scotch pulpit on week-days in the simple morning dress of a private gentleman, talking in sweet, loving tones to a church full of bright children, eagerly and trustfully listening about Jesus as their greatest Friend, their God, and their Saviour.

180. Hay Macdowall Grant of Arndilly, by Mrs Gordon (Seeley, London, 1876) p.122.
181. Recollections of Reginald Radcliffe by his wife (Morgan & Scott, London) p.37.

The good-will and wonder-working power of God were speedily revealed at these children's services; and seeing the reality of the change in all sorts of good fruits borne in their own nurseries at home and at school, the parents and teachers and the grown-up people generally began to crowd the galleries, and requests poured in to the evangelists to have the same meetings for adults at night.[182]

These meetings were commenced in Greyfriars Parish Church on 26th December. Some idea of the size of the congregation attracted is revealed in a latter of Radcliffe's dated 8th February 1859, where in an Established Church on the previous Sabbath there were 'three thousand fully, counting about five hundred children'.[183] After the impact on the children the next group to be touched were the young shop assistants, then the students.

At one of these early meetings:

Hundreds of children were assembled in one of the churches, and when he was speaking to them of Jesus and inviting them to come to Him and be saved, the Holy Spirit descended and awakened many of them to serious inquiry about the way of peace through Jesus Christ. On that evening, when the Spirit came upon them about thirty waited, in a state of anxiety, to speak to Mr. Radcliffe about their souls; and from that day onwards, numbers of dear children were convinced of sin and hopefully converted.[184]

Regular children's meetings were held in the Marywell Street school. Fortunately, we are provided with two descriptions of these, the first by David Rait, the son of the schoolmaster concerned, and the second by William Bruce, who attended as a young teenager:

My father being thus deeply interested in Revival work, and having had previous experience of such a time of blessing in Dundee:[185] it is not to be wondered at that his schoolroom in

---

182. Recollections, p.60.
183. Recollections, p.49.
184. Pamphlet 'Times of Refreshing', Aberdeen, 1859, p.18.
185. Under McCheyne and W.C. Burns.

Marywell Street became a centre for Revival and religious meetings. The outstanding feature at Marywell Street was the work among the young. On Saturdays, Mr. Reginald Radcliffe addressed crowded meetings of children in the schoolroom, and soon there was a large meeting of boys in their early teens for prayer and Bible study, at which my father acted as president; but the lads themselves carried on the work of the meeting with great zeal and devotion. Many of these lads afterwards gave themselves to the ministry, and some are still labouring in the ministerial field, while others took prominent positions in the city, and were long known for their philanthropical and missionary labours. But the work in Marywell Street schoolroom was not confined to children. There was evidence of a most gracious work amongst young men, among students, and young men in business, and practically every large establishment in town had some young men who had been influenced for good by the Revival. There was a special organization for these young men, and they were wont to meet in the schoolroom at stated intervals for prayer and study of the Bible, or to listen to addresses from one or other of the evangelists, or city ministers who were interested in the work.[186]

I was but a boy then and can speak only of the work among the young people, and in particular how it gathered in so many boys. I would be then thirteen to fourteen years of age. Some of those round me, and under the same influence of grace, were even younger; some were two or three years older. We ranged from twelve to eighteen years of age, and there were a goodly number of us. To my knowledge, there were fifty or sixty boys such as myself who all regarded ourselves as converted, and who in many ways avowed our faith.

The direction in which we showed ourselves was at the boys' prayer meetings. These were a great feature of the time. We were banded together for prayer, and we met once a week at least, and on each night a religious service was conducted by us boys

---

186. Reminiscences of the Revival of Fifty Nine and the Sixties (Aberdeen University Press, 1910) p.108

ourselves. We met for the most part in Marywell Street School; another portion met in Frederick Street School, and another in Princes Street School. Somehow I was connected with all of these; and I can well remember the first time I addressed the meeting, taking it upon me to expound the 23rd Psalm! Crude, ill digested, and ill arranged the matter was, but it was a boy's testimony to the power of the truth. At these boys' prayer meetings all was not always plain sailing. We were boys in widely different ranks in life. Some were from humble homes, others were from the homes of parents well known and esteemed throughout the city, and sometimes little jarrings occurred, and feeling over them was keen. But there were those who took a great interest in us and our meetings, who had won our affection and our confidence, and whose wise counsels often saved us from many mistakes, and served to guide us back when we had erred.

There were two men under whose influence we came, and one of whom we regarded and often spoke of as our father. The one best known among us, and often present at our meetings, was Mr. Rait, the teacher of Marywell Street School ; the other was the Rev. Dr. David Brown, then one of the Professors of the Aberdeen Free Church Divinity Hall. Mr. Rait was a man of great wisdom, of warm sympathy with young people ; a born teacher, and with something about him that set him alongside of boys as their trusted friend and counsellor. His school was always open to us and many a happy evening I have spent there with the others, who constituted our boys' prayer meeting. Dr. David Brown was less frequently among us. We looked upon him with a certain measure of awe, and we reckoned it a high occasion when he came to address us. He was in warmest sympathy with the work of grace then proceeding, and his influence with us boys went far to confirm in us the holy purpose with which we followed our Christian course. He was well known for his Christian sympathies and services, and the remembrance of what was perhaps his greatest service at the time, the Marywell Street Sabbath morning meetings, will be among the pleasantest.

One of the features of grace at that time, and one part of the great movement, was that those who had come under the power of the truth, at once set themselves to win others. So was it with us boys, we too became workers in some way. We used to arrange to go out with the preachers to the open-air gatherings - Duncan Matheson used to call us his bodyguard. Some of us specially took that work of going out with him to the street corners and standing round him. He needed no protection, but he liked to see us there, and we liked to go with him.[187]

On February 13th 1859, Mr. Grant wrote to his wife:

Yesterday...there was a meeting of children in the Marywell School, which Mr. Radcliffe addressed. I was there only half-an-hour, but found six children to speak to and an old woman...most of them dissolved in tears under a sense of sin, and believing in Jesus when this was pressed upon them as God's command, backed by His gracious promises...This morning I accompanied Mr. Radcliffe to Marywell School, which we found crowded by people of all ages, as well as children. I gave an address for twenty minutes, and then went into another room in order to converse with the anxious, and about thirty came, to each of whom I had only to say, 'Lay your sins on Jesus, and trust God's promise to pardon,' and they professed almost immediately to believe.

He then gently tells his wife he 'dare not leave' Aberdeen for another fortnight, and concludes: 'My belief is that the leaven now working in Aberdeen will leaven Scotland from one end to another.'[188]

Another reminiscence is provided by John Horne, who also furnishes us with evidence of the lasting nature of the work:

---

187. Reminiscences of the Revival of Fifty Nine and the Sixties (Aberdeen University Press, 1910) pp 136 - 8. John MacPherson's biography of Duncan Matheson (London, 1910) is of little use to us as details of places and people have been deliberately omitted. On p. 117 he uses an account given by Mrs. Bain, wife of the Free Church Minister of Garioch, who found a 'lad', one of her Bible Class, in great distress at the church door. He was taken up to the manse where Matheson led him through a time of deep distress into assurance, which resulted in a 'consistent profession'. Unfortunately we lack other details of Matheson's dealings with young people, and references to children do not appear in this biography.

188. Hay Macdowall Grant, pp 123-5.

A very remarkable feature of the movement showed itself in the case of a number of young schoolboys who started a meeting for prayer among themselves. That meeting was usually held in Marywell Street Schoolroom, and was carried on for many months. Of such youths as were at this time savingly impressed, not a few subsequently went forth as missionaries to China, India and Africa, while others filled pulpits at home.[189]

Fifty years later Rev. Rae recalls: 'in the height of the movement it was no uncommon thing to find young people continuing for four or five hours in prayer, interspersed with hymns and scripture readings,'[190] while the adults often prayed through the night. An anonymous contributor adds:

Among the children there was manifested an eagerness for prayer and Bible lessons that I have not seen equalled since then, although I have had a considerable experience of the Children's Special Service Missions, and of the Christian Endeavourers. They not only had frequent prayer meetings by themselves, but they were ever ready to attend week-evening Bible classes. Among the young men and women there was a like spirit.[191]

The work in Aberdeen was clearly not confined to any one social class. As Mrs. Radcliffe writes:

The work of conversion broke out in fresh places. At a meeting in a young gentlemen's boarding school, a few simple words were spoken, and the hearts of all were bowed down, so manifest was the power of God. Meetings were held for rough boys at Oldmill Reformatory, with remarkable results.[192]

Likewise girls of the upper class were also affected. H.M. Grant recorded on February 16th 1859:

Yesterday...I had appointed to meet Mr. Radcliffe and Professor Martin after the prayer meeting to go to a school, where Mr. R. was

189. Reminiscences, p.48-9. 190. Reminiscences, p.7.
191. Reminiscences, p.55. 192. Recollections, p.53.

to address some friends of the lady and some young people...In the drawing room, before the meeting, I attempted to say a few words to an elderly lady on a sofa, but evidently she did not relish the subject. When all were assembled in another room, I said that I would wait in the drawing-room to speak to any impressed. After I was left alone my faith began to fail, and I thought that none would come to speak, remembering the insinuations of the lady; so I prayed for help and strengthening. In about fifteen minutes Professor M. entered, leading a girl of thirteen, weeping bitterly, and when I asked her the cause she replied, 'Oh my hard, wicked heart!' I pointed her to Jesus as the Physician of souls. Hardly had she left the room, when the elderly lady mentioned above entered, and said with emotion that she had come to speak about her soul; and ere I finished talking to her, ten of different ages entered, all weeping, and deeply impressed.[193]

However, in a letter to Mrs. Radcliffe, which seems to describe the same occasion, Grant claims that 'about fifteen came in - many of them seventeen and eighteen years of age, and all weeping bitterly.'[194]

Returning to the boys, a week later Grant added:

February 23rd: Accompanied Mr. Radcliffe to the Gymnasium, Old Aberdeen. I asked Mr. Anderson if he could give us a spare room in which to speak to any individual who might desire it. He said Yes, but told me afterwards that he had not the slightest expectation that it would be required. I gave out the psalm and prayed, and then Mr. R. spoke for about fifteen minutes upon the brazen serpent, and went away into the other room, leaving me to speak further, which I did from Mark ii. Two or three boys followed Mr. R., and after a time some more, and by the time I concluded, almost all went, and then I followed to help him to speak. The boys pressed to be spoken to, many of them deeply moved. Man's work had been weakness but the Holy Spirit made it the power of God unto the salvation of immortal souls...[195]

In the same note he informs us that:

193. Hay Mcdowall Grant of Arndilly, p.104.
194. Recollections, p.51. 195. Hay Mcdowall Grant of Arndilly, p.104-5.

The conversion-work at this time in Aberdeen was largely carried on amongst children from eight to fourteen years of age, and one day about thirty-five boys asked Mr. Rait for the use of Marywell School for a prayer meeting. Afraid that order might not be kept; - he agreed to give it on the condition of being included as one of the boys himself, which was agreed to. The boys conducted the meetings always in a most orderly manner, and read the Bible and prayed delightfully. One rule was to expel from it any boy guilty of open sin; and this was carried out against one proved guilty of using bad words, who seemed to feel much his expulsion.

This presumably is the same prayer meeting referred to in a letter of 8th April 1859 held in the:

School-room every Monday and Saturday, by upwards of sixty younger lads, ranging from about ten to fourteen years of age, in which the Spirit of God is remarkably manifested. They formerly held their meetings in an attic, but the number increased so much, that they were obliged to procure a school-room, the master of which gives interesting and encouraging accounts regarding them.[196]

A similar letter asserts the multiplicity of such gatherings:

Another feature of the work to which I would advert, is the interest in divine things manifested among children. Little meetings for prayer have been found in several places throughout the town, amongst girls; and within five minutes walk from our place of residence, there are no fewer than six different meetings, composed of boys, whose ages vary from ten to fifteen years. I have been present at every one of these boys' meetings. The number present in one, was generally between fifty and sixty - in another about thirty were present, and so on of the rest. These dear boys in their meetings read God's word, that they may know his will - sing his praise and call upon his name in prayer. Their

---

196. Times of Refreshing, Aberdeen 1859, p.52-3

petitions are very simple and childlike, as they ought to be, but they come to the throne of grace with a petition; and since it is the hearer of the prayer that gives the Spirit of prayer - he who 'out of the mouth of babes and sucklings can perfect praise,' who knows but this is also of the Lord of Hosts, who is wonderful in counsel, and excellent in working.[197]

The characteristics of the Aberdeen revival are usefully summarised for us by Duncan Matheson in a letter to the editor of the British Messenger:

I never, during my life, saw more deep concern for souls than I have seen here, and the close clinging to each other, though in different churches, is refreshing, most refreshing. Groups of the young are to be found here and there, throughout the whole city meeting for prayer; and one thing has struck me more almost than anything - the holy boldness in confessing Christ, and acknowledging what He had done for their souls. Another striking thing is, that few have found Christ for themselves but they have been instrumental in the awakening of others.[198]

From Aberdeen the work spread to the surrounding district. For example, Radcliffe visited Old Meldrum for one night only, and held a meeting in the Free Church under Rev. Garioch. After a short and simple address, Radcliffe invited those who were anxious to be saved to remain, but everyone left the building, so he addressed the workers present with 'Friends, have faith in God. Let us ask God to send them back.' The congregation began returning until 'the big kirk was again one third full. Then what a night we had! There was a wondrous breakdown; boys, girls, young men and women, old gray-haired fathers and mothers, wept together like babies' according to Dr. R. McKilliam's eye-witness account.[199]

In Rhynie, Radcliffe took joint meetings between the Congregationalists and the Free Church and saw 70-80 conversions,

---

197. Times of Refreshing, Aberdeen 1859, p.52-3.
198. Quoted in T.R. 10th September 1859. 199. Recollections, p.73.

'Their age ranged from twelve to about forty years of age, with a great majority of young men' as Rev. Nicol told the Congregational Assembly in April. A similar report of youthful response was given by Rev. Noble of Laurencekirk who claimed: 'Almost every young person connected with our church was, to a greater or lesser extent, brought under the influence of the truth.'[200]

In an earlier report published in October 1859 a correspondent from Laurencekirk also traces the origin of the revival there to a joint meeting of the Congregationalists and the Free Church five weeks previously, and adds 'most of those first impressed, were young men and women who had been attending our Sabbath School and Bible Classes.'[201]

At Ballater a mother was converted, and adult prayer meetings started as a result of girls praying in Aberdeen:

At Ballater the work has begun; some young girls from there came to Aberdeen and were awakened and found Jesus. One of them invited her mother to come and see her; she promised and this daughter with three other girls united in prayer that her coming to Aberdeen might be blessed. The mother came, went to church, heard all and remained unmoved, till coming out of church a person put his hand on her shoulder, and said 'Are you saved?' It was enough, the arrow went home, she returned to Ballater and told others. There are now five or six prayer meetings.[202]

In New Deer there was 'a meeting for the young every Saturday afternoon,' and at the visit of Mr. Gordon Forlong:

A deep impression was made, and when all who desired to be spoken to individually were invited to remain behind, we were glad to find that not very many had left. For another hour, Mr. Forlong and Rev. Mr. Alexander, went about among the children and in a few cases we have good reason to believe that Christ's offer of mercy was accepted that day.[203]

In March 1859 Radcliffe went to stay with the Duchess of Gordon for a rest at Huntly:

200. S.G. 7th April 1860. 201. W.J. 22nd October 1859.
202. W.J. 7th January 1860. 203. W.J. 3rd March 1860.

It was on the 10th March when Mr. Radcliffe was visiting the school at Huntly Lodge Gates, that the power of God fell upon the hearts of many of the children.

The Duchess wrote to the Rev. Moody Stuart, Edinburgh: 'A baby of a few summers was sobbing so that Mr. Radcliffe took her in his arms to find out if she were hurt. "Oh, no; only while you were praying I felt my heart so hard I could not love Jesus." JESUS is all their cry.'

Again the Duchess wrote: 'When I went into the school the day after, I found them marching merrily, having adapted to their marching time, the hymn of which the chorus is "I love Jesus, yes, I do." Of course it will not do to allow the name of Jesus to be used lightly; but I could not at once stop the babes in their own way of rejoicing in the Lord.'[204]

The support of the Duchess of Gordon was of invaluable assistance to the revival: it was of course unusual for someone of her social status to be associated with the Free Church, but on 5th January 1860 she hosted a meeting of ministers from Inverness to Aberdeen at her Huntly home to share their experiences of the spiritual awakening.

Although this will take us ahead of ourselves geographically, it is worth pausing here to consider the reports of this meeting, which was well covered by both the Banffshire Journal and the Wynd Journal. Even confining ourselves to the extracts relating specifically to children and young people, there is a widespread evidence of spiritual concern right across the north of Scotland by the end of 1859. We quote from the Banffshire Journal of Tuesday 10th January 1860:

Religious Revival in the North of Scotland - Conference at Huntly.

A very important meeting of ministers from various parts of the North of Scotland, was held in Huntly on Thursday last, for the purpose of comparing notes, and reporting on the state of religion in their different localities... In the evening, a public meeting was held in the Free Church, at half-past seven o'clock. *Probably over 1,000 attended with 29 ministers on the platform, Rev. Williamson of Huntly was in chair introducing:*

Rev Reid, Banchory : In regard to the commencement of the work, I may mention that the first case that came under my notice was that of a little boy of fourteen years of age. He had gone to bed of a Sabbath evening, and the family had retired to rest, but about two hours afterwards he went to his mother's apartment and awoke her. She knew by his wail of distress that there was something very peculiar the matter. He said, 'Mamma, I have been thinking about my salvation, and the devil has been telling me that I cannot be saved.' She spoke to him as best she could, and they spent the whole of that night wrestling most earnestly in prayer for acceptance and salvation. Next morning - he slept none through the night - he was very much weakened, but about midday he got up and asked to be allowed to go out, and he went out into a hay loft, and there alone he wrestled with God, and there he met with the Blessed Saviour and gave himself to Christ. From all I have heard of him, I believe he is walking consistently.

Rev Fraser, Inverness reported there had been prayer meetings among young men for fifteen months. A few boys who had been a nuisance in their neighbourhood, had become little missionaries, and went through the town distributing tracts. Many had begun to enquire after salvation - old and young men and women, and little children.

Rev. Reid, Portsoy; I have had particular encouragement with regard to the young. The teachers of our Sabbath school have had a special prayer-meeting just in behalf of the children under their instructions. One evening (continued Mr Reid, after some other remarks) after addressing the children, I wished to give an opportunity to any who wished to speak with myself or their teachers. There were so many remained that I invited them to come up the following day to the manse, when thirty or forty came, and a more interesting meeting I never addressed or ever witnessed. Many of the little ones were melted into tears, and were reluctant to leave after engaging with them again and again in prayer. I may just mention a little anecdote of one of these girls. Last Sabbath, she had been three times in church. In the evening, I happened to read the closing chapter of Genesis, where it is said, 'Joseph was put into his coffin,' and I happened to make the remark that there would be not a few who would be found to have been put into their coffins before the year that had begun would close. This little girl said to herself, 'What if I should be the one that should need the coffin?' She went home that night; was suddenly taken ill; she has been at the gates of death since, when I left this morning, she still survived, but it is doubtful whether she may be among the living even now. But, be this as it may, I never stood by a sick-bed with more pleasure than I did during the last few days in visiting her. Mr. Reid concluded, after some other remarks, referring particularly to another little girl, who pleaded much with her father to attend to religious matters.

Rev McKenzie, Nairn: believed the characteristic of this revival was prayer. He could mention interesting cases of children putting their parents up during the night to pray for them, and of young persons seeking to bring others to a knowledge of religious truth.

Rev Ker, Deskford: Little children had been converted. One boy of nine years of age, going home from a meeting with his father, but who did not like to speak to him, loitered behind the rest and knelt down on the snow, when the snow was at its very deepest, and cried for mercy. They did not know of this till afterwards, and now the boy was firm in his testimony and did not care although other boys at the school scoffed at him.

Rev Campbell, Free North Church, Aberdeen: There are a great many prayer meetings, and these both amongst young men and amongst young women, and also prayer meetings amongst children.[205]

At the end of July 1860, the Duchess hosted large open air gatherings in her grounds organised by Duncan Matheson. There are discrepancies in the estimated figures of those attending, the Revival claiming 4,000 with 1,000 children attending the preceding 'Juvenile Service'[206], while the Wynd Journal states 11,000 attended and adds:

It was a great sight to see about three thousand young people assembled in the park, where the ground formed a little amphitheatre. They had short addresses between eleven and one, with prayers and psalm singing, behaving all the while with the utmost

205. Also reported in W.J. 21st January 1860.
206. T.R. 11th August 1860

propriety, though I cannot say I saw any serious impressions apparent.[207]

To this the Scottish Guardian adds these details, from the report given to the Aberdeen Free Presbytery on Friday 27th July:

On Wednesday forenoon, the main feature of the proceedings was the aggregate meeting of juveniles. The Great North of Scotland Railway Company had agreed to run special trains for children and those in charge of them besides carrying passengers at reduced fares by other trains. The total from all stations on the Great North line was - juveniles 880, adults 1,317. Of young people the number present at the place of meeting nearly approached three thousand, and altogether the assemblage would be fully five thousand.[208]

There were several addresses, prayer and refreshments provided by the Duchess of Gordon, then they were conducted back to the station.

These open air summer meetings continued for three years; two years later in a report on the Huntly open air meetings we read of a children's meeting on 25th June 1862 'attended by several hundreds of young people'.[209]

There is one other anecdote supplied by Rev George Cumming, who was converted as a completely Godless sixteen year old; regrettably he does not reveal the location:

The F.C. minister of P—and his wife, who lived about three miles from us, and in whose congregation there had been a wonderful outpouring of the Spirit, and a great awakening and ingathering into the kingdom, began to take an interest in what was then called 'dark D—', and sent ministers and evangelists to visit it. One of the first to come and preach was the late Rev Donald Grant, and, I believe, I was one of the first to come under the power of the truth. On the night he came to preach, a number of

207. W.J. 4th August 1860.
208. S.G. Saturday 28th July 1860.
209. W.J. 5th July 1862. These meetings were later continued in H.M. Grant's home at Arndilly, 14 miles south of Elgin, see T.R. 23rd August 1866.

us young people were dancing in a large barn. He had to pass this barn, on his way to the meeting hall, and he came in. He asked to be allowed to say a few words; this permission, however was refused, and he was ordered to leave the place. But before doing so, he held up his hands, his pale face beaming with a heavenly smile, and said : 'One thing is needful - the salvation of the soul,' and further, with aweful solemnity he added: 'Oh, how dreadful to see you all dancing to hell!' That was the arrow of conviction to me. From that night the movement began to spread in our parish, and a large number, especially of young men and women, came under the power of the truth.

This testimony speaks of opposition, and of him eventually being forced to leave home (to become a gardener at Huntly Lodge). We could not meet for prayer in any of our own homes, but night after night, during the dark autumn evenings, some twenty young lads met in a wood, under a large beech tree, and there poured out our hearts in prayer and song. Most delightful is the memory of those blessed meetings even now.[210]

(j) The North East Coast

The name most prominently associated with the revival along the coasts of Buchan and Banffshire is that of James Turner, a fishcurer from Peterhead. Born in 1818 he was converted after months of inner struggle in 1840 and joined the Wesleyans. On March 12th 1854 he felt the power of the Holy Spirit come on him so powerfully that 'I could not keep from weeping' and four others 'fell to the floor insensible'.[211] He began to witness, visit the sick and preach open-air. On April 10th he wrote 'I feel He is coming to save many souls in Peterhead.'[212] Over the next five years he was increasingly used in personal evangelism, and in December 1859 during a slack period in business set out on a preaching tour northwards; he arrived in St. Combs on December 6th for ten days, then went on to Inverallochy, Cairnbulg, Fraserburgh and Rosehearty returning to Peterhead by the end of the month. He set out again towards the end of January for Cullen, arriving in Portknockie on 4th February,

---

210. Reminiscences, pp 139-140.
211. James Turner, or How to reach the masses, by E. McHardie (Brown, Aberdeen, 1875) p.9. 212. James Turner, p.10.

Findochty on the 7th, Buckie on 12th (a Sabbath) and Portgordon on the 17th. He arrived in Banff for eight days on March 5th, then visited Fordyce, Portsoy and Huntly among other places before returning home in mid-April. This tour basically cost him his health, with nightly meetings often lasting from 7:00 p.m. to 4:00 a.m. He struggled on for another three years itinerating as he was able, and also leading meetings in his cooperage, which he had adapted to seat 200 and installed gas lighting, but he died in February 1863. There is a full report of his life and work by his biographer.[213] It is important to realise, however, that Turner was only one of many men sent out to preach at that time: for example, while he was in Banff Duncan Matheson was working in Macduff, and in many places the revival meetings preceded and continued long after the arrival of the evangelist, so in many of the following anecdotes we do not know who the key instrument was.

E. McHardie has preserved for us one story concerning a little girl whom Turner won for the Lord at St. Combs. Her age is not mentioned, just that she was 'so little that most people would have thought her too young to be spoken to on soul matters. James Turner did not think so.' She did not live long afterwards, but delighted to spend her time singing hymns. 'By-and-bye the summons came for this little lamb, and after taking farewell of her friends, she clapped her hands, as if in an ecstasy of delight; then waving them upwards, as if giving some one the signal that she was coming, her spirit took its triumphant flight.'[214] Accounts of the deathbed scenes of Christian children were much loved by Victorian writers, so we cannot relate them all. I have included one full account of a Portessie boy in Appendix D as a typical example of such an incident.

Three men had been praying together in Portknockie for three months, when Turner arrived at the door of one of them and asked if he could hold a meeting. James Wilson, the 15 year old son of another of these men was sent round the village with a bell to announce a meeting that night (February 4th) in the hall, to which 300 came; the next evening the Free Church was used to accommodate the even larger crowd. This lad's testimony is worth quoting in full for its description of the effect

213. James Turner, or How to reach the masses, by E. McHardie (Brown, Aberdeen, 1875). 214. James Turner, pp 49-50.

of such a meeting on teenagers, and as an example of how converts immediately went to work on behalf of others:

> The night he came, I went round with the bell, then went with many more to the hall to hear him speak from the words, 'We must all appear before the judgement-seat of Christ.' His doctrine was new and strange to us. We had never heard such things before, for in Portknockie the word conversion was not used, scarcely known, except, perhaps, by a few who had been praying for some months that God would send *some one or something* to help us.
>
> Having never heard such things before, it pressed home upon men and women with tremendous force. For myself, especially, I felt that if God were to call me that night I would be lost forever, as my sins were still upon me. I had no love to Jesus Christ in my heart. I was not a partaker of His spirit. Something I wanted, I knew not what, but get it I must or perish.
>
> A meeting was appointed for the truly anxious in J. Findlay's house, which soon filled. A prostration occurred, and the people were afraid and wanted the house cleared. The anxious ones were not willing to go, and I was in such despair about my soul that I would not go out, but I helped to put out the others by force. The ejected ones, however, would not go away, but stood round the door, and as soon as the girl got better, made their way in again.
>
> James Turner seemed moved at their persistency and said, 'Dear people, you that want to be saved may be saved *now*, so we'll all to our knees and seek the power.' And no sooner had they gone to their knees than, as quickly as to the persistent ones of old, who let their sick one down through the roof when they could find no better way, did God yield to their urgency and the power came, for, after James Turner had prayed and another man had prayed a few words, all in a moment the house was filled. I, for one, was struck down to the earth, or rather to hell, under the pressure of my sins, for I could see nothing but total darkness, and eternal hell beneath me, and I cried, 'Lord, save me!' for about fifteen or twenty minutes at the top of my voice.
>
> What a mighty struggle there was in my soul ere the king of

darkness let his captive go free. I lay on my knees about an hour unable to move - pressed down, sinking down - and just as James Turner laid his hand upon my shoulder and said 'Jesus died for you,' - in a moment, as quickly as one could turn up the gas, the light of the glorious gospel shone into my heart, and I saw one standing before me with blood streaming from His hands, His feet, and His side, and His visage 'marred more than any man's'. My heart broke within me as I looked, and I said, 'Was this done for me?' 'Yes, all for *you*, I died, that *you* might live.' And as He spoke these words the burden rolled of my soul. I started to me feet and sung at the top of my voice -

> And *now* I love the bleeding Lamb,
> *Now* I love the bleeding Lamb,
> *Now* I love the bleeding Lamb,
> Because he first loved me:
>
> By the grave I now receive!
> *I can! I will!* I *do* believe!
> *I can! I will!* I *do* believe!
> That Jesus died for me.

Then filled with inconceivable joy and gladness, I flew out of the house; knocked up the people, especially my own relatives, and kneeling down at their bedsides, told them what God had done for my soul. When morning dawned the converts were going up and down the place praising God. Portknockie had never such a sun-rising! As soon as the people had a little food, a prayer meeting was called; which, once begun, lasted all day - and every day and night also for six weeks after.

A lot of those converted about the same age as myself held meetings separate from the public meeting. We went to private houses where there were any sick, or when any other cause kept them at home. One night the house we met in was full. Had not gone on long, for we had merely sung a hymn, when some prostrations occurred. I had not been prostrated, so having the idea that I wanted something which others had received, prayed that I might get that something. So that night while I was singing, my soul was filled, and my body completely overpowered. While thinking of the words 'Behold the Lamb of God!' all at once I got another sight of Jesus, - hung up between heaven and earth as the substitute for sinners; and thus I lay, *hour* after *hour*, looking at the glorious sight, and the more I looked the more I was filled with the love of God; tears continuously running down my cheeks; *unable to move for the world.* I had merely power to ejaculate occasionally 'Blessed Jesus! blessed Jesus!' &c. Being all young people, they at last got frightened at my continuing so long in such a state, and went and got some of the older folks to come in. When they had come in, and seen the condition in which I lay, they could only say - *'This is the work of God.'* After they prayed for the young that had given their hearts to Jesus, they dismissed the meeting. And about one o'clock in the morning I was able to go home, and did so rejoicing.

After this I formed a prayer meeting for the young every Monday night in the school-room, along with two other young men about the same age as myself, and we addressed them night about from a passage of Scripture during the winter and spring months, and I had also a kind of tract society; at least, I collected a little money from those who were willing to give it, and sent for gospel tracts which I distributed among the people.[215]

Three weeks later the Banffshire Journal carried an article entitled 'Revivals in Buckie and neighbouring villages' which includes a remarkable description of the effect of revival on the local school:

Portknockie: Some three weeks ago Mr. Turner, from Peterhead, who follows the occupation of a fishcurer there, and who for a good many years has been a very earnest Methodist...came to Portknockie...The real 'striking down' commenced on the night of the 7th in a private house in Portknockie, in which a prayer meeting was held. The teacher of the female school was among the first prostrated. *Nightly prayer meetings lasted until 2, 3 and even 4 a.m.* and there is now scarcely a family in the village in

215. James Turner, pp 94-96

which there have not been cases of mental or physical prostration. Mr. Fraser, the schoolmaster of the place, was deeply
affected and *imagined* he saw visions of heaven.

The children, as in all the other villages were much affected,
and could not be tired of praying and singing hymns. One day in
the school, while devotional exercises were being gone through
previous to commencing the work of teaching, such was the
ardour with which these were entered on, that even there cases of
striking down commenced and spread very rapidly, one man, who
was sent for, reporting the result to be that when he arrived the
whole school was prostrated at one time - some twenty pupils.[216]

Meetings continued for six weeks in the village and almost all work
was suspended, not a boat went to sea, but Turner moved on to Findochty,
where Union prayer meetings had already been formed. There was a
particularly powerful breakthrough on 11th February which included
the conversion of an eleven year old boy.[217] Turner stayed with a fishing
family whose daughter had attended meetings in Fraserburgh, and had
been under conviction for four months: the lassie and her mother came
into assurance on the same day.[218]

In the next village of Portessie, there was no available hall, and
Turner spoke in an unfinished house, still without roof, despite snow on
the ground, and the rafters were full of young people. An elder of the
Free Church, who had only just come into assurance himself, came
home to find 'my little daughter, a girl of fourteen, preaching, and the
house full about her. The ablest men in the place were trying to confute
her, but in vain - only one of them, a teacher in the Sabbath school,
prayed with her and encouraged her to go on in the good ways of the
Lord.'[219]

The situation in the three villages is summed up in this article by a
'Correspondent' of the North British Daily Mail:

Port-Assie: A few young men had been attending a religious
meeting at Findochty, a village about two miles east of Port-
assie, and about fifteen miles west of Banff. So much excited

216. B.J. Tuesday 28th February 1860. 217. James Turner, p.117.
218. James Turner, pp 127-9. 219. James Turner, p.147

were they that their employer shut up his workshop - a cooper's - and headed a revival crusade, and now the greatest excitement is going on. A meeting which commenced on Friday evening at six o'clock lasted till four o'clock next morning, and was resumed at ten a.m. When I called on Saturday about 1 p.m. a scene presented itself to my view truly wonderful. Young persons stretched out on forms labouring under strange sensations might be seen - indeed were seen - supported in some cases by weeping parents or distressed brothers. One young men held his sister by one arm and raised the other before about three hundred people and appealed to Heaven for help. Men never known to pray were eloquent and unctious in devotion and some of them without the remotest pretence to education were attempting to expound portions of scripture. Even boys and girls were singing of redeeming love, and old veterans, hoary in Mammon's service, were trembling and crying for mercy. Conviction is universal and conversions seem to be numerous.

In Findochty the work is even more decided. There are about five hundred people, purely seafaring, all engaged in religious exercises. I have spoken to common fishermen who have for nearly three days and three nights been praying and singing, and exhorting their neighbours. Labour is totally suspended meantime, and has been during these five days. Even the cooking of victuals is much neglected, and everyone seems to have got the gift of tongues, for lads of fourteen and fifteen years of age and men with hoary heads have become popular mouth organs and offer up amazing intelligent petitions.

In another village called Port-Kockie, the movement has been at work. Two publicans in this place are reported 'stricken', and have pulled down their signboards in disgust, greatly to the gratification of the friends of sobriety.

Now, no villages were more destitute of spirituality prior to this change. According to the admissions of the people themselves, they were deplorably careless of divine things. A person named Turner has been visiting one or more of the above places, exhorting the people, but in no way extravagant. The work seems to be the result of Divine power. Where intemperance is arrested and destroyed, where malice and old grudges are given up, where utter worldliness gives place to spirituality, THERE there can be no mistake as to the genuineness of the movement.[220]

This account is attested by Rev. W.T. Ker of Deskford; who witnessed the situation at Portessie:

Most of the boats were at sea, and a number were absent otherwise, yet the house was full. From the number of children and infants in arms, who were present, I am sure that not one man, woman, or child left in the village was wanting.

He noted that they sang from memory, there being no hymn books; singing 'What's the news?' repeating the last verse four or five times over. *He concluded* I see an account of this work in the Guardian copied from the Mail. I believe it to be correct.[221]

And also, by Rev. Major six years later: 'on that coast...without doubt, more than a thousand persons were under conviction, and there is little doubt the numbers of the saved amounted to more than 600 persons. In Portessie alone, at least one-sixth of the entire population, or 150 persons, turned to the Lord.'[222]

Returning to Portessie the following year Turner was accompanied by children from Findochty:

Next year the horn went through the town for a meetin'. James Turner had come. Before I got to the hall it was crowded. I went in and sat down beside a woman, and when the children, some forty of them, cam' fae Findochty, and James Turner began to pray, they all began to pray th'gether. It seemed like a chorus of angels...[223]

When the representatives of the newly formed Evangelistic Association for Scotland arrived on the Moray Coast to investigate the lasting effects of this revival, they 'visited some of the fruits of the last awakening', but also found that another wave had begun at Port Gordon, and reported 'the work commenced here about the beginning of the

220. Quoted in S.G. Thursday 16th February 1860. 221. S.G. Tuesday 21st February 1860
222. James Turner, p.177. 223. James Turner, p.162

year'.[224] This time it did not attract the attention of the local press, and only one account appears headed 'Portessie, Findochty and Port-knockie':

In the second place, of 600 inhabitants,...the work began among the children...A minister was invited to come and hold a series of religious meetings. The power of God was manifest in the conversion of souls. Backsliders were reclaimed and believers were revived. Meetings were held for some weeks and about the end of the year the Spirit was poured out in the following way:-A number of young men held a prayer meeting among the rocks, and such was the deep and overpowering emotion they were under that they determined to go through their village and to speak from house to house, and to invite them out to prayer. Several joined them, and they went through the village singing a psalm. The children determined that they should hold a prayer meeting themselves, as they were not allowed into the other prayer meeting on account of want of room. They went to the walls of a Church yet unfinished. After a time they all came under deep conviction of their sinful state, and several cried out in agony of mind. With such strong crying, tears, and in 'bitterness' were they seized, that the noise of their distress reached the houses. Those of them who knew the truth prayed for the unconverted among them and then went and urged them to receive Christ. These exhortations were so blessed of God that almost everyone became affected and a general spirit of prayer was poured out. From this place they went to a hall already filled with grown up people. There also the Lord wrought graciously in pouring out such a spirit of concern that the whole place became affected. On the following day some of the young men went to an adjacent village and there also the same work was manifested. *Work stopped for 16 days in the area.*

A boy of 8 years of age once, under strong convictions, spoke in the meeting, and his words made such a deep impression that more were convicted and converted than on any other occasion. He still continues to speak, but not with his former power.

---

224. T.R. 26th February 1863.

The article concludes:

> In short the whole place professes to be converted, with the
> exception of five or six persons who keep close together and
> apart from the others. They fear contact with God's people,
> knowing that some who, in their boldness, went to drag their
> children away from the meeting have been arrested on the spot,
> and seized with overwhelming terrors, have cried out for mercy.
> One woman thus arrested remained in the place of meeting all
> night in prayer, and did not leave till she found rest in Christ.
>
> *There follows a comparison with the work of three years ago;
> while there are no physical manifestations the work is deeper.* A
> lad who had an impediment in his speech, when converted, all of
> a sudden began to pray with much fervour and fluency, and even
> addressed meetings without any indication of his defect. This
> was remarked by all, but is by no means a singular case.[225]

It is sad to have to report that it was in this area that one of the
controversies concerning the revival surfaced. The Free Church Presbytery of Fordyce appointed Messrs. Reid, Mackay, Fordyce and Ker to
investigate the happenings at Portknockie. Mr. Manson had commenced his ministry at the Free Church there at the beginning of 1860,
to find there was no public prayer meeting in the town. He instituted a
prayer meeting on Wednesday 15th January. On 8th February:

> A great many people were struck, and some children began
> singing revival hymns, for which they were rebuked by Mr.
> James Mair, and he (Mr. Manson) also said that such a proceed-
> ing was not becoming on the part of children, adding also that he
> preferred the Psalms. He heard Mr. Turner preach upon the 9th,
> and, on the 10th, he heard the children singing in the school of
> Portknockie, and certainly it was not edifying...

This was probably because they were using a street tune. Then
Methodist lay-preachers arrived from Banff, who were guilty of introducing the 'devil's error'. Mr. Manson was criticised for being

---

225. T.R. 5th March 1863.

'incompetent' for not being able 'to keep down these extravagances'.[226]

Further East along the coast at Gardenstown and Crovie the work had an independent origin, but received an added impetus from the fishermen of Portknockie. On April 7th 1860, Rev. John Munro, minister of Gardenstown, wrote to the Fraserburgh Advertiser:

> On Wednesday week, when I was in the village of Crovie baptising a child, I learned that the young men of my bible class had been holding prayer meetings, and that the females had been engaged in similar exercises. The occasion of these meetings, I was told by one of my female members, was the result of a discourse I had preached on the previous Sabbath, wherein I exhorted then to the exercise of the duties of religion. The same person informed me that, on her return home from the church, she advised her son (her husband being at the island of Lewis) to go and call together the rest of the young men in the village, and commence a prayer meeting. What she advised her son to do, she did herself with her own sex. I may here mention, as another cause of the revival in this village, the reading at the prayer meetings from time to time accounts of the work of revival in America, in Ireland, and latterly in our own country.

He relates how he met four fishermen from Portknockie in Crovie, and prayed with them, but left as it was after 9 p.m. 'I had no sooner left than they assembled the young men and the females (the male population with the exception of five persons, having all left for the Lewis islands). They began with praise singing hymns several copies of which they had with them. They then addressed the people and prayed.' At subsequent meetings there were a number of prostrations - indeed the Portknockie men claimed that 'nearly the whole assemblage were struck down at once'. The minister ceased having meetings in order to allow his people 'to let their minds reflect upon what they have heard'.

It is not easy to deduce from such a report at this one, the age of the participants, but if the 'young men' referred to had been of working age, particularly in an exclusively fishing village, presumably they would have been away to Lewis with the boats? Therefore, it may be assumed

---

226. S.G. Thursday 12th April 1860

that this was a group of younger teenage boys. It is also the only incident where a youth prayer group is started at the instigation of a parent!

The population of Buckie at this time was 3,000, and fifteen hundred of these attended the Free Church to hear Turner preach on Sunday evening 12th February. When some of the congregation were prostrated there was an uproar, and eventually Turner abandoned the meeting and adjourned to the United Presbyterian Church. During one of these meetings, two ministers who had come to investigate the work "were very much attracted by a little girl lying prostrate. While in this state she was either softly ejaculating 'Sweet Jesus, I love Thee', or praying for the ministers and people. One of the two bent down and listened with his ear close to her mouth. After a while he turned round to his brother minister and said, 'Sir, I must confess this is the work of God.'[227] An eyewitness, describing people under conviction of sin, concludes: 'Hundreds of men and women, and boys and girls, after passing through this conflict, have apparently found peace, after which their faces almost beam with joy, indicating the peace they feel within, and they then manifest great concern for the salvation of their friends.'[228]

A Christian woman in Portgordon sent her children, escorted by her servant, 'to Buckie to get the blessing. I was then a boy of 12 years, my sister and brother each two years younger.' The boy recalls his impression at length. When Turner had preached, 'Just before us a girl fell prostrate. This startled us, but some of the workers came up to her and we then had a sort of satisfied feeling as if all was right.'

'Mr. Turner then began to go through the place, speaking to the anxious. At last he came up to us. He asked where we had come from. So the girl told him the whole story - how we had been sent down to be converted, etc.' The children were asked to pray and managed to recite prayers they had learned, 'But while doing so, I will never forget how forcibly and suddenly the thought struck me - "That is not right, it is to God you should pray," so immediately I left off repeating my learned prayers, and cried to God to pardon my sins, and make me a good boy, and save my soul for Jesus' sake. Then I wept from a deep consciousness of my own wickedness, and vowed in real earnest that I would be "a revival"... I went back in the evening, and kept going to the meetings in

---

227. James Turner, p.194. 228. James Turner, p.24

Buckie all the time he was there, by which means I got my heart established in grace - confirmed in the faith, and then when Mr. Turner came over here to Portgordon, I was one of his witnesses, and by following him I got power to resist sin, and was enabled to witness for the Lord publicly.

When he left this, we kept up meetings, and the work prospered, and the people grew strong in the Lord. I started a young men's meeting here... ' [229] At these meetings as many as six boys came to the Lord in one meeting. Fifteen years later, this boy, identified only as 'D.R.' provides us with the sequel: 'About four years ago some boys were converted; these boys were taken to meetings held expressly for themselves, conducted by those who had been brought to Christ in similar juvenile gatherings. Little Susan, a girl of nine years, came to one of these meetings, and was awakened. She was pointed to the Saviour and found peace in Him; then went home to her mother rejoicing. Her mother, a converted woman, questioned her narrowly; and so fully did the Lord perfect His praise out of the mouth of this babe in Christ, that the mother was convinced the change wrought in her little daughter's heart was real, and certainly the practical results were soon such as left no room for doubt on the subject.

Her father and several other near relations were unconverted. With them little Susan began her mission by seeking to win their hearts to Jesus.' After an accident she was confined to bed for two years, from where she continued to speak for Jesus. She identified herself with the Methodist meeting, and told her father, who belonged to the Established Church, that this was because 'they set her soul in a flame by the warm way that they worshipped God,' that 'they offer a free salvation to all, and my Saviour does not want any to perish,' that they were the only people who she had ever spoken to her about her soul, 'she liked the class meetings,' and 'they loved one another'. She was carried to the meetings 'in the garret' while she was able, and managed to save two pounds to contribute towards the building of the Methodist Chapel, for which she prayed fervently. At its opening her father and five other relations were savingly converted. She then called her family together, told them, 'I have prayed to God to convert you all and make you all

229. James Turner, pp 221-3

Methodists. I have lived to see you all converted to God, and I can die now.' Her final words were, 'Weep not for me, I am going home to die no more, and I will meet you on the banks of the river - good-bye-dear-friends-I-am-going-home,' and so she died.[230]

The effect of the revival on the children of Buckie was noted by Rev. Baxter of Banff, who had to report to the U.P. Presbytery (held at Aberchirder on 20th March 1860) that 'Hundreds of neglected children are getting religious instruction at home and in the Sabbath school.'[231] This is evidenced by the following brief report:

> The Sabbath School in the United Presbyterian Church, Buckie, has increased from 50 to 200, at Portessie a Sabbath School has been opened with 180 children.[232]

The local press also draw attention to the place of children in the meetings. One article remarks on the 'physical phenomena', in Portknockie, Findochty and Portessie, compares them with similar reports from Ferryden, noting that all are fishing communities, then states:

> In Buckie, the first case of this nature occurred on Sabbath the 12th inst., under the preaching of Mr. Turner, a layman from Peterhead, who has for some time been labouring at other places on the coast, as has also Mr. Duncan Matheson, another layman from Huntly, and others. The former gentleman preached in the Free Church, Buckie, on Sabbath, to a very large audience, and again on Monday evening, to a concourse of people calculated to number several hundreds over a thousand. On the latter occasion, an adjournment was made to the hall occupied by the U.P. congregation, and daily meetings have since taken place there. The hall is opened about 11 o'clock a.m. and generally not closed till two, or even three, o'clock next morning.
>
> 'The first thing' says one of our correspondents, 'that strikes a person on entering, is the great excitement prevailing among the majority of those present. Hear we may see, at almost every

230. James Turner, pp 251-4. 231. James Turner, p.197.
232. T.R. 31st March 1860.

hour, men, women and children, labouring in the greatest bodily
distress, rending the air with shrieks and groans; while occasionally an individual might be seen falling on the floor in a fit, which,
by some observers, may be considered hysterical. Nor is it in
these meetings alone that excitement prevails. The boys and girls
pass along the streets at all hours rapturously singing hymns. The
passer-by, on our streets on Friday night, would have had his ears
assailed by a complication of such sounds. These proceeded
from a small room on the west end of the Hall, where upwards of
30 or 40 boys and girls were gathered together singing these
hymns. Many of these children have been stricken down, and
instances are not uncommon of children starting from their sleep
with these hymns in their mouths. At the time of our entrance to
the Hall on Friday night, the meeting was engaged in prayer,
conducted by a young woman, but it is no unusual circumstance
for boys of ten and twelve years of age, and even younger, to
engage in public prayer.'[233]

At this time Matheson was working in the Methodist Church in
Cullen, and the same article notes: 'Here also, cases of prostration have
occurred, chiefly among young men and girls, and one case of a young
man having seen visions is spoken of.'[234]

The following Saturday, Turner moved on to Portgordon, and his
meeting on the evening of Tuesday 21st in a packed school was
described in detail a week later:

Within, some 16 boys were standing near the schoolmaster's
desk, where the classes are exercised, all in knots of three, four,
and five, and in the centre of each a well-worn hymn book, which
they clustered around, and from which they were singing at the
top of their voices, and with much greater rapidity than regular-
ity. At first they sang 'Canaan' but soon took to hymns of a more

233. B.J. Tuesday 21st February 1860.
234. MacPherson notes that Matheson 'made his mark on the young men of the town
(Cullen)...Many of them were converted at this time; and it was pleasing to see the finest
youths of the place sitting in a company round about their father in the faith, and receiving
his counsels as from an angel of God. For the young men he had a peculiar love: they were
his joy, and as his very life' (Duncan Matheson, p.121).

exciting sort, such as 'I can, I do, I will believe', &c. *Mr. Turner was standing by the door:* The meeting, he seemed willing to inform comers was just gathering, and he was keeping the boys singing until the people should all convene....When the service commenced there were 14 men present, 55 women, mostly grown up, and about the same number of boys and girls. This quite filled the school, but the influx did not by any means cease. The place was very soon crowded. The proportion of men rather increased, but still the great bulk of the meeting was made up of women and children. The school got heated almost to suffocation...the meeting was kept up for nine and a half hours, many of the people remaining there the whole time without meat or drink.

This meeting appears to have started at 4:30 p.m. To precis the narrative a little, after quoting the prayer and comments of Turner it continues:

After this the hymn was concluded, and the last verse and the chorus repeated several times, till the audience was quite in an excited state, boys and girls holding one another by the hands and rocking and rolling with their bodies, and even beating with their feet on the floor to the time of the music. *Turner again spoke briefly.* A little boy near Mr. Turner next prayed, and after some expressions which they nearly all used such as these - 'I have been a heavy sinner. I have never prayed before, but I can pray now. Thank God I have found peace, &c.' - this little fellow went on to say 'Pour down the Holy Spirit upon my mother. She is sitting in the house. She has been here today, and she hoped she would be here tonight, but she is not here. I was walking in the broad road too long. What if I had slipped my foot and tumbled into that pit, I would have been damned for ever.' This young lad's prayer was very short, as was also the next one, offered up by a lad of the name of George Reid. He prayed, 'If there are any scoffers in this house, strike an arrow into their heart that they may feel as I feel. Pour down thy soul into this hell-deserving village, for it is a hell deserving village', and so on.

There follow quotes of other prayers by 'a girl', 'a girl', 'a young girl' and a 'young creature'.

About 9 o'clock, there had occurred a very remarkable case of striking down. It was a young lad, the 'orra man' at the farm of Leichiestown in Enzie. He had been there on the Monday night, and had then been two hours in a state of prostration...He had scarcely been an hour in the meeting until he was affected again, fell down, and as the case seemed to be rather a serious one, he was carried out, and put into a room on the opposite side of the street. He lay quite unable to move hand or foot till past 1 o'clock, about four hours, and even at 2 o'clock he was unable to rise, but was so far recovered that he joined with those around him in singing hymns... The room was generally full of men, women and children, and all joined in hymns, which they continued to sing, at short intervals, over the young lad until his recovery.[235]

Another newspaper reports the Monday meeting in the Portgordon schoolroom, simply by stating: 'A great many - old men and women - young men and boys - all ages and both sexes engaged publicly in prayer.'[236]

It was at Portgordon that one of the most remarkable incidents took place. Again we have to refer to an eyewitness account written in a letter of 1875, which gives no details of the age of the 'young girl' concerned or any other form of identification. However, it is an excellent illustration not only of the way in which God used the young, but also of the way in which the revival spread from one community to another:

Portgordon, June 16th, 1875.
A young girl belonging to this place, but in service in Portessie, was laid down in a state of complete prostration. She underwent a mighty struggle while in that state. When recovered, she said that she had received a message to Portgordon which she had to deliver there at once. Accordingly, led by her sister and another

235. B.J. Tuesday 28th February 1860, also quoted in S.G. 1st March 1860, prefaced by the comment: 'We take the following from the Banffshire Journal, with the remark by way of caution, that the Journal has not the reputation of being very friendly to earnest religious movements.' The full article covering over half a page of small print, must be one of the most complete descriptions of a revival meeting ever recorded.
236. E.M.C. 2nd March 1860.

girl (for she was perfectly blind from the time of her prostration until after the message was delivered) she came to Portgordon, and well do I remember the day - a blessed day to me that they came across.

There was a meeting in the school at the time, and the place was well filled. There was a revival going on in Portessie, and the people were expecting it over to Portgordon. The Free Church minister was preaching, and the service was about half-way through when the girl came in and sat down quietly. Patiently she waited until the service was over, then rose and asked modestly if she would be allowed to address the meeting, as she had a message from God to Portgordon.

'No, No!' said the minister hurriedly, then ran out as fast as possible. Only a very few of the people followed him. The girl then asked if she might speak to them, and of course they allowed her, knowing well that she was no imposter, but a common fisher-girl, whose parents, belonging to the same class, decent people, lived in their midst.

Her message was that of the woman of Samaria. She began speaking about the woman seeing Jesus at the well, and spoke to the point. Then she invited them all to come and 'see Jesus', whom, said she, 'I saw in Portessie, and who sent me here direct to tell you in Portgordon to come to Him. I was a great sinner, and went to scoff at the work. When spoken to about my soul, I resisted the mighty power of God, and was laid down. Then Jesus came and spoke to me, and gave me to drink of the living water, and bade me come to Portgordon with this message to the people there, that they were to come to Him.

And praise the Lord, through that message, and that weak instrument He shook Portgordon that night. The meeting place was crowded with people anxiously enquiring how they could come to Jesus, and many found the way to Him. Many backsliders also were restored, and the believers also were stirred up to more active service in the mighty harvest field.[237]

---

237. James Turner, pp243-4.

Any mass movement accompanied by such physical and emotional manifestations, is bound to attract its critics. It is therefore worth taking time to quote from a minister who had been to see the work, although this takes us beyond our immediate remit of noting the effects of the revival on children.

Rev. T. H. Baxter, United Presbyterian minister from Banff, was in Buckie and Portgordon the end of last week, and in a discourse in his own church on Sabbath evening thus gave his opinion of the movement.

He did not deny there were improprieties, but if they waited for a revival of religion without improprieties, they never would have one at all. The means, instruments, manifestations and results connected with the revival, so far as he could discern, were similar to those connected with every genuine revival since the day of Pentecost. Prayer has preceded and accompanied it. The Word of God has been resorted to in public and in private. The cardinal doctrines which ran through it - depravity of human nature, sin, redemption alone through the sacrifice of the Lord Jesus Christ, necessity of repentance, faith, and the work of the Spirit - had been insisted upon. Everywhere there had been conviction and bitter repentance, secret and even more public confession of sin that is general in conversion. He had heard indeed of one man who became so absorbed that he made confession of matters which it was believed were only visionary. Between conviction and peace there was a severe and sometimes long struggle, out of which arose mental and physical prostration. A fair proportion of all classes had been the subjects of it, from the most educated to the illiterate, the child of tender years and the hoary headed.

Repentance had in many cases been succeeded by peace in God, the most transporting joy and blessed hope ... *also self denial, reconciliation, humility.* People by no means the most regular in their habits have objected to the hours to which the meetings are continued. Were these meetings to be repeated for many weeks and conducted so on principle, the objection would be very well founded. But such irregularities are only for a short time at the beginning and arose out of the necessities of the cases. We are not ready to complain, when the interests of the body are at stake, if the nurse and physician are called at unwarrantable hours. Paul might have been condemned for preaching beyond midnight, when he dispensed the Lord's Supper to the converts at Troas. Mr. Baxter thought that the movement as a whole, ought to draw forth gratitude in every Christian and praise to God whose work he believed it to be.[238]

Another positive assertion comes from the pen of Methodist minister Thomas L. Parker, vouching for Mr. Turner's meetings:

In reference to the children, all we need to say is, that their simplicity, faith, and love, when they have found the Saviour, make them such instruments for good as God can use, and there again is the scripture fulfilled 'out of the mouths of babes and sucklings, God has perfected praise'.[239]

In Banff following news from America and Ireland, united prayer meetings began at the end of 1858. According to the Congregationalist minister, Rev. J. Murker writing on 19th June 1860:

Several young men began to feel concerned about their own souls and the souls of others. Three small prayer meetings of these young men spontaneously sprang up. Two lads commenced to pray together, in a wood near the town, after the toils of the day were over. They were joined by a third and a fourth. They made a youth of their own age a subject of prayer for some time, and then spoke to him about his soul, inviting him to their meeting in the wood. If he complied, they began to pray for another. If he did not at first join their ranks, they persevered to pray until they succeeded - which they always ultimately did. By and bye they increased to a goodly band. By intertwining the branches of adjoining trees, they constructed a comfortable booth, where they poured out their souls for a revival of religion in the place. The early storms of October, 1859, drove them from this hallowed Bethel. Their meetings were then held for a time in their different lodgings, and subsequently in the vestry of the Free Church and of

---

238. S.G. 8th March 1860. 239. I.A. Friday 16th March 1860.

the Congregational alternately. During the winter months their number increased to about forty, all earnest young men, although as yet the greater part of them had not found peace in believing. *Mr. Turner was invited to the town, and on the night of Saturday 10th March there was a protracted prayer meeting which lasted until 6 a.m. on the Sunday.* About one o'clock a spiritual power began to move the dense mass which crowded every part of the large chapel. Nine young men prayed in succession with great power and fervency, before there could be any opportunity for praise or exhortation. In their prayers they touched upon their own personal case, and the cases of their companions who had either found peace or were struggling hard after it. The scene was heart melting exceedingly. There was weeping in every part of the house. Sobs and subdued shrieks, with a few prostrations, imposed a fearful solemnity. Men, women, and children prayed in succession, in a manner altogether unusual. Young people wept upon each other's necks, while they clung together in clusters of six or seven in a group. Yet there was no confusion; all was natural and peculiarly affecting.

This report was written three months later when hardly any had fallen away, the young men had increased to one hundred, and the town of under 4,000 had sixteen prayer meetings going on at the same time. A great work is going on among the boys also, who hold prayer meetings of their own, which are exceedingly well conducted. A number of the youth between the age of twelve and seventeen give evidence of a new birth, and can pray in public with great devotion, modesty and propriety. They take a decided stand, and labour hard for the conversion of their youthful companions; nor do they labour in vain. The flower of the youth of the town are on the Lord's side. Their love to each other, their union of co-operation, although belonging to different denominations, their manly decision, excite admiration. Being a powerful and united band, they are able to bear down opposition to a great extent. Who can estimate the effect of such an increasing phalanx of ardent young people so devoted and earnest?[240]

240. James Turner, pp 259-60.

The reports carried in the newspapers are similar and add a few details. The Guardian, using the Banffshire Journal states that:

> During every night of the past week revival meetings have been held in Banff by Mr. Turner of Peterhead. After an hour of praise, prayer and preaching, there was a prayer meeting: the first finished at midnight, and after that it was two, four, and six in the morning. At every meeting, all whether men or women, were invited to engage in prayer. At the first and second meetings none engaged save clergymen, and those who had been hitherto accustomed to pray in public... Perhaps the most remarkable circumstances in the entire series of meetings occurred about one o'clock on Sabbath morning, when eight or nine young men of between sixteen and twenty years prayed nearly in succession. Their prayers were modest in tone and manner, yet in one or two cases accompanied by an elevation of sentiment and feeling that seemed to border on ecstasy. They all spoke of an inward struggle, now past, and of peace and joy secured. Nearly every one of them professed that they were averse to the public appearances they were making, but were constrained thereto by the force of their inward convictions and emotions. [241]

Towards the end of March the United Presbytery of Banffshire 'cordially passed' a report on the revival submitted by Rev. Forrester of Keith, the Moderator of the Buckie Session, who said that he was favourable to it, despite ten days of manifestations consisting of 'tears, trembling, groans, loud outcries for mercy, and failings of bodily strength,' because the result was a 'love for God's word'. [242]

John Murker himself itinerated the hinterland from Banff Congregational, and in January 1863 visited 'a parish':

> It was also cheering to find that a daily prayer meeting had been kept up for eight months by the young people attending a week-day school. This juvenile prayer meeting started during an

---

241. S.G. Thursday 15th March 1860. Also in E.C. 16th March 1860, and E.M.C. 16th March 1860.
242. S.G. Thursday 29th March 1860

awakening at one of my meetings with the scholars of that school
in March 1862. There is now beautiful fruit from the blossoms of
that spring.[243]

We are also aware of the presence of children as young as ten
attending prayer meetings in Macduff as reported by Rev. Leslie to the
Free Church Synod.[244]

Along the Moray Coast the work seems to have been contemporane-
ous with, but unrelated to, that of the Banffshire fishing villages.
Messrs. Brownlow North and Hay Macdowall Grant had been working
in the area and in a letter as early as 21st August 1858 from Hopeman
Lodge, the latter notes the effect of the gospel on younger teenage girls:

On reading over your letter, I observe that Eda is interested about
L., because she has given herself to her Saviour; so I will tell her
of a girl in T—. I had been sent for by the mother, who is a
converted person, but one who had long been given to doubting.
After some conversation the light burst into her mind more
clearly, and she said she would like me to speak to her eldest
daughter, a girl of thirteen, whose serious impressions received
last year, when Mr. North was there, seemed to have passed
away. She went to fetch her, and after some hesitation she came;
but I felt at a loss how to speak to her, and hardly know now what
I did say. Next day I received a message to ask me to come and
see her, if it were but for ten minutes. I went, and found her very
anxious; so I set before her the way of going to Jesus. Two days
later she found peace, and seemed to grow in grace rapidly whilst
I was there. One morning this girl brought a friend of hers, aged
fourteen, to see me. 'Well,' I asked, 'what have you got to tell
me?' 'I wish to say that I am very happy.' 'What makes you
happy?' 'My sins are all forgiven.' 'How do you know that?'
'Because I believe God's Word, which tells me so.' I afterwards
learned that the first use the former girl had made of her reconciliation to God was to write to this second girl, and press on her to
seek Christ - and see the result! Before I left, she had been

243. T.R. 18th February 1864 from Scottish Congregational Magazine.
244. B.J. Tuesday 17th April 1860.

speaking strongly to a cousin of her own, and brought her to me two or three times. It is pleasant to see the young thus wide awake to their responsibilities and God blessing their simple faith.[245]

A year later in August 1859 Radcliffe met with Grant at his home in Arndilly, and preached in the Free Church at Rothes, and then commenced open air meetings the following day:

A great crowd was soon gathered in the open air. A deep impression was made on the people that night; especially among young men, which was the beginning of a considerable movement in that place.[246]

Before the end of 1859 we read from a letter:

In Elgin there is a movement among the boys of the Academy. They have organised both public and private prayer meetings. In Keith and Nairn, children, apprentices, and maidservants have their stated prayer meetings.[247]

Regrettably, further details of these are lacking.

Up on the coast at Hopeman:

The awakening began in the district payer meetings organised by the Free Church. It began Monday last, in the house of Mr. Sclater, a fish curer, where the prayer meeting lasted till 3 a.m.[248]

This would refer to Monday 5th March. On the following Friday afternoon there was a meeting in the Free Church schoolroom, where God's chief instrument was an unknown boy of ten:

While sighs and groans were rising from many in the schoolroom a boy (said to be about ten years of age) voluntarily stood up and prayed with great fluency and intense earnestness - confessing his own sins, beseeching an outpouring of the Holy Spirit and

---

245. Hay MacDowall Grant, pp 105-6. 246. Hay MacDowall Grant, p.130.
247. S.G. 13th December 1859 and T.R. 24th December 1859.
248. S.G. Tuesday 20th March 1860.

pleading for a number of his relatives. An eye-witness says the impression made by this prayer was thrilling, and the greater part of the audience were manifestly much affected. The proceedings during the subsequent part of the evening were solemnly impressive. Cries for mercy rose from almost every part of the schoolroom; a number fell down, and lay in a state of entire prostration, and had to be removed by their friends. All, or nearly all, present seemed to be impressed with a sense of their sin, and a deep WAIL filled the building. It is impossible to convey to the reader a correct idea of the state of matters throughout the evening; cries for mercy, exhortations to come to the Saviour; prayers for the Spirit, confessions of sin, people falling down in a state of entire prostration, and in some cases exclamations of joy at 'having found Christ.' Hymns were sung at intervals on this as on other occasions and during the singing all was perfect quiet, but as soon as the singing closed, the excitement was resumed. This was continued throughout the night and during the greater part of Saturday.[249]

Daily prayer meetings continued until the following Wednesday, and the Courier provides us with this attestation of the work:

When not engaged in public worship in the Church, the minister visited the people in their houses - and found a very large number of young and old, but especially the young, under deep and serious impressions, and some in great agony of spirit...It is proper to state that, as far as we can learn, no attempts were made to 'get up' this movement. There were no special 'revival meetings'; the movement seems to have been purely spontaneous, whatever the ultimate result may be.[250]

In neighbouring Burghead:

Young men and young women in particular appeared to be under serious impressions, and in many houses throughout the village,

249. E.M.C. 16th March 1860 also in S.G. 20th March 1860, T.R. 31st March 1860 and T.F. 4th April 1860.
250. E.M.C. 16th March 1860.

the whole of the younger members of the family were found engaged in earnest and almost continuous prayer.[251]

On Sunday 18th two young men affected at Hopeman were in Burghead, where there was a special prayer meeting, and then during a service in the Free Church a young man of sixteen cried out:

Oh how great sinners we are: we have one foot on earth and another in hell and yet we will not come to Jesus.[252]

Is this the same sixteen year old referred to in this account from the Guardian?

Burghead: Mr. Fraser of Rosskeen preached again on the fore-noon of Sabbath...As soon as the English service was concluded, Mr. McLeod addressed the Gaelic speaking portion of that community in that language. No sooner was the Gaelic over than many of the congregation met for prayer in the church, in which duty many took part. During these exercises, which were of a very exciting nature, we were deeply moved by a lad of sixteen years or so, who completely gave way under the influence of his feelings, and between convulsive sobs we could plainly hear the short but impressive prayer, 'Lord Jesus, have mercy on my soul.'[253]

On the same evening in the United Presbyterian Session House:

A boy of about thirteen years of age cried out 'Oh Lord, I am a sinner, a great sinner. I feel my sins pressing on me like a mountain. Oh for one drop of Jesus' blood to melt them away.' Many young persons have been struck in the street. Two young lads, brothers, were deeply convicted at the same time in the street, and both immediately ran home. One went into the room, fell on his knees, the other knelt down by his mother's side and poured out his soul in prayer.[254]

---

251. E.M.C. 16th March 1860.
252. E.C. Friday 23rd March 1860.
253. S.G. Tuesday 27th March 1860.
254. E.C. Friday 23rd March 1860.

The Guardian also tells us that:

> It is the fishing population chiefly that are affected, and it is
> impossible to go into any house almost, day or night, in which
> you do not find the family, or some of them, engaged in prayer.[255]

The Guardian notes a couple of weeks later 'the increased attendance at
Sabbath Schools in Burghead.'[256]

The first report from Lossiemouth, dated Thursday 15th March also
traces the movement's origin to Hopeman, and notes the effects on
children who were obviously present at the meetings:

> The movement began here on the first of this week, by three
> fishermen from Hopeman, and prayer meetings continue to be
> held at all hours, by day and by night. Cases of 'striking' are
> common, chiefly among the fishing class, however, as well as
> prayers - rather incoherent - and the most awe-striking ejacula-
> tions imaginable. This is the case among males and females, from
> those of adult age down to the lisping child.[257]

These meetings were held in the United Presbyterian Church, and
the same report suggests that Rev. Vassey had to come over from Elgin
to restore order to them. Another report, dated Wednesday 21st, but
describing the previous Thursday's prayer meeting at the U.P.C. said
that 'here both males and females of full age, as also those of very tender
years successfully engaged in prayer ... (and that) ... More private
meetings continue to be held among young and old by day and by night.'
The Courier concludes with the comment:

> We have some doubts as to the propriety of young boys taking a
> leading part in public devotions in the Churches at least. Every-
> thing should be done decently and in order; and there is a solemn
> reverence due in addressing the Deity, so that our words ought to
> be few and well ordered. And though, certainly, through the
> Spirit of God the youngest child may speak with a new tongue;

255. S.G. 20th March 1860. 256. S.G. 3rd April 1860.
257. S.G. Tuesday 20th March 1860 and E.M.C. Friday 16th March 1860.

yet from what we saw and heard we would beg merely to throw
out the suggestion for the consideration of more sensible people
than ourselves, without presuming to dictate.[258]

This is a mild foretaste of the subsequent press criticism about to
break out over later meetings in both Lossiemouth and Elgin.
After the meeting on the Thursday evening:

A number adjourned to the Free Church schoolroom, where both
male and female, some of them even mere children, engaged in
prayer, the intervals being occupied by singing hymns.[259]

It was at the Free Church that there were the first special meetings for
the children:

On Saturday afternoon Mr. Tulloch gave short addresses to such
of the young persons who felt anxious, and an opportunity
afforded to such as wished to engage in prayer was embraced by
three or four parties, chiefly boys.[260]

Although the Courant repeats the caution of the Courier, it concludes
approvingly:

We may add with pleasure that very many parties seem deeply
convinced of a sense of their guilt, and we should gladly record
several most hopeful cases of genuine conversion. This extra-
ordinary movement forms a new era in our history.[261]

The same paper also reports that during the following week 'On
Wednesday afternoon there was again a meeting for the young, and at
7:30 a public one' [262] in the Free Church. It is the Courier of the following
week which reports from Lossiemouth dated Tuesday 27th:

We were present at juvenile meetings held in the Free Church

---

258. E.M.C. Friday 23rd March 1860.
259. E.C. Friday 23rd March 1860.
260. E.C. Friday 23rd March 1860.
261. E.C. Friday 23rd March 1860.
262. E.C. Friday 23rd March 1860.

school on Thursday and Friday evenings, and we must be allowed to say that the scenes here were most irreverent...Two much respected parties here respectively pointed out the more common errors in which the young people were persisting, and tendered them much seasonable and pious advice, showing them at the same time the impropriety of protracting their meetings to such unsuitable hours. So determined were these ardent youths, however, on their own way, that they carried it out heedlessly, and even prayed vehemently for those paternal advisers, that 'their hearts might be softened, and that they might be forgiven for trying to shut the doors of mercy upon them.'[263]

A week later the 'Correspondent' of the Courant writes from Lossiemouth bemoaning the fact that:

Juvenile meetings continue to be held in the Free Church...(and)...It is a very common thing to hear also in our streets here, among the young folks, such expressions as, 'this one was converted at this meeting, and that one at the other meeting': the liberal and imprudent use of the word 'converted' in this way is too obvious to require comment. Others, again, of a peculiarly loquacious turn of mind, and who are evidently bent, in season and out of season, on using, as they think, every possible opportunity, seem to take an infinite delight in asking every person they meet in our streets their usual question, 'Have you found Jesus?' The motives of such may be pure, but it is for the intelligent public to judge as to the propriety of such a course.[264]

The final report from Lossiemouth is dated Thursday 12th April, and is quite dismissive:

Revival meetings are still kept up here, but are now comparatively thinly attended...The public meetings all along have been confined for the most part to the Free Church and Free Church school. At those in the church formerly, the novelty of hearing boys and women praying attracted great crowds, evidently from

263. E.M.C. 30th March 1860 and quoted in S.G. 3rd April 1860.
264. E.C. 6th April 1860.

curiosity; but the stringent restoration of order - for these irregularities are unwarrantable on the part of women at least - has tended much to separate the chaff from what wheat there may be; as these meetings are now attended but by apparently an anxious few... Meetings are still held, however, at which excitement seems to be the leading principle, encouraged by parties with whom we can by no means sympathise. Here boys and women still persist in engaging in prayer in the most frantic like and irreverent manner, and in singing hymns, beating time to the music with their feet, etc., altogether making one fancy that he beholds a company of wild bacchanalians.[265]

Nevertheless, it was the young people of Lossiemouth, who brought the revival to Elgin, on the weekend of 24th/25th March. The account in the Courant is more of an editorial than a report, and the full transcript is included in Appendix E. The Courier's headline is 'Extra-ordinary Proceedings' and is equally hostile. In both cases the main cause of offence seems to be no more than the children singing lively hymns instead of the metrical psalms!

Extra-ordinary Proceedings: Some very unseemly scenes occurred here, in the name of religion, on Saturday and Sabbath last. A juvenile prayer meeting was held on Saturday evening in the Free High Church, at which several young people appeared from Lossiemouth, by the invitation of some person or persons of more advanced years. The proceedings, though apparently not much calculated to edify, were on the whole conducted with comparative propriety. At the close of the services in that church, about ten o'clock at night, a large number of the juveniles and others adjourned to the Baptist Chapel in Reidhaven Street. While that chapel was being lighted, the youngsters struck up on the public road, the ranting hymn, 'What's the news?', and the doors of the chapel were no sooner opened that it was filled chiefly by children, but a good many adults were also present. The services, such as they were, were then proceeded with, and in the course of the evening, a number of boys and girls engaged

265. E.C. 13th April 1860.

in prayer, each prayer being followed by the singing of one of such hymns as 'I can, I will, I do believe,' 'What's the news?', &c. This was kept up until about four on Sabbath morning. Like services were again commenced in the Baptist Chapel on Sabbath and kept up during a great part of the day, to the great grief and annoyance of many worthy people who worship there. Similar scenes were enacted in some private houses in the course of Sabbath and Monday evenings. These proceedings are felt by the great bulk of the community to be an outrage of public decency and Christian propriety; but the blame lies not with these children, but with those who sought to make them and their services a public spectacle; and who, forgetting the sacredness of the services, and the decorum befitting a place of Christian worship, sanctioned these proceedings. But, as a regard for Christian decency and propriety has begun to assert its supremacy, and as at least some of those who at first encouraged these excesses have felt it necessary to disown and discourage them, and as this is tantamount to an acknowledgement of the error committed, we forbear publishing names and details.[266]

The Forres Gazette adds the detail that at the Saturday night meeting in the Baptist Church:

Three girls from Lossiemouth were engaged in prayer, as also four or five boys. A young woman in the audience screamed out while one of the girls was engaged in prayer, and caused a good deal of commotion.[267]

In complete contrast the Banffshire Journal has nothing but praise for the effect of the visit of the Lossiemouth youngsters to the village of Kingston, whose population it notes belongs 'almost exclusively to the Free Church':

With most sincere and unbounded gratitude to God, we have now to state that a movement bearing very strong marks of being a

266. E.M.C. 30th March 1860 and S.G. 3rd April 1860.
267. Quoted in I.A. Friday 30th March 1860

genuine revival of religion has begun among us...It seemed, indeed, as if we were to be passed by...About a fortnight ago a few boys from Kingston, under an impulse which we would characterise as certainly in the right direction, brought from Lossiemouth some young people of their acquaintance who professed to have benefited by the revival there. These remained here for a day or two, and doubtless by their presence and conversation, produced a certain impression of the reality and greatness of the work going on, which must have intensified the already prevalent desire for an outpouring of the Spirit. Among the young especially this influence seems to have been very decidedly felt.[268]

Further west, Thomas Davidson, then teaching at Forres, wrote:

The movement has reached our port, Findhorn, a village of one thousand inhabitants, among whom there are already one hundred and seventy to two hundred cases of deep conviction of sin. For some days the work of the school there...could not be carried on. The excitement broke out among the boys, and that still more remarkably than among the adults - forty cases among them. The teacher...has been very active in the work, and has aided the minister very much. I thoroughly believe in the genuineness of it all; it is the most remarkable event in the history of Christianity since Pentecost.[269]

This is dated for us by the Forres Gazette, which states that 'The religious excitement reached Findhorn last week...meetings are held daily...and by young people in the schoolroom.'[270]

(k) The Far North

In August 1859 H.M. Grant took his teenage nephew, Hay Aitken, with him as co-worker on a tour of the North of Scotland. Here is his description of the response of children in Thurso, and the testimony of a Sunday School teacher taught to pray out loud by the children:

268. B.J. 10th April 1860.
269. Couper, p.137.
270. Quoted in I.A. Friday 30th March 1860.

It was shortly after this that my uncle informed me of his intention to pay a visit to the extreme north of Scotland. Mr. Brownlow North was to have accompanied him; as my uncle believed it to be a right thing that two should go together. This arrangement, however, fell through, and my uncle invited me to be his companion. I was then only seventeen years of age, and felt the responsibility of assisting in so important a work a heavy one; but he encouraged me in his own kind way. On the 23rd of August we found ourselves at Thurso, the most northerly town in Scotland. Here we commenced holding services in the Free and Independent Churches. Mr. Grant addressed the grown-up people, and I took the children, amongst whom a considerable work soon began. Many a little face brightened up as the "tidings of great joy" seemed to reach their hearts. After the meeting was dismissed, I remember, a little girl, whose heart was very full, found her way down to a quiet spot behind some trees by the river-side, followed by two or three companions, and there knelt down and poured out her soul in prayer. Two or three rough boys from the streets offered her some molestation, but the little maid was not to be diverted, and only prayed for them. Two elders of the Free Church stole up behind the trees, and their testimony was: - 'Weel, we've heard mony a minister pray in our time, but never did we listen to sic a prayer as cam fra that wee lassie.'

I remember that, a little later, an earnest Christian lady, whose timidity prevented her from opening her lips in prayer before others, had occasion to visit some of her Sunday scholars. She was surprised to hear that they were 'upstairs praying'. She crept in silently and knelt down. When the last had prayed, the eldest girl looked up timidly, and said, 'Won't you pray?' 'I couldn't refuse,' the teacher afterwards said, - 'so I threw myself upon God, for words and power. The difficulty vanished and I have never suffered from it since.'[271]

Three months later, Mr. Grant preached in Tain in the absence of the minister. A letter dated 12th November 1859 tells of a similar response there among the children:

271. Hay McDowall Grant, pp 130-1. MacRae records Grant's previous visit to Thurso with Brownlow North in 1858, with Rev. Taylor's letter reporting progress of the Bible Class and the class 'of female house-servants' probably teenagers (MacRae, p.170).

It was particularly gratifying to see so many children eagerly inquiring the way Zionward. We had a deeply interesting scene in the Sabbath School; uncommon stillness and awe pervaded our meeting, and many of the little ones were bathed in tears. Surely this is the work of the Holy Spirit: it is sin to doubt it.[272]

In October 1859 there were Union Prayer Meetings in both Wick and Thurso. According to Rev. George Stevenson's own account at Pulteneytown on Sunday 15th January, 'The Holy Spirit came down with great power on the congregation.'[273] His subsequent description of the work among the children is worth quoting in full, as another example of an entire school shut down by the work of the Holy Spirit, and also the instantaneous way the children organised themselves into prayer meetings:

The first open movement among the children took place in the congregational school on the forenoon of Monday, the 6th February. Early in that forenoon a request was sent to me, by the teacher, to come to the school, as several of the children were in distress about their souls. It began in the following manner:- At a prayer meeting in the church on Sabbath evening I read, from a proof copy sent me by the Editor, a portion of Part II. of 'Records of Revival,' containing three striking cases of conversion. A little girl in the school, after the Bible Lesson in the morning, began to speak of these cases to her companions; and immediately those who were listening to her began to weep aloud about their sins. After I arrived and addressed the school, the concern among the children rapidly spread, and, before I ended, there was loud weeping in all parts of the school. It had become a Bochim. When dismissed, the children went home weeping, and, when asked by friends the cause, one said, 'For the load of sin that is on my soul'; another, 'For Jesus to come to my soul'; another, 'For fear they should be taken and I left'; with other similar replies. Upwards of a dozen boys held a prayer meeting together before going back to school in the afternoon. Since then

---

272. T.R. 12th November 1859.
273. MacRae p.155

several prayer meetings have been established both among boys and girls. At one time there were about a dozen separate children's meetings, some of them very large, numbering forty or fifty, who met to pray together; some of them small meetings, where five or six more timid little ones met to pray together. There are not now quite so many of these meetings, some of them being merged into others. This impulse to pray together was quite a spontaneous movement on the part of the children, and took their parents and teachers by surprise. Extra week-day meetings, for instructing the children who were anxious, were also readily attended by them.

On the last Sabbath of March I preached a sermon to the children in the evening. There were upwards of 200 children present. The deepest solemnity pervaded the congregation, and the young people were evidently greatly impressed during the sermon. At the close of the service they could no longer contain their feelings. A loud weeping began among the children. Almost all the young people, both boys and girls, were soon weeping aloud. They were exhorted, prayed with, and invited to join in singing by turns, but they could not be quieted. Three or four times I had pronounced the blessing, but had again to address them. For more than an hour and a half after the regular service was ended this continued, and the House of God became a place of weeping and supplication. The boys began to pray aloud for mercy to their souls, and their earnest petitions were heard all over the church. The prayers of several elders, whom I asked at this time to conduct the devotions, were drowned in the petitions of the boys. One boy's voice I heard above the others, where I was standing in the pulpit, earnestly praying, 'Come, blessed Jesus, this very night into my soul,' etc. It was with the greatest difficulty that the children could be persuaded to leave the church, and it was not till I had promised to preach to them the following evening that they retired. I learned from relatives that numbers of the children that night went to their closets as soon as they entered their homes, and some of them continued the most of the night in prayer. Many were, I believe, savingly impressed that evening. One boy of twelve years, who had to be helped home by a neighbour, kept saying to her by the way, 'Woman, can there be any mercy for a sinner like me?' This boy continued praying earnestly for his soul, and, on the fifth day after he was awakened, he found peace. When I saw him last he said (among other things) to me, 'I feel as if one were beating me when I hear them swearing.' Formerly he had been quite careless, now he fears the Lord. A youth of about fifteen years of age was, that night, brought under very great concern of soul. He used to spend the Sabbath, for the most part, in walking in the fields with other ungodly companions. When I saw him, three days after, I was struck with the uncommon solemnity of his countenance. He felt his sins to be like a load upon him, but he continued praying for mercy, and at last he found peace. He is now attending a boys' prayer meeting, the Sabbath School, and the church. He was from home for a few weeks lately, and he went up to a boys' prayer meeting in the place, and took the lead in it while there. A girl, between seven and eight years of age, who went home crying, was asked why she cried. Her reply was, 'For the Holy Spirit'; and, when asked what she wished the Holy Spirit to do, she said, 'To give me a new heart.'

For several weeks after this Sabbath evening I continued to find out fresh cases of boys and girls awakened during the discourse...A striking feature of the work, which reminded me of early times, was the grace of God bestowed upon *families*. There are instances of whole households who have been awakened and brought to rejoice in the Lord.[274]

Minor details can be added from the Christian Press of the day. The first is a letter dated 10th February 1860 which describes the scene in the school, then adds:

About a dozen boys held a prayer meeting together before going back to the school in the afternoon. They have had evening meetings of their own for prayer every night since. The boy's prayer meeting numbers above thirty, the girls above fifty. The meeting in this way to pray together has been quite a spontaneous

---

274. MacRae pp 160-4

movement on the part of the children, and has taken their friends by surprise. Truly it may be asked regarding these little ones 'Who are these that fly as a cloud, and as doves to their windows?'[275]

With reference to the last Sunday in March, the "Northern Ensign" covers the story thus:

Wick and Pulteneytown. On Sabbath evening in the Free Church of Pulteneytown, when the Rev. Mr. Stevenson was preaching to the young, a scene of deep solemnity was witnessed. Many individuals were much moved, and gave expression to their feelings in cries and tears. This was particularly the case with a number of young individuals, who continued crying for a considerable time. One boy, about thirteen years of age, prayed with great earnestness for an outpouring of the Spirit. Mr. Stevenson several times attempted to bring the service to a close, but could not succeed until nearly ten o'clock, after which time he was engaged in dealing privately with some of the anxious.[276]

There was considerable contact between the fishing communities of Caithness and those of the Banff and Moray coasts, the latter shared their blessings, sometimes deliberately and sometimes by force of circumstances. For example, three crews of Buckie fishermen were forced to shelter in the harbour at Lybster, resulting in 'A revival similar to that in the coast towns of the south shore of the Moray firth has begun in Lybster.' And 'In the school there was a scene characterised by all the usual exciting features.'[277]

A police sergeant in Govan wrote to the Wynd Journal to give details of events in Dunbeath:

A respected elder of the Free Church in the village of Dunbeath, informs me that a wonderful movement has taken place within the last eight to ten days. *Nightly prayer meetings were held in the*

275. W.J. 18th February 1860.
276. S.G. 3rd April 1860.
277. S.G. Tuesday 17th April 1860 quoting W.H.J. of Friday 13th April 1860.

Free Church: Both Church and School are crowded to overflowing from six at night to four or five in the morning, and numbers struck down both at the meetings, and in their own houses. Boys from six to twelve years of age stand up to pray uninvited and can scarcely be got to desist. A number have found the Saviour, and not a few of them the most debased in the place.[278]

The same Journal continues the story from Pulteneytown by stating: 'a great awakening continues among the young. Mr. Stevenson had been preaching to them not only on Sabbath evening, but during the week,' and it notes that children recognisably from tinker backgrounds were present.

One further anecdote was related by Stevenson to William Reid, and reveals quite remarkable religious sentiments expressed by a very young child early in 1860:

On January 2nd a man was awakened and converted, his wife six weeks later. The second child of the family, a girl between four and five years of age, has something very remarkable about her. One day she said to her mother, when her mother was still unwakened, 'O, mother, my heart is sore.' Her mother asked her, 'Why is it sore, my child?' She replied, 'It is sore for the love of Jesus.' About a fortnight after, as they rose from family worship, she said, 'O Father, if I could get a drop of that love.' He asked, 'What love?' - 'The Love of Jesus' was her reply. Another night when her mother was putting her to bed, she said, 'My heart is sore for God,' and next morning, whenever she awoke, she exclaimed, 'O mother, my heart was sore, sore for God last night.' One day she was overheard praying by herself in a corner of the room, 'Oh, wash me in that GRAND fountain.'

This account also adds that between January and March people were awakened every Sabbath and prayer meeting.[279]

The July 1861 issue of The Revivalist published a report from J.T. in Wick (probably John Thirkhill):

---

278. W.J. 7th April 1860 also T.F. 18th April 1860.
279. Reid pp 434-5.

In the neighbourhood of Helmsdale many have given themselves up to God and His service, among whom are a great number of youths. Fault-finders have also sprung up, like so many fungus roots, growing out of a rank heap of corruption, and complained of boys and girls crying 'Hosanna, hosanna,' but if *these* should hold their peace, the *stones* would cry out.

(l) The Northern Isles
Sanday
On 7 October, Rev Matthew Armour (Free Church, Sanday) intimated that on the afternoon of the following Sunday, the 14th, they should 'set themselves as a congregation to wait for the promise of the Father'. This they did, and one member recently appointed deacon stood up, raised his hands and prayed, 'for the Spirit to come down and revive the whole congregation'. Their prayers were answered and many went home weeping.

When the children assembled for the Sabbath School, the same individual who had prayed in the church gathered them at the door and addressed them with great earnestness, and during all the time many of them were crying bitterly, and during the whole time of the Sabbath School the weeping and crying continued.[280]

On 11th November it was Communion in the Free Church on Sanday. Mr Armour was assisted by Rev N P Rose of Rousay. The morning service was protracted with preaching by Mr Rose and a further address by Mr Armour. When the ministers returned to the church after the interval the scene was 'perfectly indescribable'. People were leaning against the walls outside crying for mercy, while inside many lay prostrate and hundreds wept. The meeting broke up between 4 and 5 a.m. and they went home - to pray!

It was remarked that some of the most deeply affected were young men who had formerly been cold and even careless about religious matters. Little children were observed with clasped

280. Orkney Herald, 20th November 1860

hands and eyes uplifted praying 'Come, Lord Jesus', 'Come, sweet Jesus', their countenances at the same time beaming with a brightness that seemed seraphic.[281]

In the same paper a Kirkwall correspondent contributed a letter dated 16th November 1860 about this meeting:

One young girl apparently not ten years old was very conspicuous. Mr Armour, Mr Rose and I were standing in the desk speaking together when she came to a gentleman seated near us whom she knew. 'Oh Mr —, have you found Jesus. Come and find him; do pray, pray; come and I will pray with you'. She pleaded with him a long time, and he was deeply affected. Her actions, the expressions of her beautiful face, beaming as it were with a halo of joy, was inimitable.

On the Tuesday they met at 4 p.m. in the Established Church, where 'young men seemed to be more brought under the power of the Spirit', and that meeting continued to 4 a.m. Wednesday. John Thirkhill recorded that 'Mr. Rose delivered an address, especially designed for the young,' but was forced to give up because of so many people crying out.[282]

On Wednesday 21st November the Free Church was full by 5 p.m., and people were prostrate in the session house, in galleries, between pews, etc. Rev. John Paul of Sanday witnessed this:[283]

I have seen two or three little girls apparently about eight years of age, kneeling on the floor with their faces on the seat board, and one of their number, about the same age, praying most earnestly over them and for them; and there were many such instances of juvenile earnestness.

This is picked up in the United Presbyterian Missionary Record of January 1st 1861 which adds:

---

281. Orkney Herald, 20th November 1860.
282. Letter from Wick, 2nd December 1860, to the Revivalist in London, published in January 1861 issue.
283. In letter dated 26th November to Rev. Dr. Paterson of Kirkwall describing Mr. Armour's meetings - also quoted in S.G. 20th December 1860, and Orkney Herald 4th December 1860.

In the corner of the back garden there issued forth a girl's voice evidently, greatly suppressed at first, but gradually waxing louder, and she was bewailing the sins and shortcomings of herself and her companions, some of whom were likely with her, from the way in which she spoke - 'Oh Lord, how thoughtless and sinful we have been, in neglecting and misimproving our precious privileges'...the movement is now universal, all denominations attending.[284]

Westray

An eyewitness account submitted by Rev James Ingram of the United Presbyterian Church, Eday, of the outbreak of revival in the Baptist chapel at Pierowall, Westray, where he was presiding at a joint meeting tells of conversions (especially amongst the young) on Edary and Pharray (now Eday and Farray):

About 50 persons, adherents of all the churches in the island, were as deeply affected under the conviction of sin as any I had seen before. Some, especially the young men, trembled violently, readily acknowledging their guilt, and cried for pardon; others were earnest but less demonstrative, but considerable numbers wept loudly.[285]

The same meeting was described by a Westray correspondent:

At first they only sobbed but their pent-up feelings soon found vent in cries not loud but deep-toned and unmistakably expressing deep sorrow of heart...[286]

Other reports add:

Quiet meetings for prayer among the young are common.[287]

Westside, Westray: '...The house filled with young people'- *it had been suggested by an older person that they should meet by*

---

284. Also reported in T.R. 29th December 1860.
285. Orkney Herald, 8th January 1861.
286. Orkney Herald, 8th January 1861.
287. Orkney Herald, 15th January 1861.

themselves - 'A number of young men and lads who had never before opened their mouths in public led the devotions. This meeting is also kept up weekly. A number of our young women have united together for prayer by themselves ...'.[288]

Monday 14th January was observed as New Year's Day in Westray (an old tradition now abandoned, when Christmas was the 7th):

The aspect of the day was completely changed from its usual appearance. The present religious movement has so far influenced the youth of both sexes that no amusement of any kind was engaged in. Presently the salvation of the soul is the great object of attention ... In the evening prayer meetings were held all through the island. Mr Reid invited the young people and others in his own congregation ... to meet ... *The room was too crowded for personal conversation with individuals anxious about their souls, which had been his intention.* ... after some had engaged in prayer piercing cries were heard, not strange here now. Mr Reid then left the meeting and retired to the manse inviting such as wished to converse with him to follow. Now both males and females were seen in twos and threes moving towards the door to take advantage of the privilege. During the minister's absence the meeting was conducted by an elder and to the inexpressible joy of all several young lads engaged in prayer *(for an outpouring of the Spirit on other islands). The meeting drew to an end after some discussion and singing. It was by then very late, but as soon as it had broken up,* a party of youth of both sexes entered the room and there in the dead of night poured out their supplications to the Hearer and Answerer of prayer.[289]

The school too experienced a move of God:

The following communication has been received from one of the teachers who has laboured among the young between twenty and thirty years: -

288. Orkney Herald, 15th January 1861.
289. Orkney Herald, 22nd January 1861

I have for some time kept a Sabbath-school in the class-room on Sabbath evenings, and in it there are four large classes. My class consists chiefly of young women from fourteen to eighteen years of age. I believe that nearly all my class, which is a large one, have become serious. Some of them I trust had received Christ before this. Several have had very powerful convictions, and have had great anguish of soul for some time. I feel it pleasant now to speak to them about the way of salvation; every ear is attentive, and their countenances beam with joy while we speak of that Saviour in whom they have found peace. A number of females have been exceedingly useful since the revival began. They commenced a prayer meeting, and thus became a centre around which others collected. They are ever ready to pour the balm of consolation into wounded hearts, and these are numerous. Several young men in our Sabbath-school, who attended with us several years ago, have evidently undergone a saving change, and are uniting with others in prayer meetings. To my delight I have heard several of them pouring out their supplications with all the fervour of first love. Did space permit, I could tell of others that attended me formerly but were become so careless that they were looked upon as nuisances to society, and have been wonderfully struck during this movement, and are become praying persons.

The revival has extended to every society and to every class of persons, especially to the young. The most respectable among us, and those reared in religious families have been brought low under the conviction of sin: while the careless and profane have been arrested in their career of sin, and it is believed that God is worshipped in many families where the voice of praise and prayer was never heard before. For some time past I felt as if God was converting sinners all around and was passing by the children of this school. After the Christmas recess, a boy who had appeared to be proof against religious impressions returned, to all appearance a changed character; shortly afterwards a few young girls were brought under the conviction of sin and earnestly sought refuge in Christ. We had also in the school some more advanced females who had evidently tasted that God is gracious. All these clung together in a little band and had become the objects of scorn to others. Two small prayer meetings were voluntarily and quietly formed, one for boys and the other for girls. On the 24th of January 1861, about 1 o'clock pm, while the scholars were repeating their ordinary Scripture task in John 3: 13-14, I observed an unusual appearance of silent weeping among a number of boys who had previously been careless. Though I had seen symptoms of seriousness in the early part of the day, I had paid no attention to it until now, and I could no longer conceal that I was aware of their state of mind, and I began to tell them so. Then almost all instantly gave vent to their anguish of soul. Tears flowed freely over their young blooming faces, while their deep-toned cries revealed their agony of soul. Now a scene exceedingly affecting and one that cannot be described took place. The little band at once found work congenial to their nature. With tears of sympathy flowing freely they ran to their afflicted school-fellows with their Bibles in their hands, entwining their arms around their necks, and whispering into their ears the invitations of the gospel - the very words which gave themselves comfort. I felt the scene before me uncommonly affecting. I tried to pray with them, but from my deep emotion I could hardly utter a word. I sent for Mr Reid, who came in to witness the solemn scene. He was also deeply affected. He spoke to them and prayed with them. We spent the rest of our time in directing them to suitable passages of Scripture, and when the hour of dismission came they asked leave to remain to hold a prayer meeting. On this occasion two boys were absent, and, to my surprise, next morning they were both struck with deep conviction of sin, which being observed (for they seem to know this by instinct) they ran to them and embraced them.[290]

Shapinsay

Three reports are available mentioning children on Shapinsay:

One of the most interesting features of the revival here is that persons of all ages are brought within its blessed influence. Boys, of not more than ten or eleven years of age are evincing great

---

290. Orkney Herald, 5th February 1861.

anxiety about their souls and earnestly desire to serve the Lord.[291]

The young converts are generally seen in small groups, either telling each other their experiences and giving glory to God for his unspeakable kindness to them, or singing hymns expressive of Christ's all-sufficiency, of his great love to sinners or of their inability to do anything for themselves.[292]

There are now several district prayer meetings composed entirely of boys, and conducted by them. We understand there are also two of young girls. It is very gratifying to see such a movement among the young. We would mention what we consider some of the fruits of these revival meetings–evidences of the good done by them–namely a marked improvement in the speech and behaviour of the children attending the various schools in this island. We have reason to believe that the very acceptable services of Mr John Thomson here have been blessed to the good of many souls.[293]

Orkney mainland

Rev, Mr. Souter of Firth who had officiated on February 10th at St. Andrews spoke on a Sunday by invitation in Deerness and for 3 nights following. Every evening the church was crowded with an eager audience, listening with the deepest interest to the preaching of the gospel.

Even the children were deeply moved and attended in large numbers, besides being addressed by themselves during the day. Some of them have given pleasing evidence of their having found Jesus...[294]

In the nearby parish of Holm the school was brought to a standstill by the revival:

One Wednesday afternoon when the ordinary business was proceeding in the Subscription School, one of the boys, who had formerly been noted for his love of play commenced weeping

291. Orkney Herald, 22nd January 1861.
292. Orkney Herald, 12th February 1861.
293. Orkney Herald, 26th February 1861.
294. Orkney Herald, 26th February 1861. Also in W.J. of 9th March 1861.

without any apparent cause. In a few minutes a dozen of others who were seated at a desk a few yards off began to weep all at nearly the same time, but some more violently than others. In the course of twenty minutes more nearly all the boys and girls in the school were weeping... After a little some of the scholars took up their Bibles and turned up passages, some in the Old and some in the New Testament and some in the psalms. For nearly an hour there was almost perfect silence, and the teacher found it necessary to have a chapter of John's Gospel read and make some remarks on it, after which the school was dismissed at the usual time...[295]

On February 26th in Birsay on the other side of the island:

Mr Souter gave a narrative of what had come under his observation in Sanday and Deerness. A very deep impression seemed to be made...several were in tears. Many young people were present and some of the boys seemed much moved.[296]

There is a letter from an unnamed correspondent in Sandwick:

I have heard also of considerable indications of seriousness among the young and of prayer meetings held by them among themselves or under the superintendence of their seniors.[297]

Papa Westray
Finally, there is a report of children praying on this small island in a letter from Rev. John Peddie of the Free Church:

Last week young men and women have commenced prayer meetings of their own. The little children too meet in different parts of the island to pour out their young hearts to the Lord...I have been informed that some of the children on their way home from school have prayed together in boats on the beach and by the dykeside...[298]

---

295. Orkney Herald, 5th March 1861. 296. Orkney Herald, 5th March 1861.
297. Orkney Herald, 2nd April 1861. 298. Orkney Herald, 5th March 1861.

All the general accounts from the parishes where revival took place indicate that the younger people of the community were particularly affected, and their conversation and their behaviour changed, becoming especially active in prayer.

Shetland

A revival in Shetland was reported to the Congregational Union in 1864 but contained no references to children.[299]

299. T.R. 28th July 1864

4. The Era of Mass Evangelism 1864-1904

(a) The Aftermath of 1859

When did the revival that commenced in 1859 come to an end? No clear answer can be given, but its effects clearly continued right up until the first visit to Scotland of Moody, and it released a flood of evangelistic activity that continued into this present century, for example the Evangelistic Association of Scotland which was constituted early in 1863.[1] Two of their workers on a visit to the Borders found in Greenlaw

> Abundant evidence in a goodly number of earnest and prayerful young men and young women who are, we believe, destined to have a healthy influence on those around them.[2]

Richard Weaver returned to Scotland twice that year. From February until April he worked in Edinburgh, Perth, Aberdeen, and Glasgow with extensive results but no mention of children, but during his later work in Inverness, Major Conran of Elgin reported:

> In one case a little boy of ten years of age came very early in the morning to a City Mission in deep anxiety about his soul, beseeching in most affecting earnestness to be told 'What he must do to be saved'.[3]

Weaver then joined Harrison Ord for a fortnight's campaign in Glasgow, the latter 'winning souls to Christ, especially among the young'. Ord held meetings for 'those converted during the revival of the last five years', and gave opportunity for testimony.

> Among those who spoke last night, one was a boy about eleven, who was made anxious about salvation under Weaver's addresses, and brought to rest in Christ by the text 'the wages of sin is death but the gift of God is eternal life through Jesus Christ'. *He was followed by a young man* . After these two had spoken an

---

1. See T.R. 26th February 1863 for details.
2. T.R. 7th April 1864, report of Dr. Craig and Captain MacKenzie.
3. T.R. 17th November 1864, letter dated 11th November.

invitation was given to about two hundred young persons from eight up to twenty years of age, who occupied the centre of the circus, that such of them as knew they had received a sensible blessing, might hold up their hands, when about half the number did so.[4]

About the same time, Duncan Matheson was holding nightly meetings in Glasgow at the Circus:

at which the regular attendance of about two hundred children, the majority of whom appear to be sincere lovers of Jesus, and to have their greatest delight in the exercises of such meetings, is a remarkable feature.[5]

On Saturday 10 June 1865 the annual meeting of the Sunday School Unions of Carrubbers' Close Mission were told that:

The most interesting feature of the past year was a movement chiefly among the elder boys, a considerable number of whom are now holding prayer meetings among themselves, and in their own houses in different parts of the town.[6]

Otherwise, it appears to have been a barren year. Harrison Ord did use 'a little girl' to give her testimony at a meeting on Glasgow Green[7] and later in the year visited a Ragged School Reformatory in Inverness 'but saw little signs of blessing'.[8] The Free Church Assembly of 1866 were told that in the preceding year the only evidence of the revival movement was in Banff and in two Glasgow churches.[9]

However, at this very time, The Revival discovered 'Awakenings in the North of Scotland', where at Nairn:

During the last three weeks a very decided movement has commenced among the little boys and girls from the age of ten to fourteen years. Some of them truly seem to have laid hold of Jesus, and have little prayer meetings among themselves.[10]

---

4. T.R. 1st December 1864. 5. T.R. 8th December 1864.
6. T.R. 22nd June 1865. 7. T.R. 17th August 1865.
8. T.R. 5th October 1865. 9. T.R. 7th June 1866. 10. T.R. 17th May 1866.

It also tells us that Capt Otter and Mr Adam on Wednesday 25 July on Mull:

> visited the girls school, where, as they were telling the children of Jesus and His love to all, the first indications of the glorious work that God has done among us appeared.[11]

Infuriatingly it gives no further details! A month later The Revival talks about an awakening in Kilsyth with crowded nightly meetings in both the Independent and Wesleyan Churches.[12] By the end of the year the tide of blessing was being noted again, for example Alex Taylor from Strathaven reported on the work of two young English evangelists, Thomas Holt and George Geddes:

> The blessed result has been a widespread awakening, still going on, especially among the young.[13]

Northrop was conducting meetings in Aberdeen's Music Hall:

> There was a children's meeting this afternoon with a large attendance and considerable impression, several desiring to find Christ. One little girl about ten with whom I conversed, and on whom I was urging God's claim, replied so sweetly and quietly when I pressed her to give her heart to the Lord, 'I did it last Sabbath evening'.[14]

Duncan Matheson could write of his campaign in Forfar: 'It has gone quietly on and has taken hold chiefly of the young, specially about twenty years of age.'[15] The year concludes with a letter from Thomas Holt dated 18th December:

> Until I came to Scotland, about twelve months ago, with brother Geddes, I had not seen any work of this kind and was not aware that children could be converted at so early an age. We visited Newburgh in March, where many children attended the meetings

---

11. T.R. 16th August 1866. 12. TR. 13th September 1866 and 11th October 1866. 13. T.R. 25th October 1866. 14. T.R. 8th November 1866. 15. T.R. 15th November 1866.

and were impressed and some professed to find 'peace in believing', *and as a result a Band of Hope was formed with 130 children in it.* We had children's meetings in Hamilton and about 100 on an average attended, some few were impressed... At Wishaw the Lord blessed a number of children, and they labour amongst others of their own age. A sister holds a meeting for them in a cottage and a little fellow about nine years of age, who was there one night, opened with prayer. The presence of the Lord was amongst them; many were very anxious and quite broken down, and a number of them professed to find peace in Jesus. At Larkhall we had about 200 children... At Stonehouse the children were much impressed; nearly 400 attended. We had two churches open nightly, one for children, the other for adults: a vast number of these dear little ones were blessed. I have seen as many as thirty or forty weeping at once.. A teacher in one of the day schools writes... 'I counted sixty in the school yesterday, who give good evidence of being converted, and that does not include the little ones in the first, second, third and fourth books, many of whom I believe are lambs of the flock.' *He ends with the story of an eight year old in Lanark Free Church, who had been converted the previous night, but who had been anxious* ever since she heard Richard Weaver last year in the City Halls, Glasgow.[16]

1867 opens with widespread reports of results across the country, starting on the Moray Coast, where Rev T Major reports the opening of the Portessie Methodist Chapel on 23rd December 1866 by the Rev H J Pope of Glasgow.

On the Tuesday evening, Mr Pope again preached in Portessie, and on the Wednesday evening in a neighbouring village. On each of these occasions, souls were saved. Never was a work more clearly seen to be of God. It commenced with the children, and reached the grey-haired; children of seven and old men of seventy are among its subjects.[17]

---

16. T.R. 27th December 1866. 17. T.R. 17th January 1867: Taken from the Methodist Recorder. For further details see 'The Romance of Banffshire Methodism' by Wesley F. Swift, (1927, Banffshire Journal Ltd.)

Similarly for the past two and a half months in Portknockie a 'very marked work of the Spirit has been progressing here.' 'The majority of the converts have been young men and women but some of very tender years ... have also felt the power of the gospel.'[18]

For some reason this part of the Scottish coast continued to witness pulses of revival, under the ministry of John Mangles in the Methodist churches in 1869-70, then:

This year, 1871, begins with a descent of the Holy Ghost upon the people of Findochty. The first was a stirring amongst God's people. The next was a desire with the ungodly for the means of grace. In a very little time many became anxious and by-and-bye got savingly converted to God. The Spirit wrought mightily and many souls were saved...

One thing especially that took all considerate Christians by surprise was the dance. It was never for once dreamed of and at first seemed to many very unseemly... Its first appearance was among the children, and then among persons more advanced in life, and perhaps stranger still many advanced in the Christian life also came under its power and in many cases irresistible power. And the persons thus engaged showed symptoms of the greatest joy - and truly their very appearance bespoke them to be under a high divine impulse... An impression came that they must visit the neighbouring villages. *Thus they processed with banners to Portessie, then Buckie, preaching the gospel as they went.*[19]

This became known as the Dancing Revival. When James McKendrick later visited Findochty he discovered:

A beautiful custom in that place is that when a person is converted they at once go to the homes of their relatives and tell them of the change. Their friends rejoice with the converts and engage in praise and prayer. A favourite custom, when a number of then

18. T.R. 4th April 1867. 19. Turner, p.137.

are thus gathered is to join hands and sing a hymn with a rhythmic air, to which they keep time with their feet.[20]

Some trace of this has continued for a century: when Graeme Young was converted as a nine year old in 1959 among the Brethren in Portessie he remembers being taken first to one relative's house where prayer was offered, and then at a second relative's house they immediately gathered together to sing and rejoice over his salvation.

Rice Hopkins was conducting a very successful campaign in many of the Orkney islands. One Sunday evening he preached to 1200 in Stromness, and also reported:

> The Lord has been working among the children. We had two children's meetings, attended by about three hundred, and several of these seem to be awakened and converted.[21]
> *On Westray:* On Wednesday I had a meeting at twelve for children. Of course many others came, and the place was full. We remained until four, speaking to the anxious.[22]

He then writes from 'Edary' (Eday), that:

> a great spirit of anxiety was manifested; about twenty professed, among them the two children of Mr Tait, Baptist Minister.[23]

It is sad to have to record that by the time Hopkins returned the following year he had become set in Brethren views, advocating withdrawal from existing churches, and causing much division.

Meanwhile E P Hammond had returned to Scotland and was revisiting Annan, where, from 1861 he found:

> Hundreds, who in those days, used to be seen weeping for their sins, now appear at the meetings with happy faces, and during these six years have maintained a consistent Christian walk.[24]

---

20. Seen and Heard, by J. McKendrick, Pickering & Inglis, 1933, p.127. McKendrick describes an extensive revival move along the Moray and Banff coasts in 1893-6, but apart from references to gangs of youths, makes no reference to children.

21. T.R. 14th February 1867. 22. The Latter Rain, 1st February 1867 (letter undated). 23. T.R. 28th March 1867. 24. T.R. 14th March 1867.

We also have a report that in Johnstone: 'men, women and children have been led to our precious Saviour.'[25]

In March 1868, from Finnieston, Andrew Bonar records in his Diary for Wednesday 25th 'this week the Lord is working remarkably in our congregation among the children under Mr Hammond.' The following Tuesday (31st March) he states: 'The awakening going on, tonight both Isabella and Marjory came home truly speaking of their having been enabled to rest on Christ. What a joyful time this has been!' His daughters were then aged 17 and 13 respectively. By 30th May he is able to note 'There have been of late a good many conversions among us, among the children, and among the young people of my classes.' And on Saturday 27th June reported 'last Sabbath evening, my sermon to the Sabbath scholars was a season of unusual power; I felt the words going forth and coming down with strength. A good many were impressed.'[26]

In 1867 the Bible Class in Linlithgow Town Mission Hall rose from about twenty to:

> At present 105 and the attendance is between 80 and 90. Often very great earnestness prevails among the children, and as an evidence that the Holy Spirit is quickening their young hearts, about six weeks ago five of their number formed a prayer meeting, and meet every Sabbath night, after the Bible Class is dismissed, for prayer. Their number has gone on increasing, and now there are ten who have joined themselves to the Lord, and each engages in prayer. Their ages are from eleven to fourteen years.[27]

Since Richard Weaver's visit to Bathgate 'a youth of seventeen years from Glasgow has been labouring for ten days, holding meetings every night', with twelve conversions on the Sunday.[28]

In Arbroath: 'A great many of the young have been brought to know the Saviour and are showing this by their walk and conversation. There are about thirty-four young men who meet for prayer every Friday; their ages are from eleven to eighteen.'[29]

---

25. T.R. 14th March 1867.
26. This was obviously a regular practice for Bonar: two years later 'the children were strangely still as I preached of Christ calming the storm, and the little ships sharing in the calm' also on a Sabbath evening. Diary 25th September 1870.
27. T.R. 4th April 1867. 28. T.R. 16th May 1867. 29. T.R. 13th June 1867.

Meetings by evangelist Mr Adam and local minister Rev Goldie in Tullibody led to 'over one hundred anxious inquirers, exclusive of children, of whom there was a considerable number.'[30] Children were reported at his subsequent meetings in Ferryden.[31]

In Peterhead Rev. Wilson 'has held a series of children's meetings in Maiden Street Hall and some of the little ones have been converted'.[32]

With the setting up of the Children's Special Service Mission (now 'Scripture Union') in June 1867 by Josiah Spiers,[33] but strongly influenced by Hammond, we can trace the origins of special evangelistic activity aimed at children. It would be impossible to record every instance of child conversion available to us, as well as being tedious to the reader, but it should be noted that hereafter, to a large extent we are looking at the phenomenon of highly successful children's evangelism, rather than children being affected by revival. Therefore we shall restrict ourselves to a few of the more spectacular examples. Children were now on the church's agenda.

In April 1868 C H Spurgeon, the great London preacher but of no small influence within Scotland, devoted the editorial of his magazine 'The Sword and the Trowel' to the subject 'Can Nothing More Be Done for the Young?' After advocating lively meetings for children, with short talks, revival hymns and 'The liberty of clapping their hands and cheering every now and then, there will be no fear of their going to sleep.' Even more interesting than this amazing statement, he goes on to advocate children's prayer meetings:

'Prayer meetings for boys and girls, judiciously conducted, will be of abundant service. There should always be an experienced lover of children at their head, and then the fewer grown-up persons tolerated in the room the better. When there are half a dozen praying children present, their earnest prayers and tears will be with those of their own age the most potent instrumentality imaginable. Never fear precocity, there is much more danger

30. T.R. 26th September 1867.
31. T.R. 14th November 1867. 32. T.R. 28th November 1867.
33. For a history of the CSSM see article 'Suffer little children' in the Revival Times of London, 18th August, 1905, from Spiers' first mission in Llandudno, to sixty seaside towns by 1905.

> of indifference and levity. Let wisdom and love preside. The fact
> of not being able to pray will often, by the blessing of the Holy
> Spirit, force home conviction upon the young conscience and
> lead to the best results...We know classes where the young
> believers have multiplied till they have become the majority and
> then they have, of their own accord, formed a sort of religious
> society for bringing in others of their playmates and relatives, for
> looking after absentees, for writing to the unsaved, and for
> generally seeking the glory of God within the bounds of the class.
> Fine education, this, for future church members.'

Towards the end, Spurgeon concludes: 'We have never developed the
capabilities of youth as we should have done.'[34]

(b) The 1870's and Moody's first visit

Before analysing Moody's work in Scotland, it is worth pausing to
record a significant conversion of a twelve year old boy on holiday with
his parents in Arran in the summer of 1873. That boy was John George
Govan, later to become founder of the Faith Mission. His biographer
states:

> Testimony was neither enjoyed nor practised in those days, when
> religion was more awe-ful than joy-ful, and it was six months
> before he confided in one of his sisters. Then he began his first bit
> of Christian service, inviting boys to the 'Schoolboys' Meet-
> ings', which had been started by an elder brother and some
> friends in the Queen's Rooms, Glasgow, at the suggestion of his
> mother. He attended the Schoolboys' Prayer Meeting in the
> Gibson's house on Friday nights.[35]

This piece of information, given in passing, is of value to us in
providing evidence of another group of children regularly meeting
together to pray, outside of a time of revival.

The story of how D L Moody came to be in Britain need not concern
us here. Suffice it to say that while he was in Newcastle Rev John

---

34. C.H. Spurgeon 'The Sword and the Trowel' April 1868. London, p.149-50.
35. Spirit of Revival, a biography of J.G. Govan by I.R. Govan, Faith Mission, 1938, p.17

Kelman of Leith took upon himself to invite Moody to Scotland, and he arrived in Edinburgh on Saturday 22nd November 1873. Moody and Sankey held their first meeting in the Music Hall on the Sunday evening and several thousands had to be turned away.[36] Kelman provides the first report of the meetings with 'hundreds...brought under serious impressions' then adds in a postscript, 'since the above was written, the noon day prayer meeting of today has been held. Upwards of 1700 were present, including many children, who have no school to attend on Saturday. A blessed meeting.'[37] Later in the campaign that Saturday noon meeting was to become specifically for the children, but references to them in the early accounts are few. There is a passing reference to 'young men from the public schools' being at a meeting for Young Men in the Free Assembly Hall on Friday 19th December attended by two thousand[38] and the story of Margaret Lindsay, aged 17, on her way home from the Free Church Normal Seminary in Edinburgh by train, and involved in the Manuel railway disaster, who while trapped and suffering from two broken legs and a cut face, said: 'will you tell Mr Moody from me, how much I owe under God to him?'. She subsequently died of her injuries.[39]

The 'Times of Blessing' was a 'Weekly Record containing Full and Authorised Accounts of the Present Religious Movement', but did not commence publication until the day after Moody ended his Glasgow campaign. Nevertheless it gives comprehensive coverage of news from around Scotland. The report from Edinburgh has a paragraph headed 'The Children's Saturday Meeting' which:

Is by far the most crowded and popular of the mid-day prayer meetings. Saturday forenoon has always been appropriated to the young. It is a striking sight to see them gathering to it and still more so to see the meeting dispersing at one o'clock. The whole slope of the Mound is darkened by the mass of little gures, with their parents and friends; or if, a few minutes after, you are walking in the opposite direction, you meet them on George IV Bridge, you observe them crossing the Meadows, you find them in Princes Street or Lothian Road or Leith Walk, knowing where

---

36. T.C. 18th December 1873. 37. T.C. 11th December 1873. 38. T.C. 1st January 1874.
39. T.C. 5th February 1874.

they have been by the hymn-books which they are carrying in their hands. Nothing can be more remarkable than the interest and affection which the young people have for this meeting. Even the standing room in the Assembly Hall is occupied on Saturdays; you require to go early to secure a seat. The love of Jesus for the young is the great theme of these meetings. The hymns are sung with relish that never abates, and there is a wonderful attraction in the spirit of the place.

There follows a report of the Monday evening meeting for converts and inquirers, numbering 600-700 weekly, which states that:

Many of those who attend are among the more advanced pupils at the various public schools. In a number of cases, nurses, parents, or others accompany those who are too young to go out alone at night.[40]

At the end of the volume there is an appendix on Edinburgh, entitled 'Narrative of Awakening', which adds a few more details:

Dr Thomson, in a letter described inquirers in Moody's early Edinburgh meetings : I was much struck by the variety among the inquirers. There were present from the old man of seventy-five to the youth of eleven, soldiers, students, ... *There were daily meetings in the Christmas holidays for the children.* From the very beginning of the work a large proportion of the conversions were among young people brought up in Christian families, or who had received Christian instruction; and on Saturdays, when the meeting was reserved for children, from 1200 to 1400 often assembled...On New Years' Day both Assembly Halls were filled. Many young people and mere children look back to that day as their birthday for eternity.

It also records that at his watchnight service 'a young girl' Maggie Lindsay was converted: she was killed a month later as a result of the Railway collision at Manuel, 'in great suffering but with hymns of praise on her lips'.

---

40. T.B. 18th April 1874

John MacPherson also attests Thomson's statements:

The immense number of the children of Christian parents and other young persons religiously trained who were converted was a striking feature of this revival. The majority of converts probably consisted of this class.[41]

On January 16th Moody held a farewell meeting for those converted in the previous two months and 1400 applied for tickets.

One further contemporary report exists of these Edinburgh meetings. Mrs Peddie writes: 'On the Saturdays the services of the noon prayer meeting have been specially adapted for children. By the most simple presentation of gospel truth, by illustrative incident, by the most direct appeals to the conscience, and by the most fervid and winning entreaties to receive Christ NOW, as a personal Saviour, Mr Moody has, on all these occasions, sought to win these young souls to Christ, and we understand with much blessing and success.'[42] To which is added the comment: 'Mr Sankey's sweet service of sacred song always seemed peculiarly attractive to the youthful audiences and doubtless contributed its good share to the blessing experienced on these occasions both by the young and by many others.' Later she includes another account: 'The noon meeting in the Free Church Assembly Hall on Saturday was devoted to children, and addresses suited to their intelligence were made to them by Mr William Dickson who at the request of Mr Moody, took charge of the meeting at the outset, and by Lord Cavan, Mr Sankey, and Mr Moody afterwards. The attendance was very large, especially of the young.'[43]

Moody did not confine himself to centralised meetings, but worked in different parts of the city. 'The Rev Mr Robertson of Newington, at one of the noonday meetings, stated some facts in regards to the special

41. MacPherson, Revival p.45.

42. 'A Consecutive Narrative of the Remarkable Awakening in Edinburgh' by Mrs. R. Peddie, Religious Tract Society, Edinburgh, 1874, p.27. According to MacPherson (p.56) Sankey's decision to give himself to communicating the Gospel through music, came when visiting one of his Sabbath school pupils dying of burns after the great fire of Chicago, having had a revelation of assurance while singing 'Jesus loves even me' the previous Thursday.

43. Peddie p.71

services held by Messrs Moody and Sankey in his church during last week. ... there had been not a few little children, both boys and girls, perhaps chiefly boys, who were seeking rest and not able to get it until they found it in the Saviour; and then going away rejoicing, having found the pearl of great price.'[44]

Moody's impact on Edinburgh lasted long after he left the city for a fortnight in Dundee on January 21st. In Edinburgh University a daily prayer meeting was 'attended by a considerable number' and:

> Similar meetings have been held in several of the schools. We could tell of institutions where the pupils appear en masse to have been impressed and changed. The Children's Church for the waifs of the Canongate has experienced great benefit from a wonderful accession of spiritual life and power which has come on the pupils, male and females, of the Training College in Moray House... We could tell of equally remarkable changes in connection with various gatherings of young persons, where the influence seems to have passed on four-fifths or five-sixths of the whole.[45]

Simultaneously there was also a flood of Christian activity throughout the country. For example in Berwick upon Tweed, during a second week of special evangelistic meetings:

> the number of inquirers is very great. At first they belonged chiefly to the Sabbath Schools and Bible Classes, but now many of riper years are among their number.[46]

There is a first hand account of the Dundee meetings given by John MacPherson, dated 30th January 1874:

> *In Dundee*...parents and children are seen together in the same attitude of earnestly seeking after Jesus ... Very affecting was it to find a whole family of six seeking the way to the feet of Jesus. The oldest, a grown up girl, was rejoicing in Christ; the others, three girls and two boys, in age ranging from eight to sixteen,

44. Peddie p.71-2.
45. T.B. 18th April 1874.
46. T.C. 29th January 1874.

were weeping most bitterly and entreating the Lord to convert them. *All reached assurance in the inquiry room.*[47]

One of our esteemed brethren in the ministry found among the inquirers a boy of some fourteen years. His anxiety was great, but he could not weep, he could not pray, his heart was like stone. The way of salvation was opened up to him. When he understood that Jesus died for sinners, and that eternal life is the free gift of God through Christ, his heart was melted, he burst into tears, and offered thanksgiving to the Lord in a very affecting manner. Before he saw the cross not a tear could he shed, not a prayer could he offer; but on obtaining a glimpse of Jesus and the finished work, penitence and prayer and praise flowed from heart and lips in a stream.[48]

An anonymous letter from Dundee is quoted following Moody's first visit there:

There has been a very manifest work of grace in the Sunday School here, large numbers of the children remaining to be spoken to. Those who are saved have been holding a prayer meeting.[49]

Also of Dundee Rev Reid says 'many little children have felt the sharp arrows of the King in their hearts, and yielded to His sceptre' and 'young people are crowding round their ministers and crying for work'.[50]

An unsought bi-product of the tour of Moody with Sankey was the popularising of the singing of hymns. A letter of 'JM' to The Christian dated 6th February 1874 gave examples of children singing gospel songs: a three year old's singing reduced her father to tears and a Jemima Annan was singing Sankey's songs as she died of scarlatina.[51]

From MacPherson we learn that this seven year old girl:

47. T.C. 5th February 1874 and MacPherson p.288.
48. T.C. 5th February 1874.
49. T.B. 16th July 1874.
50. T.B. 18th April 1874.
51. T.C. 12th February 1874

A little child of bright complexion and sparkling intelligence is sitting in the Union prayer meeting held by the American evangelists in Dundee early in 1874. Seated beside her mother, she sings 'Sweet Hour of Prayer' with a warmth that attracts attention. 'Does your child understand what she is singing?' was the question of a lady who was struck with the fervour of the little singer. 'Yes, she understands it,' was the Mother's reply; 'she is a child who loves prayer.' On the day following she was taken ill of scarlatina. It was near the hour of midnight on Sabbath when her uncle took me to see her. Throughout her three days illness she continued to sing. 'I feel like singing all the time' was often on her lips. She spoke much of heaven and loved to sing 'In the land beyond the shadows'. One she had learned from Mr Sankey, 'I am so glad Jesus loves me', she continued to sing as long as consciousness remained. ... 'I am going to Jesus, Mother,' she said; 'I am not afraid to die, because I am going to see Jesus.'[52]

In another instance: Mrs Barbour reports from Edinburgh on 28th March:

In several districts of this town a most cheering satisfactory work is going on in Sabbath Schools and among the poorest and wildest boys. For some time past the errand boys and others have gone humming or whilstling through the streets the airs of their favourite hymns...[53]

Moody commenced his work in Glasgow on Sunday 8th February by addressing 3000 Sunday School teachers in the City Hall, giving a clear indication of the importance he attached to youth work. It is strange that John Pollock in his recent biography of Moody[54] should have a chapter entitled 'Friend of Children' with reference to his early work in America, but make no mention at all of the place of children and youth in Moody's British meetings. One of Moody's key supporters

---

52. MacPherson p282-3. He also recounts other instances of children dying in full assurance of faith in pages 286-8.
53. T.C. 2nd April 1874.
54. Moody without Sankey, Hodder and Stoughton, London 1963.

during his ten weeks in Glasgow was Rev Andrew Bonar who supplied several reports. Referring to 14th February he writes:

> On Saturday the meeting (as usual on that day) was specially for children - a lively and impressive meeting. The church was filled with young people, and there had been decided conversions in connection with these gatherings for the young.[55]

All the same, he appears to contradict himself three weeks later with the statement dated 9th March:

> There is a children's meeting held every Saturday ... as yet there is no very general movement among the young though there are many cases of decided conversion in several of our Sabbath Schools.[56]

Bonar's Diary for Saturday May 16th 1874 states 'in our Sabbath-School there have been not less than one hundred awakened, and most of them very hopeful', plus 70 adults in his congregation. He records for us the conversion of 15 year old Lizzie Hamilton on March 20th, who went down with scarlet fever later the same evening and died soon afterwards.[57] Dr George Jefferey also describes the conversion of girls aged 10 and 15 during the campaign[58] although Moody seemed to have a special appeal to young men. Rev James Wells reporting from the Free Barony Church in Glasgow noted this special response among the young men and said that in one church:

> Among the inquirers in that district there had been about two young men for every young woman and two boys for one girl.

At East Campbell Street UPC Rev Dr Wallace on Tuesday 24th March noted 'fully a hundred young men remained to the inquiry meeting' and by the Friday 300 of the 2000 present remained. He 'spoke to three young lads and it has never been his privilege to witness such evident tokens of the melting power of the Divine Spirit. He has met them several times since and their "joy still abounds".'[59]

---

55. T.C. 26th February 1874. 56. T.C. 12th March 1874. 57.T.C. 25th March 1874. 58. T.C. 16th April 1874. 59. T.B. 18th April 1874.

MacPherson observes:

The next remarkable point in the progress of the movement was the extra-ordinary work among the young men of Glasgow, and the call from that city for prayer on behalf of the youth of Scotland. This well-timed call was joyfully responded to throughout the country. ... We can recall how, at this time, in the late evening hours, we found groups of young men and boys at the street corners engaged in absorbing and warm discussion of the gospel, some rejoicing in the Saviour, some enquiring, and some simply stunned, not knowing what to think or say.[60]

A little later he again affords a personal anecdote:

I have seen a group of little children, the oldest not more than twelve, engaged in solemn converse upon the street, and overheard one explaining to the rest the plan of salvation by Jesus who died for sinners.[61]

After one of the Glasgow breakfast meetings a lady noticed a man pacing up and down in an anxious state. As she tried to point him to salvation, he protested that he must do something in order to be saved. 'As he was saying this, a little boy (of about eleven years of age) who had been seeking out a passage in his Bible, touched the lady and holding the Bible open, said, "please read that to him". It was Romans 4:5: "but to him that worketh not, but believeth on Him who justifieth the ungodly, his faith is counted for righteousness". The lady read it. The man listened most attentively ... and the word entered his soul.'[62]

From Glasgow Moody and Sankey were over in Greenock:

On Saturday the daily meeting was reserved specially for children and the hall was again densely crowded with children, their parents and friends. Mr Sankey sang 'Jesus loves me', 'Room

60. MacPherson, Revival, p.40.
61. MacPherson, Revival, p.43.
62. MacPherson, Revival, p.83.

among the Angels', 'Hold the Fort', etc ... On Sunday a special
general meeting of the Greenock Working Boys' and Girls
Religious Society was held in the Town Hall at 11 O'Clock. Mr
Macphail presided and Mr Sankey conducted the praise. There
were about 1200 boys and girls present, and the remaining parts
of the hall were again crowded with grown people.[63]

Before he left Glasgow[64], Moody held a conference on Thursday 23
April with 2000 leaders to discuss how to forward the work. Prof
Charteris from Edinburgh recommended regular Sunday afternoon
services conducted at least in part by the minister 'so that the children
might come to think the minister and the church had a real and direct
relation to them. Children's Churches are an excellent stepping-stone to
this and might still be used; but the pastor of Christ's flock is as much
bound to feed the lambs as to feed the sheep.'

> Mr Moody said Scotland needed a John Wesley, not for his
> doctrine, but his power of organisation. The Church in Scotland
> is a first-class mob. He would suggest that all girls under fifteen
> years of age who had been converted should be put under the
> charge of a godly mother, with whom they should have meetings
> once a week or so. Then Christian boys under fifteen and seven-
> teen should be taken charge of and formed into a class by some
> godly man, who should encourage them and teach them to work.
> In every church some such organisation should be instituted and
> reports given in to the elders every week or every month.

Rev David Russell, Glasgow 'said inquiry meetings should become
normal - connected with every congregation, every Bible class, every
Sabbath School'. Dr D McEwan of Glasgow proposed 'a great amend-
ment and extension of the Sabbath-school system was needed. An
hour's teaching at an inconvenient hour, in ill-ventilated school rooms,
on one day of the week was not enough to counteract the influences of
the rest of the week.' In the afternoon session of questions Moody was

63. T.B. 18th April 1874.
64. His Glasgow meetings terminated on 17th April to go to Paisley, Greenock and
Ayrshire, returning through Glasgow. (Coupar, p.146).

asked what more can be done for children? He replied: 'First put up buildings for them. I have not seen a decent building for Sabbath school children in Scotland. Your Sabbath schools are dark and dingy, with high, hard seats. You must remedy this.'[65]

At a Monday noon meeting in Glasgow Rev Wells reported on a Sunday evening meeting led by Mr Mackeith of the Foundry Boys' Society, where 'about fifty of the senior boys and girls remained to be talked to. They seemed all deeply impressed.' Mr Sloan told of a meeting which had been held in the Queen's Rooms for the boys in the West End schools. There were about 800 or 900 present and about 70 anxious remained; some seemed to get into rest'. 'Mr Miller told of a work of grace amongst the young in Finnieston Mission Schools.'[66]

Also in Glasgow, James Scott records:

> Every Saturday from 12 to 1 o'clock, Wellington Street UP Church, which holds about twelve or fifteen hundred, is crowded with boys and girls. Sometimes Ewing Place church is also filled. *Last Saturday* our meeting was held in the City Hall which holds several thousands. Mr Sankey, who is immensely popular with the children, was also present. It is marvellous to see the hearty manner in which even the smallest of the children join in the service of praise.[67]

The work did not finish when Moody moved on from Glasgow, calling back at Edinburgh en route for Perth, Montrose and Aberdeen, and provision was made for follow-up work.

> *At the weekly meeting for young converts in Ewing Place church* one or two very young lads spoke so simply, modestly and withal clearly, as to convey the most intense conviction that none other than the Holy Spirit could have prompted the utterance.[68]

Evangelism also continued, including a special attempt to reach the miners around Glasgow. A Glasgow miner relates how:

65. T.B. 25th April 1874. 66. T.B. 30th April 1874.
67. T.B. 7th May 1874. 68. T.B. 4th June 1874.

The death of a little child of four years, who gave evidence of loving the Lord, produced a deep impression upon the father, who had been bound up in that child. After the funeral, some friends spoke to him of Christ, who heals the broken heart, and pointed him to the cross. His eyes were opened on Christ and that very week he began to be a cheerful worker for his Lord. *During the third week of meetings among the mining villages on the west side of Glasgow* a work began to appear among the young people. A great number of boys and girls have been awakened.[69]

Paisley too had been included in the itinerary from Glasgow: Rev A Henderson from Paisley UPC writes:

In addition to the 200 inquirers who waited in the Free High Church at the close of Mr Moody's meeting on the 10th, there were also 44 boys, who met in one of the rooms connected with the church. Several of these seem to have laid hold of the truth. ... Among them there was a lame boy, whose limbs are so weak that he can scarcely get along even with the help of crutches. As the church is situated on a hill, one of his companions, at the close, took him up on his back, and carried him home, and another performed a similar service in bringing him to the mid-day meeting for the young on Saturday.[70]

Rev George Clazy told the Reformed Presbyterian Synod meeting in Glasgow on Tuesday 8th May:

The impression produced in Paisley had been very profound and that this was especially the case among the young. He had had meetings of about forty or fifty young boys and he knew that many of them spent a part of their play-hour in singing hymns and praying.[71]

There is evidence of lasting results, notably in the schools as JAH of Paisley writes on 29th June 1874:

Here, as in many other places, the school-boys have been wonder-

---

69. T.B. 11th June 1874. 70. T.B. 25th April 1874. 71. T.B. 14th May 1874.

fully stirred. There are boys' prayer meetings connected with our two principal schools. There are about 36 boys connected with one of these schools who meet regularly twice a week for prayer and reading of the Scriptures.[72]

Meanwhile, back in the east side of the country Prof Charteris commenting on the Religious Movement in Edinburgh, quotes a minister noticing:

during the last six or eight months growing interest in spiritual things, especially among the young, so that he was not surprised by the general movement.[73]

A Young Men's evening meeting in Edinburgh were informed:

Eleven boys in our school have decided for Christ: we mean to go to the University next year.[74]

Mrs Barbour reports from Edinburgh:

Yet are whole schools bending under the influence of the Almighty Spirit, the ragged school children, and those of the first boarding-schools are yielding up their hearts to the Lord of Love.
At one Sabbath school all the boys and all the girls separated to go into different rooms when the Superintendent gave an invitation - in the absence of all the other teachers who were attending Communion.[75]

An eyewitness at a fortnight's meetings for the young held two months previously in the Stockbridge area of Edinburgh, reports 30 anxious on the first evening, and 60 on the second.

72. T.B. 2nd July 1874
73. T.C. 16th April 1874. See also T.B. 30th April 1874 for a description of Saturday children's meetings held in Edinburgh on 18th and 25th April. A similar description of a Glasgow children's meeting run by George Stewart is found in T.C. 9th April 1874.
74. T.C. 23rd April 1875.
75. T.C. 7th May 1874.

Many, if not all, were deeply convinced of sin. There was no special preaching to that effect; and yet, such was the state of the case. We have seen the head bent low, the lips quivering and the eyes wet with tears, because of a sense of sin. But when Christ was set forth as the sinner's substitute, we have seen the eyes gleaming through the tears, and what flowed indicating a sense of sin, flowed on in joy for rest and peace found in a Saviour's love....Many of these elder boys and girls are to be seen with little groups of the younger ones with them on the street, telling them about eternal things.[76]

At the annual meeting of the Congregational Union held in Edinburgh last week *Mr McMunn* said that all the churches and Sabbath schools had felt the awakening and the work seemed to be spreading among the young like leaven - nothing could account for it - it must be of God.[77]

From April 1874 onwards reports appear from all over Scotland, and from every denomination, of a wide-spread awakening,[78] for example in the south-east, Rev. Dr. Ritchie reports from Duns a regular united evangelistic meeting every Sunday evening, and:

The youth of our town and neighbourhood are at length deeply stirred to anxious inquiry about salvation, and not a few of them have, we trust, been brought to Christ.[79]

The difficulty in analysing this report, as with so many others, is to know what is meant by the term 'youth'. It most probably refers to those over 15 rather than under, but again emphasises the effect of the Gospel at this time on the young adults of Scotland, many miles from the scenes of Moody's direct labours.

In the centre of the country Moody was not free to visit Dollar, but three weeks of meetings were held in the Academy. According to Rev G H Knight:

---

76. T.C. 2nd July 1874.
77. T.B. 30th April 1874.
78. In. T.C. 19th March 1874 Bonar cites awakening across Scotland from Locherbie to Aberuthven.
79. T.B. 25th April 1874.

The movement took a deep hold of the boys and girls attending the Academy; and at a closing meeting for those alone who professed to have accepted Christ and His salvation during the three weeks of our meetings, more than 180 gathered together confessing their Saviour. ... The boys have started a prayer meeting once a week amongst themselves in one of the class-rooms; and the girls have a similar meeting weekly in a private house. I was present one evening lately at the meeting of the boys, and felt it exceedingly interesting to hear their simple artless prayers for their companions still unsaved, and for themselves that they might all be kept stedfast and grow Christ like.[80]

From Fife, William Gibson reports on a week of meetings for the young, at Abbotshall Free Church, Kirkcaldy:

I was greatly touched at the deep feeling manifested by some of the young persons. So many were the anxious, that sometimes they could only be spoken to in groups. In a young women's Bible class, at least 70 have been awakened and many of these have been brought to Christ.[81]

And in Cellardyke, a daily prayer meeting commenced during the last week of 1873 and after five weeks:

Some anxiety, especially among the young, began to be manifested. A number of the Sabbath school children remained at the close of the meetings to be spoken to, and not a few professed to have found Christ. *Then a nightly prayer meeting attracted up to 400.* Another very remarkable feature of the work is, that from twenty to forty young children have met together for religious instruction for nearly six months every night. The meeting is conducted by two of the Sabbath school teachers.[82]

Further north the Rev S R Macphail reports on four weeks of meetings in Elgin:

---

80. T.B. 18th April 1874.
81. T.B. 21st May 1874.
82. T.B. 18th June 1874.

fully twenty every night remaining in spiritual concern. These
have been to a very considerable extent our Sabbath scholars and
members of Bible Classes. It has been noted by some of us that
scarcely a teacher has been stirred up in reference to his or her class
to desire and aim at immediate conversion without a considerable
blessing following. Some classes have been almost entirely, as we
hope, savingly impressed, especially among the senior pupils; and
in others a large proportion have given similar evidence...All the
Sabbath schools in town have shared in this blessing...we trust that
several hundreds have derived lasting benefit.[83]

From Inverurie J B Johnstone reports:

In a senior class of girls connected with the Free Church Sabbath
School, fourteen out of sixteen state that they have decided for
Christ, *and special services for children* were largely attended,
and from time to time at the close many remained to be spoken
with about their souls.[84]

Regrettably, the following location remains unidentified:

We met this week another Highland minister who told us ... that
his son had been brought to Jesus during the winter, at meetings
held in a small town in the south. About forty boys attending an
educational establishment there meet regularly for prayer.[85]

On a sadder note, John MacPherson writes from Dundee on 13th June:

During the last three months many of the little ones have been
carried away by scarlatina. I have often of late heard the children
in their last moments speak of the things of God with an intelligence and a simplicity of faith which has been both a lessons and
a reproof to older Christians. Beyond measure affecting is it to
hear the little ones sing their sweet gospel hymns with their dying
breath. He *then instances two sisters aged 7 and 3.*[86]

---

83. T.B. 30th April 1874. 84. T.B. 4th June 1874. 85. T.C. 9th July 1874.
86. T.C. 18th June 1874, also recorded in MacPherson, Revival, p.286.

In Perth preparatory meetings were held before the arrival of Moody and Sankey:

> There was a cheering work amongst the children. Professor Martin from Aberdeen held meetings for five weeks and in those meetings many little ones gave their hearts to Jesus.[87]

On Saturday 30th May at 3pm William Robertson of Edinburgh addressed a crowded City hall in Perth full of children, of whom thirty remained for personal conversation afterwards. Moody arrived that evening in the city.

> Every evening during the week, meetings for children have been held. They have been largely attended, and most interesting - our report stating that in some cases, nearly 200 remained to the inquiry meeting, many being in tears. A large number have professed to find peace.[88]
>
> At the children's meeting there was an unusually large attendance, many of the little ones, who had given their hearts to Jesus during the week, had brought their companions to seek Him.[89]

Similarly in Aberdeen the moving of the Holy Spirit preceded the arrival of the American evangelists on 14 June by several months. A report by John Sloan from Aberdeen informs us of a week of meetings for children in early February attended by 800 nightly, with 150 responding to an appeal on the Saturday evening.

> These meetings for the young have subsequently been held in the Free High church, and with equal evidence of the Spirit's presence. Frequently from 150 to 200 children, professing to be anxious about their souls, have remained to the inquirer's meeting; and this, it is to be noticed, night after night and week after week. No doubt in many cases the children were the same, but new faces also among the anxious were continually appearing.[90]

---

87. T.C. 11th June 1874. 88. T.B. 11th June 1874.
89. T.C. 18th June 1874. 90. T.B. 25th April 1874.

Another report of these meetings appears in The Christian. Mr Daniells had led a week of children's meetings in Free South Church and then a week in the High Church daily at 6pm, attracting 600-700.

On Saturday there was an after meeting for anxious children, when many remained, a number being under deep concern, and several professing to be eager to receive Christ, and trust Him as their Saviour. *(dated 26th February).*[91]

John Ross reports on 27th March also from Aberdeen of:

the remarkable work of grace that has broken out in one of our large industrial schools here. About a fortnight ago, after an address on Sabbath afternoon, out of about 270 boys, 170 held up their hands as wishing to give themselves to Christ, and among about 60 girls, 20 were under deep concern, and these among the worst behaved in the school. Many have professed since, and the testimony of the teachers is that there has been a corresponding change in their conduct.[92]

This phenomenon was also noticed at Gartley (south of Huntly) where special meetings began on Sunday April 5th.

On the Monday, all left the Church except three or four. Having spoken to them for about fifteen minutes we looked round and saw the door open and a number of anxious faces looking in. Thinking that they were perhaps more curious than anxious, I went hurriedly to the door, and in an abrupt stern tone said: 'If you wish to come in, you had better do it at once; if not, I am to shut the door.' Scarcely were the words spoken, when about thirty of them, mostly young people from twelve to twenty-five years, poured into the Church; and such a scene of weeping followed as I have seldom or never witnessed - it was indeed a Bochim. The work was now begun in earnest...On Wednesday, seven girls from the female school near by took advantage of the short interval between school hours to come to the manse to get a word

91. T.C. 5th March 1874.
92. T.C. 9th April 1874.

about their souls and to request that thanks be given to God, in the meeting of that evening, for having given them Christ as their own Saviour. *Overall a third of the parish responded as inquirers. Parents noticed* the marked change in the tempers, and habits and tastes of their children *and the minister, Rev Hugh McIntosh, knew* of children, who in general thought little about spiritual things previously, pleading with their school companions to come to the meetings and to accept of Christ, and in return for much abuse and mockery only putting in requests that their persecutors might be converted and made happy in Jesus. *The minister's Bible class increased from 90 to 120. (Report dated 26th June 1874).*[93]

Prayer meetings were started by the minister, Alexander Forbes, in the Aberdeenshire village of Drumblade, with nightly conversions in the spring of 1874 until some 200 people had professed faith.

With only two or three exceptions, all the young men and women of the congregation were among those who professed to have obtained mercy. Some forty of the children also were among the young converts. In several instances it was after the conversion of their little children that fathers and mothers, no longer able to hold out against the wonder-working grace of God, surrendered to the Lord Jesus. 'Oh, father, just trust Him!' said a little believing boy of twelve to his father, who had returned from the meeting in a state of such anxiety that he could not conceal it from his family. 'Just trust Him, father,' said the little disciple, thus commending the great Master. Curiously enough, what all the teachings, counsels, and prayers of ministers and others in the inquiry room had failed to accomplish, was effected by the words of the child. The father was enabled to trust Jesus, and now he and his family are rejoicing in the Lord.[94]

There was a deep awakening in the Free Church in Cornhill (Banffs) with a prayer meeting of forty young men.

---

93. T.B. 9th July 1874.
94. MacPherson, p.114.

Nor were the children left outside the good influence, many of the little ones in the Sabbath-school receiving, it is believed, the grace of God. 'Why are you so happy?' said a minister to a little girl with a beaming countenance. 'Because I believe Jesus loves me' was the prompt reply 'and has taken away my sins'. In some instances the blessing enjoyed by the children produced the deepest anxiety in their parents. One father, whose children had all received the blessing, was found 'in great distress' as he realised that he lacked what they had found.[95]

'Young women and boys and girls' are noted as having responded to Moody's invitation when he visited Peterhead on Monday June 22, and at the noon meeting in Aberdeen on the Friday following a man 'from the Country ... gave thanks for his own conversion and that of his wife and eight children.'[96]

In Aberdeen an estimated 25,000 gathered in the open air for Moody's last meeting on Sunday 28 June. The next afternoon a crowd of at least 12,000 gathered in Huntly to welcome Moody and Sankey. Tuesday saw them in Montrose and Wednesday in Brechin where:

> The School Board also gave the children attending the schools and their teachers a holiday, that they too might have an opportunity of hearing the strangers from America.

They took another meeting in Forfar that evening, Arbroath on the Thursday, and back to Dundee on the Friday.[97]

On Sunday 5th July Moody and Sankey saw a crowd of 7000 in the open air at Blairgowrie, and on the evening of the 7th arrived in Inverness.[98] A brief report of the children's meeting held Saturday 11th July in Inverness Music Hall with 400 children describes it as 'interesting and encouraging'. From Inverness they visited Tain and Strathpeffer.[99]

Their last meeting in Inverness was on the 20th, Nairn on the 21st, Elgin on 22nd and 23rd and Forres on 24th, but no mention of children

---

95. MacPherson p.111.
96. T.B. 2nd July 1874. 97. T.B. 9th July 1874
98. T.B. 16th July 1874. 99. T.B. 23rd July 1874

occurs in any of these towns.[100] On to Elgin on Sunday 26th, Grantown on Spey 27th, Keith 28th and 29th and back to Elgin on 30th where at the end of the open air meeting Moody specifically addressed the children for the last fifteen minutes, but the results are not recorded.[101] We also know that 'a large number of young people had professed conversion in Elgin before Moody's visit, because of five months of prayer'.[102] They continued on to Banff to preach from Sunday 2nd to Thursday 6th August and were due to land in Wick on Tuesday 11th. A rough sea not only made Moody violently sea-sick, but prevented them from landing and they were diverted to Thurso, but ran aground off Scrabster and had to be off-loaded into a small boat, catch a Coach to Thurso and thence by train to Wick, by which time they were too late for the meeting! Rev W R Taylor of Kelvinside was in Caithness at the time, and wrote on Friday 14th:

> Today, at the close of a service for the young, many of the young people waited to be conversed with and seemed to welcome gladly the Saviour's call to children. *He also noted a response among the young men in their twenties.*[103]

At the conclusion of the meeting in the Established Church in Thurso on Tuesday 18th, the children were separated off for specialist counselling in the vestry and the same happened after his farewell meeting on Friday 21st August.[104] One wonders if this is the first time children had been prepared for in this way?

The remainder of Moody's first Scottish itinerary appears to lack further references to children so is beyond our scope here. He sailed down the Caledonian Canal, preached in Campbeltown and to a crowd of 2000-3000 in the open-air in Rothesay before sailing for Belfast in September. On Saturday 31st October 5000 children attended their meeting in the Exhibition Palace in Dublin.[105]

Couper summarizes Moody's work thus:

---

100. T.B. 30th July 1874. 101. T.B. 6th August 1874.
102. MacRae, p.115.
103. T.B. 20th August 1874.
104. T.B. 27th August 1874. 105. T.B.. 5th November 1874.

Perhaps the most striking features of the whole mission was the way it seized upon young men.

Moody chose Henry Drummond, then a student at New College to assist him, 'and Drummond was soon addressing meetings for young men and children who attended in thousands.'[106] Many of these young men began their own evangelistic activity. Here are two examples:

A team from the Edinburgh Young Men's Committee working in Comrie noted at their thrice weekly children's meetings 'warm interest and deep impression and anxiety manifested'.[107]

A fortnight ago two of the Edinburgh Young Men went to Aberfeldy:

On the first night, when the anxious were invited to stay behind for conversation and prayer with clergymen and others, several young girls without any hesitation remained. Some of them were in deep distress because of their sins. A meeting specially intended for children was held regularly in the congregational Chapel at 7 o'clock *and* averaged about 130 and the interest excited was so keen that they were continued night after night at the desire of the children themselves.[108]

Other evangelists were reaping a harvest too: when Brownlow North gave an appeal for commitment in Dumbarton, between three and four hundred responded. One third of these were young, 'say from 12 to 24 years of age'.[109]

William Tulloch of the Baptist Home Mission of Scotland sent this Report of an evangelistic tour of Orkney and Caithness in June.

Sunday 20th on Burray: In the afternoon, when an address was given to the young, the hearts of some were touched, and they were willing to be conversed with personally about the great matters of their souls' salvation. One or two professed to give themselves to the Lord, and a number remained as inquirers. *On Eday* between thirty and forty young people profess to have been converted *in recent months*.[110]

106. Couper p.148.
107. T.B. 4th June 1874. 108. T.B. 25th June 1874.
109. T.C. 23rd July 1874. 110. T.B. 13th August 1874.

On 13th August K Moody-Stewart wrote from Moffat that over six months there had been an awakening in Annandale:

The classes mainly impressed have been children and young persons (say from 15 to 25); and while many cases of deep and apparently genuine conviction of sin may have stopped short of saving conversion ... we cannot but rejoice over a considerable number who give every evidence, so far as we can judge, of having really given themselves to the Lord. ...In the case of children of tender years, we can only commit them to the Saviour, trusting that impressions made when the heart was melted under a sense of sin may be preserved or revived and believing that some, at least, of the good seed sown in young hearts, ploughed with the furrows of conviction, will bring forth fruit to everlasting life.[111]

A month later we read from Dumfries:

It is true we had no general awakening, yet daily we met with men and women and children seeking salvation. The young, and especially the little children, were particularly interesting. I suppose this was because the little ones had not yet, as older people, learned the art of concealing their feelings. When the teachers took them aside and spoke to them about their souls, and set before them the simple gospel, they seemed to embrace it so readily that we often wondered if their answers were real. But then there was such a distinctness and clearness in their answers and such brightness in their very countenances, that we were constrained to accept their statement whenever we remembered what the Master said, 'suffer the little children to come unto me, and forbid them not, for of such is the Kingdom of God'. *In mid-August Messrs Dunn and Scroggie began a campaign, resulting in* a large number of young men and women and little children too, are taking their stand on the Lord's side.[112]

111. T.B. 20th August 1874
112. T.B. 24th September 1874

Reports of children's meetings and conversion continue to pour in from all over the country. From Stonehaven we are told that Mr Daniel's children's meetings were 'particularly interesting and profitable'.[113] A number of girls are converted in a Shetland Sunday School.[114] There are brief notes about Sunday afternoon meetings for children on Glasgow Green in the gospel tent, with 'many children among the seeking ones'[115], and the later comment 'the children turn out in considerable numbers. Many of them show by their looks that they are not strangers to hunger'.[116] Back in June the Times of Blessing ran an article headed 'Blessing on the Young' quoting numerous instances of child conversion, but as no names or places are given, to narrate them all would be tedious and profitless.[117] There are also accounts of the death of Christian children like these under 'Incidents of Blessing' a four column article describing the death of 15 year old Rebecca the previous year. When her mother said 'My poor Rebecca, how sorry I am to see you suffer so', she replied, 'I'm not poor, mother; I'm rich. Jesus died for me; my treasure is in heaven and Christ suffered far more for me. Oh mother, don't lay up your treasure on earth, where moth and rust can corrupt; lay it up in heaven, where it will be safe.' At her death she asked John 14 to be read and spoke of Jesus having gone to prepare a place for her. Her mother asked her 'Where are you going, Rebecca?', to which she replied, 'to my home in heaven', which were her last words. This is immediately followed by the story of Johnnie, a 'young boy' dying in Edinburgh, who told his visitors to 'O, speak to my mother and pray with her. I'm wearying to go home. I'm so happy to go. The only thing that grieves me is to see mother not willing to part with me. Oh mother, just say that you'll let me go to Jesus, and promise, mother, to follow me there, and my joy will be full.'[118]

On the last Sabbath of September there was an awakening in a large boy's boarding school (of undisclosed location), with thirty anxious inquirers, and another forty the following Thursday.[119] 'There is a very decided movement among the young' in Turriff with a weekly chil-

---

113. T.B. 24th September 1874. 114. T.B. 10th September 1874.

115. T.B. 23rd July 1874. 116. T.B. 27th August 1874.

117. T.B. 18th June 1874. 118. T.B. 17th September 1874.

119. T.C. 10th December 1874

dren's meeting held since July in addition to the Sabbath Schools, so as to allow for an inquiry meeting and 'a very successful "Praise meeting" has also been held'.[120] In the Free Church in Dunbar 'many young people have been awakened and to all appearance savingly converted to God' in a series of meetings led by William Stoddart of Kelso.[121] Finally, at Galston, Ayrshire, 'some interesting cases could be reported in connection with a children's meeting begun in July with an attendance of between one and three hundred,'[122] later described as 'a great work amongst the children'.[123]

Couper is adamant that an awakening that touched the Western Isles at the same time was not linked to work on the mainland.[124] In Tiree the harvest was so plentiful that Rev Alex Lee of the Free Church at Port Ellen on Islay, was sent over to assist. In September he wrote: 'among the anxious there are of all ages and classes and of both sexes - boys of fourteen and old men of sixty; young girls in their teens, mothers with infants in their arms...'.[125] The number converted was estimated at 300.[126]

One other work remains to be recorded at this period: the labours of the Brethren evangelists in the Highlands. Donald Ross had joined the Brethren in 1871 and held several successful missions in upper Speyside, forming the Assemblies in Aberlour and Craigellachie in 1873. One of his associates, Andrew Allan, wrote from Craigellachie on May 3rd 1873:

> The Lord has saved a few fine young men - praise be to His Name; and He is begun in the school. A few of the scholars, from ten years old to fourteen, have got Jesus, and the school is in an uproar. It is only yet being made known round about.

This is attested by a letter from 'M' at Aberlour on May 14th re Craigellachie, stating that:

---

120. T.B. 19th November 1874. 121. T.B. 10th December 1874.
122. T.B. 24th December 1874. 123. T.B. 18th February 1875.
124. Couper, p.156.
125. T.B. 22nd October 1874 and MacRae p.62.
126. T.B. 7th January 1875 and MacRae p.63.

Several young men are now praising God for the salvation of their precious souls; also a good many young boys and girls. It is really fine to hear them singing the hymns; how heartily they praise God; the most are very fine cases.[127]

Alexander Anderson, later a medical missionary in China was converted under Donald Ross in 1873 at the age of ten in Rhynie, under hell-fire preaching.[128] A few months later two other Brethren evangelists William Murray and John Scott, had a revival in Rhynie and an Assembly was formed. Anderson got permission from his father to attend and he presented himself at the door of the house where the breaking of bread was being held. He was asked if he wished to break bread and he replied 'yes', and so it came about. 'The admission of a child to Communion shows the way in which conventions are suspended during revivals. Later, once the Brethren had become more formalised it wouldn't have been so easy.' [129]

To summarise this period we may use part of William Dicksons's report on Sabbath Schools given to the General Assembly of the Free Church. He chides his audience for their lack of expectancy of child conversions, then quotes from a minister, unfortunately anonymous, describing some of the children of his congregation:

They have betaken themselves, in a way they never did before, to reading the scriptures and prayer. Many of them have passed through deep convictions of sin, and were seen for nights weeping like to break their little hearts. But in course of time they found peace, and are now rejoicing in Christ. A strong attachment to one another has sprung up among them, and they seem to be very watchful over themselves, as well as over each other, lest they should do anything inconsistent with the profession they make. In short, I have as much hope of these dear lambs of the flock as I have of those of maturer years brought to Christ at the same time.

127. The Northern Assemblies, June 1st 1873, pp23-4 (both letters).
128. Autobiography of John A. Anderson, M.D., Aberdeen 1948, p.16.
129. Neil Dickson, Brethren historian, from personal correspondence.

And in another account:[130]

> A boy of twelve years' old was the means of the conversion on his father. Seeing his father in a state of anxiety, he said to him. 'Oh Father, just trust Him'. His father was enabled to 'trust Him', and now he and all his house six in number, are rejoicing in the Lord.

In another:

> The great work of grace has been very blessedly present in our Sabbath school and Bible classes. Upwards of 80 have professed to surrender to Christ; and several have been the means of bringing others to the meetings and to Christ. One girl I know of has been the means of blessing to twenty of her companions in the town. These children are the best home-mission workers we have; their faith and energy know no bounds. Upon the whole, our best scholars have got most of the blessing.

He concludes:

> One of the most touching petitions for thanksgiving ever given in at the noon-day meeting in this hall was the following, in March last: A Sabbath school teacher desires to give thanks for the conversion of her whole class, seven in number, none of them more than twelve years of age, all since her own conversion within the last six weeks.[131]

At the National Sabbath School Convention held in mid August in Edinburgh:

> Mr Mitchell ... called attention to the evangelistic meetings which had been organised for the young in Stockbridge district and mentioned that the interest had been so great that they had been compelled to continue them for a fortnight. Mr Martin

---

130. Possibly the same as footnote 94 above.
131. T.B. 18th June 1874.

mentioned that a number of meetings for children had been held in Grange Free Church and that the anxiety which had been manifested was most refreshing.

Mr Anderson of Greenock .. alluded to the Glasgow and Greenock Foundry Boys' Society and stated that there must now be no fewer than 20,000 of the youth of the working classes meeting every Sunday for the purpose of worshipping. *Mr McPhail of Greenock* said many poor children who attended children's churches were better acquainted with Bible truth than the children of church members.[132]

One of the lasting effects of the 1874 revival was to awaken the Church in Scotland to the plight of the urban poor and to stimulate social concern. In an article on reaching whole families based on the work of the Grove Street Home Mission Glasgow, the Times of Blessing states:

In connection with the foundries there is a vast population of boys - wild thoughtless lads, who literally care neither for God or man ... Between ten and twelve they enter the foundries, which are the academies of sin and blasphemy, where the current is all downwards, and where the juvenile rivalry is to outvie the roughest of their men-models in evil words and deeds. Many of them have one hour's feeble teaching in the Sunday school, but that is all which the church of Christ is doing to combat the degrading effects of a week of sin.[133]

The Wynd Church had already tried to grapple with the needs on its own doorstep and had run a Medical Mission for three years,[134] but Moody's abiding legacy to Glasgow was to enable the churches to combine their resources in the formation of the Glasgow United Evangelistic Association. From its inception it offered free breakfasts on a Sunday[135] and by 1880 was providing Sunday dinner for 1500 children, besides feeding 300 daily and housing forty in its home in Saltcoates[136].

---

132. T.B. 8th October 1874. 133. T.B. 5th November 1874.
134. MacColl p.211 and 215-6.
135. G.U.E.A. Annual Report for 1875 has article on 'Work among Neglected Children' and describes those attending the Tent Breakfast Meetings.
136. G.U.E.A. 1880 report

Among the spiritual provisions it undertook was the continuation of the children's Saturday prayer meeting for a number of years:

> The children's prayer meeting is held in the same place as the daily prayer meeting. Interesting and instructive addresses are given by clergymen and others. Parents, guardians and teachers are asked to use their influence in getting the children to attend this meeting *(presumably held in West Campbell Street?).*[137]

However, that which may be termed 'revival' really ceased at the end of 1874. The Rev John MacPherson, surveying the work among children in that year in Dundee decides 'we have never before seen so much precious fruit in the same space of time.'[138]

We conclude this section with an anecdote about some praying children in a Perthshire village, where the schoolmaster was assisted by his niece who spoke to the children about Jesus and His love.

> First one girl and then another sought and found Him... The number of these praying children at last increased to fourteen or fifteen, who met with their young teacher during the noon play-hour, to pray and sing sweet hymns together. All are girls, whose ages range from fifteen to six or seven. *One seven year old, called 'little Janet' was in deep distress until she found Jesus. Her mother then beat her for praying and singing, but eventually was convicted by her testimony.*[139]

(c) The 1880's and Moody's second visit

We have already traced the origins of specific attempts to evangelise children to the work of Hammond in the 1860's and the boost it received at the time of Moody's first campaign when he set aside the Saturday noon meetings for children. By the 1880's special meetings for the young were commonplace. For example early in 1881 Dr D A Moxey writes at the end of a campaign held in the capital by Messrs Whittle and McGranahan:

---

137. G.U.E.A. 1878.
138. T.B. 4th February 1875, also in MacPherson, Revival, p.76.
139. T.B. 18th February 1875.

Edinburgh is in the presence of what we believe will be a great revival. ...On Friday February 11th, the children's night, the area of the hall was crammed with the little ones. ...At the conclusion Major Mossman met the girls who were anxious in one room, and Major Whittle met the boys in another. A deep impression had been produced and many gave their young hearts to Jesus.[140]

However the only claim to revival at this time was made by The Christian which reported that Stornoway had seen a limited awakening and revival with the arrival of the east coast fishermen in May and June of the previous year, then the arrival of The Evangelisation Society in the autumn. It concludes 'the blessing seems to be all around, Inverness, Oban, Mull are sharing in it.'[141] Despite these claims, it cannot be said that Scotland witnessed any widespread revival in this decade.

Moody arrived in Liverpool on 6th October, 1881, visited London, and began work in Newcastle before coming up to Scotland on 17th November. His actual campaign began in Edinburgh on Nov 23rd, and Glasgow on 7th January following, where he worked for five months. R W Dale made a critical but by no means hostile comparison of these first and second visits:

When Mr. Moody was in Birmingham early last year, I was struck by the change in the general tone of his preaching. He insisted very much on Repentance. ...Now observe the effect of this. He was just as earnest, as vigorous, as impressive as before. People were as deeply moved. Hundreds went into the inquiry room every night. But the results, as far as I can learn, have been inconsiderable. ...I have seen nothing of the shining faces that used to come to me after his former visit. From first to last in 1875, I received about two hundred Moody converts in to Communion and I reckon that 75% of these have stood well. As yet I have not received a dozen as a result of his last visit. In 1875 ... he exulted in the free grace of God. The grace was to lead men to repentance - to a complete change of life. His joy was contagious. Men leaped out of darkness into light and lived a Christian life

140. T.C. 24th February 1881. 141. T.C. 7th April 1881.

afterwards. The 'do penance' preaching has had no such results.[142]

Whether Moody had changed his theology, or if he was just trying too hard to produce repentance, or if 1873-5 was accompanied by a deeper moving of the Spirit than 1881-2, would be unwise for us a century later to try to assess. He certainly attracted vast crowds and these included children as evidenced in this report from Edinburgh;

> Mr Moody held meetings in the Corn Exchange which secured many nights in succession vast audiences filling the Corn Exchange from end to end. The people who have flocked in thousands are not the church-goers or what are generally regarded as the respectable classes in the community. During the past week (December 18-24) it is estimated that between four and five thousand people - men, women and children - assembled nightly in the exchange. Stormy or cold weather had no deterrent effect.[143]

The idea of Saturday meetings for children was continued from his earlier visit, and apparently Moody 'was highly delighted with the conduct of the children and with the interest they manifested in the meeting ...'[144] which were held in an overflowing Free Assembly Hall. But however successful they were, it can not be described as 'revival' and we must pass on.

'An immense gathering' of children met with Sankey in Kirkcaldy[145] and a noon children's meeting with Moody in Campbeltown was 'largely attended'[146] while in Hawick Moody moved his planned open air meeting 'to avoid the distraction caused on such occasions by a fringe of noisy children and curious onlookers ... to the grounds of Wilton Lodge'[147] on Monday 14th August - one might comment that this was an odd move for someone committed to reaching the masses?

---

142. Letter to Rev. Dr. Wace of Llandudno, dated 25th January 1884, and quoted in 'Life of R.W. Dale' by A.W.W. Dale (Hodder & Stoughton, London, 1898, p.530).
143. T.C. Thursday 5th January 1882
144. See T.C. 12th January 1882 for details
145. T.C. 20th July 1882, probably referring to Monday 10th July.
146. T.C. 17th August 1882 held on Tuesday 8th August
147. T.C. 24th August 1882

The Christian Press reported in detail several Question and Answer sessions held by the American and some of these reveal problems thrown up by the presence of children in the Churches. To quote but two:

'How shall we interest the children in the regular church services?' - 'Let them feel they are part of the church. ...Many ministers are now giving a five or ten minute talk in their sermons to the children. They like that kind of minister who will tell them an interesting story or give them something specially for themselves. Let the minister speak kindly to them and notice them in the street. It is a good thing to have a meeting for the children, say once a month, and have the parents come with them. Let them feel they are part of the church.'[148]

'Would you admit very young persons to church Membership?' - 'Certainly if they have given good evidence of being converted. Mr Spurgeon has said that he has had less trouble with the young people who have joined his church than anyone else; there is less backsliding among them. If they are looked after, they make the best Christian workers; but it is cruel to take them into membership of the church, and then neglect them by preaching right over their heads. It is not fair to starve them out and then complain because they backslide.'[149]

Perhaps the Church in Scotland has still to learn this lesson?

The description and content of one of Moody's talks to children, given on Friday 28th July on his last day in Aberdeen, has been recorded for us in detail, but the effect of it, or its results, were not mentioned.[150] Similarly, testimonies of children at this period may also be studied.[151]

In Greenock J M Scroggie continued Moody's campaign:

---

148. T.C. 24th August 1882.
149. T.C. 17th August 1882.
150. T.C. 10th August 1882, continued in 17th August 1882. Similarly Moody's address to 6,000 children in St. Andrew's Hall, Glasgow, is described in T.C. 20th April 1882, and the claim made 'I fancy it has never been done in the country before...In all my life I have never seen such an audience. The children were swarming in dense seething clusters in every available corner, wedged around the galleries...'
151. T.C. 16th November 1882, also with less detail in 1st June 1882.

The children are also being greatly blessed, and it is moving to see many of them, both at their own special meeting and at the ordinary evangelistic service, with the tears of penitence trickling down their cheeks, professing to come to the Saviour.[152]

And Mr. Mackeith followed him:

Mr Alexander Mackeith has had crowded audiences of young people...every night since Mr Scroggie left and has won their hearts by his simple and tender way of speaking the gospel to them. Many have given their hearts to the Saviour, and it is touching to see their anxiety to get their companions spoken to by the workers. Hundreds have remained during the week, professedly anxious about their souls, and the unbelief of many was rebuked by the results of the meeting.[153]

Alexander Mackeith was probably the most significant figure in children's evangelism in Scotland at the end of the Nineteenth century, by November 1882 he was addressing crowds of 2000 children in Glasgow.[154] He remained a well-known business-man, with a tea importing business, and lived at 105 Douglas Street. He was an elder in Andrew Bonar's church in Finnieston, but devoted his time to the evangelism of the young, most notably with the Glasgow Foundry Boys' Religious Society, which had commenced in 1865. In August 1882 he claimed: 'I have been in such work since 1858 and I never remember seeing such a stir in spiritual matters among the children as there is in the present day.'[155] Here are a selection of reports of his meetings taken from The Christian:

For well nigh three weeks, in Cunningham Free Church, Glasgow, evangelistic services have been held for the young, conducted by Mr Alexander Mackeith, Mr Steele and others, under the auspices of the Foundry Boys' Religious Society and Sabbath School Union. They have been in every way very

152. T.C. 3rd August 1882. 153. T.C. 17th August 1882.
154. T.C. 9th November 1882. 155. T.C. 24th August 1882.

successful. From 400 up to 1,100 have been in attendance, filling both church and hall. Wonderful order and quietness, and sometimes wonderful remarkable solemnity, prevailed. Two after meetings were held - one for young believers, and the other for anxious inquirers. I have seen about 120 in the hall professing to have received the Lord Jesus and on being dealt with singly it was intensely interesting to hear how they came to see and feel their need of a Saviour, and how they were led to embrace him as theirs and give their young lives to his service.

On passing out of the hall into the church, a deeply interesting sight was to be seen: the whole area occupied with little groups of twos and threes, being spoken to in regard to the 'great salvation' and the importance of their early decision for the Lord" (Andrew Alexander, minister).[156]

David Lowe, minister of London Road Free Church Glasgow writes on 1st December to report eight united children's meetings in the east end of Glasgow, held in his church by A. Mackeith, attended by over 1000 nightly:

One after meeting was limited to those who professed to receive eternal life at the services ... *and* was attended by over 250. Perhaps more than 300 in all have made this confession.[157]

Glasgow: in the beginning of the month, Mr Mackeith gave the course (Pilgrim's Progress) in Dr Andrew Bonar's church. Every night about a thousand children were present and often older persons. Of these generally two hundred waited to be conversed with at a second meeting. These were almost all young persons, who had an intelligent knowledge of scripture, being members of Sabbath Schools. At the last meeting Mr Mackeith invited all who professed to have received the Saviour to meet in the adjoining hall; 102 boys and 107 girls responded to the invitation. The majority of these were about the age of eleven or twelve.[158]

---

156. T.C. 12th October 1882
157. T.C. 7th December 1882
158. T.C. 1st February 1883. 'The course' referred to was a lantern slide presentation in serial form.

A series of meetings for the young have been held in Downvale Free Church, Partick, by Mr Alexander Mackeith. The church was filled each night, the number never being less than 1100 and the hearers were deeply impressed. ... It was very remarkable to see the deep earnestness and soul experience of even very young children. At the close of the series 369 passed from the church to the hall below, professing to be saved, and having the knowledge of it from God's word. These received valuable counsel as to keeping in the way of life, and on work for Jesus, suited to their years.[159]

At Helensburgh U.P. 1000 young people attended four nights of meetings led by Messrs Mackeith, Steel and Pratt:

A large number responded, varying in age from about ten to about sixteen years ... it was evident from their faces that the great majority were most deeply in earnest.[160]

In the south-east of Glasgow a remarkable series of meetings has been brought to a close. *1700 children attended nightly with Messrs. Mackeith, Pratt and Steel.* At the close of every public meeting an opportunity was given for anxious inquirers remaining behind for personal dealing; but the numbers who waited were so large that personal dealing became impossible. On the last night 116 boys and 140 girls wanted the second meeting. Many among them were evidently impressed ... (A C Fullarton)[161]

Many other attempts were being made concurrently to bring the Gospel to the younger generation by many others. The second fortnight in July 1882 saw Rev Pentecost and Mr Stebbins holding meetings in Dumbarton, with children's meetings in the Burgh Hall every evening led by Mrs Denny and Miss Pentecost, in which 'many of the boys and girls have been much impressed and give evidence of being made new creatures'.[162] Three months later, Rev Collins of Bonhill reports a regular children's meeting with a weekly attendance of 300.[163]

---

159. T.C. 22nd February 1883. 160. T.C. 19th April 1883.
161. T.C. 27th December 1883. 162. T.C. 10th August 1882.
163. T.C. 26th October 1882.

In the south-west Henry Drummond held nightly meetings fo children at 5pm in Dumfries South Free Church, where 'many of th young people have given their hearts to the Saviour'.[164] While at Mintlaw in the north-east nine weeks of meetings had been held and a 'meeting for prayer and Bible Reading ... for young people under the direction o an elder of the Free Church' commenced.[165]

In March 1885 Hammond returned to lead a ten week campaign i Glasgow before moving on to the Vale of Leven.[166] By April 2nd The Christian was claiming 'During the twenty-six days Mr Hammond has been here, over seventeen hundred young people have been examine and re-examined by Christians appointed for the work and have pro fessed to have found Christ'. A fortnight earlier they had stated 'in al our experience we have never seen such a deep work among the young people in Glasgow'.[167] The farewell meeting took place on Saturday 16th May and there was a time of testimony in the Christian Institute after the inquiry meeting, where 'many were melted to tears. One said he believed that he had been the worst boy in Glasgow. He had beer twice imprisoned for stealing; but when Mr Hammond was speaking o the great love of Christ, he felt the burden of his sins and was led to trust in Christ. Since then he had been as happy as the day long.'[168]

In a survey of Hammond's work, Rev A C Fullarton noted 'Many young persons who had previously been more or less awakened to concern about salvation came to Mr Hammond's meetings, and found a blessed wave of spiritual power that floated them into the harbour o assured safety.'[169] The same edition tells us of the 500 who had pro fessed conversion in Alexandria and of the mother of a 'little boy' in Glasgow (who had been killed by a kick from a horse). She told his teacher that her son 'has been like a recruiting sergeant ... among his companions, trying to get them to the meetings.'[170]

In recognising the need to effectively follow up this youthful re sponse to the Gospel, the Glasgow United Evangelistic Association

---

164. T.C. 31st August 1882. 165. T.C. 19th April 1883.
166. Weekly reports appear in T.C. from 5th March to 21st May 1885.
167. T.C. 19th March 1885 also instances the conversion of a German girl, and a lady previously converted under Hammond at the age of 17 bringing her son to the meetings.
168. T.C. 21st May 1885. 169. T.C. 4th June 1885.
170. T.C. 4th June 1885

osted a regular 'Boys and Girls Fellowship Meeting'.

The boys and girls meeting held in the Gymnasium of the Christian Institute every Friday night was begun during Mr Moody's visit in May last; it is especially intended for the young people from twelve to fifteen years of age, who made profession of their faith in Christ at that time or since. The special aim of the meeting is to encourage, advise or stimulate the young people in the Christian life. The attendance has been very encouraging and there is much reason to be thankful that so many have been led to give their hearts to Jesus in the morning of their youth. It is cheering to hear the humble yet firm testimony which they can give of the hope that is in them.[171]

They also recognised the difficulties encountered by those unable to read and in their James Morrison Street Hall Sabbath School provided a class for non-readers aged four to nine. By 1889 the following activities for children can be tabulated, many of which were based on the Christian Institute at 70 Bothwell Street:

Children's Sabbath Dinner and Bible lessons 'for 1500 hungry bairns'.
Children's Gospel Temperance meeting - 873 had signed the pledge.
Children's Pilgrim's Progress meeting.
Children's Daily Bible Reading Union.
Children's Present Help mission, Day Refuge and Home for Destitute (Saltcoates).[172]

Meantime on the other side of the Atlantic a young minister was struggling to find the appropriate form of nurture for his young people, and eventually founded a society that was to have a major impact on evangelical church life in Scotland for several generations:
The first Christian Endeavour Society had been founded on February 2nd, 1881 in Portland, Maine, USA 'to harvest the fruits of a notable

---

171. G.U.E.A. report 1883
172. G.U.E.A. 1889

work of grace among his young people'[173] by Rev Francis E Clark at the Williston Congregational church. He commenced his pastorate in this mission hall in November 1876 and in two years saw the membership increase from fifty to four hundred. The basic idea was to offer a training ground in Christian service for young people, based on a weekly prayer meeting at which everyone who attended was expected to take some part. Nearly one hundred attended the first meeting. The idea spread to other churches and eventually around the world.[174]

In Scotland at the Bell Street United Presbyterian Church, Dundee in March 1887, the Rev T S Dickson, MA formed a Christian Endeavour Society, which maintained a useful existence for about three years, but there being no other society north of the Cheviots, it declined in numbers and influence and to quote its originator, 'died of isolation'[175] leaving Crown Terrace Baptist Church in Aberdeen as the first registered Scottish Society in 1891.[176]

Another lasting legacy of the '80's, but this time birthed within Scotland, was the foundation of the Faith Mission, with the deliberate aim of taking the Gospel to the unreached villages. In 1885 John Govan at the age of 24 resigned from business to preach the gospel full-time. His meetings were lively and informal and he saw particular success at Irvine where there was a deep sense of conviction at the end of one meeting, so that no-one moved until an invitation was given to move downstairs to an inquiry room, when 'there was a movement and then the people poured out of their seats and downstairs until the hall was crammed. It was a night of salvation. "Revival started, Hallelujah" he entered in his diary when he went home. Before long there were hundreds of young people, marching the streets, full of exuberance and the joy of a wonderful salvation.'[177]

Prayer meetings were formed and they went out on visitation and to

---

173. The British Manual of Christian Endeavour, by Rev. John Pollock (Eighth Edition, C.E. London, 1932, p.1).

174. Fifty Years of Christian Endeavour, by Knight Chaplin & Jennie Street, C.E. London, 1931, p.21.

175. Fifty Years of Christian Endeavour, by Knight Chaplin & Jennie Street, C.E. London, 1931, p.32.

176. Fifty Years of Christian Endeavour, by Knight Chaplin & Jennie Street, C.E. London, 1931, p.35.

177. Spirit of Revival, I.R. Govan, Faith Mission, Edinburgh, 1938, p.32.

take kitchen meetings. The following years the Faith Mission was more formally constituted and by 1887 had taken on 'sister pilgrims', or lady evangelists.[178] From the outset, the workers were all young adults; some barely out of their teens. In 1889 the pilgrims witnessed local revivals on Bute and Islay where 'the children sang the hymns in the streets'.[179] A couple of years later, there is a report from an unnamed island, where a little girl who had only been saved that morning was asked to sing 'The grace of God so rich and free': the effect was profound and rows of adults came out to kneel at the front of the meeting.[180]

In February 1886, Alex Harper from the North-east Coast Mission visited Cannisbay in Caithness. His Friday evening meeting for children produced such a noted effect that he was invited to preach on the Sunday in the Free Church and stayed on for a fortnight's mission, which saw eighty professions of conversion.[181] Such a large response in a scattered rural community could justifiably be labelled as a revival.

Finally, perhaps passing reference ought to be made to the Boy's Brigade, founded in Glasgow in 1883 by Sir William A Smith, described as 'the world's first successful *voluntary* uniformed youth organisation'.[182] Its interest to us is that it was probably a product, or better still a bi-product of the revival movement and did become an influential adjunct to youth evangelism. Springhall suggests a number of contributory factors to its inception: These may be listed as:

* Quarrier's Working Boys' Brigades of the 1860's (Shoe-black, News and Parcels Brigades).

* The Glasgow Foundry Boys' Religious Society. Because boys began work in the foundries between the ages of 10 and 12, a young factory girl, Mary Anne Clough got the use of a room in

---

178. Lady evangelists were not unknown in Victorian Scotland. For a background study to this fascinating topic see Olive Anderson's article in the Historical Journal for 1969 on 'Women evangelists in the 1860's'.

179. Govan, p.77

180. Govan p.98-99

181. MacRae, p175-6

182. 'Sure and Stedfast: The History of the Boy's Brigade, 1883-1983' by John Springhall, Collins, Glasgow 1983, p.13. I am indebted to him for the information in this section, and also recommend this work for further background on the period.

one of the Foundries to hold a Sunday afternoon meeting, which some 50 boys attended. After she emigrated to New Zealand in 1862 four Glasgow businessmen took up the idea and formed the GFBRS in 1865, starting work in Cowcaddens. They were William Hunter, William Martin, James Hunter and Alexander Mackeith. They had four aims: religious, educational, social reform and provident. Until 1870 when Girls were admitted (there was also a Glasgow Mill Girls religious Society) drill and uniform formed part of the programme. Membership reached a peak in 1886 with 16000 boys and 2000 leaders listed.

* The Volunteer Force, formed in 1859 to guard against the possibility of French Invasion, which the invention of the steamship had appeared to bring nearer!

* The Young Mens Christian Association, which catered for those of seventeen and upwards, founded 1844.

*The Band of Hope which commenced as the children's section of the Leeds Temperence Society and spread rapidly catering for children from 5-14, with a Scottish union founded in 1871.

*To all these must be added the Sunday school movement and the influence of D L Moody.[183]

Smith had come to Glasgow from Thurso at the age of 14 to enter his uncle's business on the death of his father. At the age of 18 he joined the YMCA and at 20 the Volunteer Force , in 1874, the same year that he

183. On p.22 Springhall states: 'Dwight L. Moody's evangelical influence on William Smith and his business colleagues at the College Free Church in Glasgow's West End can certainly be detected after the 1874 campaign in the city. This is not to agree with those who claim that it was Moody who actually inspired Smith to start the Boy's Brigade, but there is no doubt that the progress of youth work in Glasgow owed a great deal to revivalist encouragement of social work among the young. Indirectly, the building of the North Woodside Mission, the birthplace of the Boy's Brigade, by its wealthy Free Church patron owed much to the inspiration of Dwight Moody's preaching, even if the actual idea of building mission churches in the tenement areas of Glasgow preceded the evangelist's visit.'

heard Moody and Sankey, which led him to leave the Established Church and join the College Free Church. He began teaching Sunday School in the North Woodside Mission. In a later interview with the Boys Own Paper in 1898 he admitted:

In Sunday School they too often came to amuse themselves and the whole effort of the teacher was spent in keeping order, in quelling riots, subduing irrelevant remarks, minimising attacks upon the person, and protecting his Sunday hat from destruction. The boys would not listen for two consecutive minutes. What was to be done?

To plug the gap between Sunday School and the YMCA in the summer of 1883 Smith asked the Rev George Reith if Sunday School boys aged twelve and over could be formed into a Brigade. It was started as an experiment on 4th October, meeting on Thursday evenings at 8pm, to which a Sunday Bible Class was added in December 1884. The stated aim was 'The advancement of Christ's Kingdom among Boys, and the promotion of habits of Reverence, Discipline, Self-respect and all that tends towards a true Christian manliness' to which 'Obedience' was added in 1893. Fifty nine boys turned up on the first evening and thirty five became members, mainly lads from skilled working class backgrounds.

The movement was non-denominational, but took root mainly among the non-Established churches. The second Brigade in Glasgow was at the Berkeley Street UPC's mission in North Street, near Charing Cross and the third in the St Clair Street Baptist mission, until the parent church's deacons in Adelaide Place objected to 'anything that tends to foster a war-like spirit in the boys'. By the first annual meeting on 12th October 1885 there were twelve companies in Glasgow and three in Edinburgh, the first Edinburgh one being at Stockbridge UF. By 1900 75,000 were enlisted both at home and overseas. In a survey of 409 officers that year, 50% of them were found to have a background in Sunday School work and other religious organisations, and 62% were either ex-Army or Volunteer Force.

(d) From Moody's third visit to the turn of the Century

An invitation 160 feet long and containing 2500 signatures was sent to Moody in August 1891 to invite him to return to Scotland that autumn.[184] He arrived in London in November, travelled to Glasgow via Edinburgh, and began work in Campbeltown's United Presbyterian Church with the deliberate intention of reaching the smaller towns. He moved through Ayrshire and on up to Inverness.[185] On this tour only in Ross-shire are children's meetings recorded and also the story of a thirteen year old boy who 'showed considerable anxiety' in a public meeting, but when a worker tried to speak with him his father said 'don't you think he is 'most too young?'[186] Moody worked in Tain, Cromarty, Nairn then up to Caithness and was in Elgin for Sunday 27th December. In a series of articles headed 'The Revival in Scotland' his movements are traced via Huntly to Aberdeen, down the East Coast, through Kirkcaldy to Edinburgh, then Stirling, Alloa, Falkirk, and Strathclyde returning to Edinburgh by mid March. He visited East Lothian and the Borders and ended with 'three monster gatherings in Edinburgh' on 31st March.[187] His work was continued in many places by the campaigns of John McNeill.

Among all the reports of these meetings, only two need detain us further:

> *In Crieff on Wednesday:* an interesting fact was the presence at the evening meeting of a little band of very intelligent youths, who are boarding at the local Academy, who came with their master in charge. Those who were conversed with showed a very hopeful interest in the truths that had been proclaimed.[188]

The crowds flocking through Coatbridge at 9am on the Sunday morning headed for Coats Parish Church comprised 'a seemingly endless stream of people, mostly of the poorer orders judging by their dress, with a large proportion of young boys and girls...'[189]

Meanwhile other evangelistic work aimed specifically at children continued. Mackeith was attracting 2000 children to the Tent Hall on

---

184. T.C. 27th August 1891. 185. T.C. 19th November 1891.
186. T.C. 17th December 1891. 187. T.C. 7th April 1892.
188. T.C. 4th February 1892. 189. T.C. 25th February 1892.

Sunday afternoons[190] and the Glasgow Foundry Boys' Society claimed that a total of 15000 attended meetings across the city every Sunday morning, out of a total 22000 children on their roll.[191]

However, despite these mammoth efforts, it was not until 1897 that evidences of revival began to reappear. As Rev Alex Bain reported to the Free Church General Assembly of 1897, it began in the mining village of Drumlemble near Campbeltown on 21st March. A characteristic was the prayerfulness of young Christians. Many of the young converts joined the Christian Endeavour which increased from 25 to 80 members.

> To hear these young men and women pray - so humbly, reverently and earnestly - would do good to the heart of any man who had in his breast a spark of the love of Christ.[192]

Something similar happened on the nearby island of Arran on a visit by Mr Corsie the same year:

> Quite a number of young people, particularly at Slidderie and Shiskine professed to have undergone a saving change. The number was over fifty.[193]

A localised awakening occurred in Inverness when a New College student, Alex Fraser preached in Queen Street Free Church, Inverness in September 1898 where 'the converts were mostly young men and women'.[194]

> In the autumn of 1900 Mr Duncan McColl, Glasgow, conducted a series of evangelistic meetings in Ullapool, when a very serious impression was made on a number of young people, *followed by work by the Rev John Mackay, which led to* the institution of a weekly prayer meeting in English which is still largely attended by the young people of the town.[195]

---

190. T.C. 17th January 1890. A description of one of his meetings is included here and another in T.C. 7th February 1890.
191. T.C. 28th February 1890.
192. MacRae pp 50-51. 193. MacRae, p.36.
194. MacRae, p.130. 195. MacRae, pp 79-80.

In the autumn of 1899 another Glasgow based Christian journal appeared entitled The Campaign Weekly, giving extensive reports of evangelistic activity across the country. Here are some selected extracts:

A week of meetings was held in Parkhead UP from 16-20 October by Mr Kerr and the Christian Endeavour of Gorballs Cross Mission, with over one thousand present nightly and some turned away. We cannot tabulate numbers but we are confident a very large number made intelligent decision for Jesus Christ.

On Friday evening at quarter past six, a very interesting meeting was convened for those who had professed to trust Jesus Christ as their own personal Saviour. Upwards of 400 were present, the majority being from twelve to fourteen years of age...

While in Cathcart Parish Church: Between fifty and sixty gave in their names as having given their heart to Jesus. *Also testimonies are quoted from Springburn.*[196]

In Finnieston: The after meetings were well attended ... with boys and girls who were manifestly anxious to know the Saviour. As the mission went on the interest deepened, and the climax came when on Thursday of last week over a hundred boys and girls responded at the early hour of 6.45pm to the invitation to a meeting for those who had accepted the Saviour during the mission.[197]

At Trinity Free Church over one hundred children gave in their names as having made a decision to live for Christ.[198]
According to Rev John Coutts at the children's meetings in Dalmarnock Road UP and Whiteinch FC admission was by ticket and at the latter from fifty to a hundred came to the front each evening all seemingly in earnest and many deeply impressed.[199]

In an article headed 'A night with Mr W Thomson' at Portland Street: We saw fourteen boys going to their knees on the front seat. We do not know how many girls afterwards.[200]
And at Gorballs FC also with Mr Thomson: As the result of

---

196. C.W. 4th November 1899. 197. C.W. 18th November 1899.
198. C.W. 18th November 1899. 199. C.W. 16th December 1899.
200. C.W. 23rd December 1899.

one week 108 children over twelve years of age gave in their names as being anxious to know more of these things, the number below that age would have been as great but we did not take their names. It was pathetic to have boys of twelve and thirteen coming back saying that they could not give up smoking.[201]

In the first fortnight of the 1900 Mr Mackeith dealt with 2178 children. These were mainly children of eleven years and upwards. That made 10,765 from the start. ...They had commenced a meeting in Anderston for bigger lads.

In Carntyne FC Mr Van de Venter was working among the young: The first meeting lasts for only 35 minutes. More waited than could be dealt with, so they had to be broken up into smaller groups. That was done by their ages. For instance, those aged ten, twelve and thirteen were asked to go into the side. The younger in the centre were then sent home. In this way over 300 were dealt personally, some that I myself dealt with were under manifest conviction of sin, they saw clearly the way of salvation.[202]

In the Opening Editorial entitled 'God turning to the Little Ones' on 3rd March 1900 Rev James Paterson of White Memorial Free Church says 'God is turning to our little ones. What else could He do? He has for many a long day, continued to make His offer of reconciliation to us who are grown up ... but we are all so busy ...' In a fortnight's campaign William Thomson took the 9-14's at 5.30 (boys first week, girls second week) and the over 14's at 8pm. Between six hundred and a thousand attended and those who responded had to be counselled in groups due to lack of workers. They recorded the names of 220 boys of 12 and 13, and didn't collect those younger. 'Of these, a large proportion were from homes which had no connection with any church or mission.' The meetings for the older teens were attended by between 250 and 400 and 161 names taken.

He points out that Jewish boys took on the responsibility of the Law at twelve, yet we encourage 'the evasion of personal responsibility in things pertaining to God' if we leave it till nineteen or twenty. 'I know of nothing more trying than to speak to a large class of boys, full of life,

201. C.W. 30th December 1899 By 'A.I'. 202. C.W. 3rd February 1900

in the ordinary Sabbath school class. To catch and hold the attention of them all is almost an impossibility. It was not so in the inquiry meeting. The other evening I had no fewer than seventeen. There wasn't an unattentive or uninterested face in all the group.' Six months later he adds: 'I do not know that we are appreciating the vastness of the movement among the young. God in His saving Providence is once again turning His hand upon the little ones. Only children over nine are admitted to the meetings. A large number are 13,14,15 and 16 years of age. and when all the churches are taken into account, it is found that there are some nine, or ten thousand at the meetings night after night.'

'And the attendance is not the only hopeful element. There is found among the children a very deep conviction of sin. It is not too much to say they are weeping their way by hundreds to the foot of the cross. As an example of what is going on in this way, reference may be made to the meeting in the Kent Road UPC on the evening of Monday last. It was a wonderful meeting. Though it was the first of the mission, between two and three hundred stayed behind to be spoken to about salvation. Those dealt with were under the deepest convictions. A very large number were anxiously seeking the Saviour.'

Meanwhile Mackeith and Stewart were at Langside: 'Grace is sweeping in great mighty waves through the crowds of Glasgow's young people. It is a time for which Christian parents with trembling gratefulness should pour out their thanks to God.'[203]

In February 1903 Dr Torrey conducted a four week mission in Edinburgh. During the third week of the campaign:

> Fresh ground was opened up by the evangelists on Friday after-noon, when the Central Hall, Tollcross, was packed from floor to ceiling with young people from all ages and classes. The scripture lesson consisted of memorising Isaiah 53 v 5, and after this had been done 'our' was changed to 'my' and 'I am' substituted for 'we are' causing the teaching to be of the most personal character.

> One touching reference was to a meeting at which a man had protested against children of ten or twelve being encouraged to go into the inquiry room; but found his own nine year old girl weeping and begging for leave

---

203. C.W. 2nd September 1900

to go in, because 'He was wounded for my transgressions'.

Dr Torrey's points were:

1. That children can be Christians
2. That children can pray
3. That they can live beautiful Christian lives
4. That they can give testimony for Christ
5. That they can plead with others.

After every precaution had been taken to prevent the boys and girls from simply following one another impulsively, about three hundred professed to accept the Lord Jesus Christ as Saviour, Lord and Master. Telling this to a crowded adult meeting in the evening, Torrey said he believed this meant much more than the conversion of the same number of adults. After comparing the average length of service which may reasonably be expected from a child of ten and a grown man converted at the same time, he said he had been told a man CAN do so much more, but in his experience a Christian child did much more than most Christian men. Men will go to Church and go to Church and nothing for the good of others will come of it because they never open their mouths for Christ. On the other hand he had never known a converted child who did not get to work.[204]

Other examples of highly successful evangelism may also be cited. When William Oates of Glasgow led a mission in Keith 'during the week 400 or 500 children met in this hall and many professed to find the Lord Jesus'.[205] At a children's mission held in King Street, Govan 'altogether about sixty have been dealt with, all over twelve years of age'.[206] Thus there is considerable evidence of a heightened awareness of and response to the gospel at the turn of the century, well before news of the Welsh revival broke at the end of 1904.[207]

---

204. T.C. Thursday 26th February 1903. 205. T.C. 10th March 1904.

206. T.C. 9th June 1904

207. First mention of the Welsh Revival occurs in T.C. 24th November 1904. By 22nd December 1904 it was described as 'a young people's movement', corroborated by F.B. Meyer who wrote: 'It is pre-eminently a young people's movement. Boys and girls, young men and women, crowd the chapels' (T.C. 11th May 1905).

5. The Twentieth Century

(a) The Pre-War Period

Although the opening decade of the Twentieth Century is associated in most people's minds with the Welsh revival and its subsequent manifestations in India[1], South Africa and indeed many parts of the world within a couple of years, the Scottish story in fact begins in the Northern Isles. In the spring of 1902 an evangelist, Charles Robertson, went to Orkney to assist the Baptist minister on Burray, A Campbell Seivewright: 'The interest rapidly spread beyond the limits of the church until the whole island was stirred' and 'some of the children of the school were amongst the first to experience blessing in the revival of 1902'[2] which was attributed to 'a little band of faithful and devoted teachers'. Robertson was followed by Edinburgh based evangelist A Y McGregor who visited many of the islands. Albert Griffiths described the effect of his visit on his church:

> We were compelled to stand still and see the salvation of God as we saw in our Westray Baptist Chapel more than 300 people, of all ages, leave their pews, walk up the aisles, and go into the inquiry room to seek and find their Saviour. ... The Movement began with the young, and gradually extended to the old.[3]

In a letter he wrote 'young boys and girls moved by the same power, come forward and accept the Saviour as their all in all.'[4] After visiting the island in August, F B Meyer estimated the number converted through McGregor's mission as 400.[5] On Sanday Seivewright estimated the numbers converted as 'over seventy at the very least'[6], and in Kirkwall during a mission led by Dr Henry; it was estimated that half the population must have been reached by the services where 'there were

1. See The Revival Times (London) 1905-6.
2. Burray Baptist Church Minute Book, 1904.
3. Scottish Baptist Year Book, 1905, p.A16.
4. T.C. 14th January 1904.
5. T.C. 1st September 1904.
6. Scottish Baptist Year Book, 1905, p.A19.

some beautiful cases of conversion among the children and young people.'[7] McGregor returned to Westray in November 1907 and the pastor reported 'young people converted'.[8] Subsequent reports include references to children being baptised: on December 29th 'three sisters and two brothers (one twelve years old)' and on September 5th 1908 'six of the senior Sunday School scholars were baptised - the youngest 12 and the oldest 16 years of age - all girls.'[9]

There is no doubt that news of events in Wales stimulated interest in prayer and evangelism in Scotland, although it cannot be claimed that there was a widespread awakening. William Oates was one of the Scottish leaders who witnessed the Welsh revival first hand and on the Sunday evening of a mission organised by Blairgowrie YMCA attracted 1400 out of the total population of 7000 into a packed UF Church; 'the work was specially fruitful among lads and girls, young men and young women, a large number of whom made public profession of their surrender to the Lord.'[10]

Also early in 1905 Dr Henry conducted a mission in Berwick-upon-Tweed where 'over 150 of those over twelve years of age were dealt with personally in reference to their salvation; later they confessed Jesus as their Saviour and King.'[11]

> *In Leith:* For six weeks without a break, except Saturdays, revival prayer meetings have been held in Ebenezer United Free Church ... addressed by young people of both sexes, many of whom have been converted only recently ... At another centre in the town (North Leith Baptist) meetings are also in progress and have been for seven weeks past, attended by conversions at almost every meeting.[12]

However, it was in Charlotte Chapel, Edinburgh, that the revival reached its climax and lasted the longest. Their pastor, Joseph Kemp had been sent to Bournemouth to regain his health in January 1905, but after one day had seen so many wheelchairs that he fled to Wales! He can

---

7. T.C. 14th July 1904. 8. SBYB 1909, p.182.
9. SBYB 1909, p.183. 10. T.C. 26th January 1905.
11. T.C. 16th March 1905. 12. T.C. 23rd May 1905.

be said to have brought back the revival with him and Charlotte Chapel began a series of nightly prayer meetings. Conversions took place at every meeting, and often on a Sunday there would be no preaching as the spirit of prayer rested on the services. William White states that 'one thousand were converted in that year alone.'[13]

Mrs Kemp recorded that:

> Children, too, were sharers in the blessing. A work of grace commenced in the Sunday School and many of the children were brought to Him. One teacher told in one of the meetings that twelve of her fourteen scholars had decided for Christ; and at a meeting for young people a number of the older children were brought to the Lord. So keen were the children that they started prayer meetings of their own and a sympathetic leader was appointed to guide them.[14]

In summarizing the revival moves Mr Kemp records 'at one baptismal service as many as ten children were baptised on the profession of their faith in Christ.'[15] After the second wave of blessing over the New Year period of 1907 a fourteen year old girl wrote 'I feel so overflowing with joy that I have to write and tell you of the marvellous blessing God has poured down upon me.'[16]

Special provision was made for the nurture of the young people. Mr Kemp started a 'School of Bible Study' meeting at 3.15pm on Sundays. 'From a Bible Class of seven a little over three years ago, our membership has risen to 222, with a regular attendance of quite 230, and often a higher figure' by April 1906.[17] New rules introduced in March 1908 denied enrolment to anyone under fifteen, which suggests that younger members had attended previously.[18] By the following December Junior classes had been formed to cater for the 14-17's.[19]

---

13. Revival in Rose Street, William White, p.35.
14. Joseph W. Kemp, by his wife, M.M. & S., 1935, p.31.
15. Charlotte Chapel Record, Feb 1907, p.20.
16. Charlotte Chapel Record, Feb 1907, p.23.
17. Kemp p.45.
18. Charlotte Chapel Record, March 1908.
19. Charlotte Chapel Record, Dec 1909, p.178.

The first to go to the mission field from the Bible class, after training at the BTI in Glasgow were Jean Scott and Laura Gray who went to China and India respectively. Andrew MacBeath, who later witnessed revival on the mission field at Bolobo in the Congo, wrote in February 1935 of his boyhood memories and impressions:

> With great vividness I recall the scenes on a Sunday night when I used as a lad to sit on the pulpit steps, and how wonderingly and yearningly I watched men and women coming through 'the valley of decision'. First I saw faces strained and gloomed with the desire to resist the Saviour and after a sharp conflict I saw the decision made and a man stand up, yielding to the Saviour. If I can at all disentangle the threads of motive that determined my future career, I would say that very much is due to those nights when Mr Kemp drew in the net ,and eager elders and deacons watched for souls as the crowd dispersed."[20]

Another later missionary was Annie Wighton, later of Nigeria:

> As a girl of thirteen she was attracted to Charlotte Chapel by the singing at the open air meeting, and followed the workers indoors. She sat spellbound, for the Spirit of God was working in her heart. Some weeks afterwards she answered the appeal for decision, and entered into the assurance of salvation, as a lady worker dealt with her. Her home was a mining village of Lanarkshire where she had a father and mother, five sisters, and three brothers all unconverted. Her greatest desire was now to see her family saved, and for this she set herself to pray earnestly. ....She has had the joy of seeing her prayers answered in the conversion of members of her family. Her brother, Robert, has been discharging a soul-saving ministry in a Baptist Church in Coatbridge. One sister is married to a minister in Canada. Her youngest sister, while in training for the mission field as a nurse in Glasgow, was instrumental in bringing many of her fellow-workers to the Lord, before going out to the New Hebrides.·[21]

---

20. Kemp p. 78
21. Kemp p. 79

Blessing on the children's work continued into 1909 as this extract from the church magazine reveals:

> Rev A A Milne, commenced a two weeks' mission in the Chapel on Lord's Day, 7th March. The first week was devoted to children, when Mr Milne gave gospel addresses, illustrated by lantern views. The attendance of the children has been good, with manifest interest, and there is evidence of a work of grace in the hearts of many of the young people.[22]

The same journal reports an Awakening among the United Free churches of Islay in the winter of 1907 with children entering the inquiry room in Port Charlotte and in Bowmore; 'fifteen young people decided for Christ at one meeting.'[23]

One other agency of revival at this period should be noted. The mission yacht 'Albatross' had a significant ministry in the north of the country. When it visited Wick in February 1905, 500 were converted and 'school-children were led to Christ.'[24] There was also a significant movement of prayer in Easter Ross and the Black Isle:

> In one village on the edge of Ross-shire, at the request of some young people, a prayer meeting was arranged for at seven o'clock in the morning. This went on, with only a break on Saturdays, for eleven weeks. As many as twenty-one were present, the average number being above fourteen. Almost all were young men and women. Some rose at 4.30am to be able to get through work and be present. Others went breakfastless to work rather than be away.[25]
>
> The movement, as might be expected, reached principally the young people.[26]

Rev A J MacNicol dates the outbreak of revival in Cromarty as 17th September 1905, and states:

22. Charlotte Chapel Record, April 1909 p.49.
23. Charlotte Chapel Record, May 1907, p.68.
24. MacRae, p.198.
25. 'A wave of blessing in Black Isle and Easter Ross', Scottish Bible and Book Society, Glasgow, 1906, p.14 . 26. Wave of Blessing, p.16.

> Young and old were drawn in, parents with their children, ... children seeking their classmates with the invitation, 'Come and See'. [27]

The greatest response was among the 18-25 age group, and of the numbers converted he says 'including children, the total must have crept into three figures.'[28]

The work in Dingwall was chronicled by Rev J R MacPherson and a six week mission in the winter of 1906 included 'a few children's services':

> The mission proved to be a fruitful one from the very beginning. But the more striking work seemed to commence one afternoon at the close of a children's service. We were all rather troubled about some young boys and girls who waited to be talked to without apparently any real desire after Christ; but just as we were wondering about this, the spark was lighted among a few of the older girls and there was no mistaking its bright reality. One girl followed another; a girl's prayer meeting became a new centre of work and these young women and bigger girls have, from that afternoon, been the brightest spot in Dingwall. They have helped one another and they have brought in others; they have been the mainstay of the Christian Endeavour movement among us, but they have not been content with that. Their eagerness, their brightness, have helped us all onwards, week after week. *MacPherson concludes very honestly that* the work has been a great one. It did not reach the height of revival; it was a most successful mission *largely reaching* the young people of our Christian homes, the church-going lads and girls.[29]

However, the Revival Times, in one of its few references to Scotland, noted 'much blessing in connection with evangelistic services in different parts of Scotland - a new interest ... a greater readiness ... to respond' and refers to crowded meetings in Glasgow, Motherwell and Forfar.[30]

27 Wave of Blessing p. 23. 28 Wave of Blessing p.24. 29 Wave of Blessing pp. 42-43. 30. Revival Times, 15th May 1905 – The Revival Times started as a monthly newssheet until 16th June 1905 when it became an illustrated weekly, covering all aspects of revival worldwide.

(b) The 1920's

Hints of a renewed interest in the Gospel following the First World War are found in the 1920 report of the Baptist Home Missionary Society for Scotland, which notes an 'improvement in Sunday School attendance and in some places a quickened interest'.[31] Edward Hogg reported 'there are many anxious ones at this time' among the young people of Westray.[32] The following year Rev W H Millard of Wick claimed 'the church has had a touch of revival in the coming of the Pilgrim Preachers at the beginning of September'.[33]

More extensive revival broke out in East Anglia in 1921 through the ministry of Douglas Brown who visited Lowestoft at the end of February, and from where the work spread to Yarmouth and Ipswich. At the opposite end of the country a Welshman, Pastor Fred Clarke conducted a mission in Cairnbulg Gospel Hall which was extended for four months longer than intended because of the response:

> Conversions were most evident amongst the 16 to 18 years age group. Young folk who attended the dance hall which was next to the gospel hall came to disturb the meeting. One night Pastor Clarke stated, 'the Devil's agents are in our midst tonight, but we are claiming them for Jesus.' So many young folk were saved the dance hall had to close.[34]

Towards the end of December 1921 the Aberdeen Daily Journal claimed that over '10,000 people have already experienced the force of the evangelical hurricane now sweeping over the fishing ports of the north'. The Fraserburgh Herald reporter complained that:

> On entering Cairnbulg ... the motor car had to be drawn up to avoid collision with a party of 17 boys and girls who were kneeling in a circle in the middle of the roadway outside the school. Under the leadership of an older child, they were repeating a prayer, a recurring phrase in which was 'O God, save mammy and daddy'. Every sermonette that is preached to them

31. BHMS (1920) p.9 referring to the previous year. 32. BHMS (1920) p.12.
33. BHMS (1921) p.21. 34. Ritchie, p21.

has as its theme the imminent second coming of the Messiah and the end of the world.[35]

As an act of separation from worldly goods and in anticipation of the Second Coming children's games were publicly burnt:

On Saturday night there was a bonfire of a great variety of articles that had stood between the converts and grace. A huge pile containing such things as cigarettes and pipes, playing cards, draughts boards, ludo, tiddle-de-winks, snakes and ladders, dancing pumps, etc, was fired, and fanned by a high wind, was speedily devoured while their former owners knelt around the conflagration in the ring and sang and prayed.[36]

It was at this time that most of the Scottish fishing community were in Yarmouth and Lowestoft, and Jock Troup began open-air meetings in the former place. On the third Saturday in October people crashed to the ground under conviction of sin. Troup a 25 year old cooper from Wick gave up his employment to preach full-time, and then in the middle of the revival had a vision of a man in Fraserburgh praying for him to come up to that town, so he left the next day.[37] When he arrived he began an open-air meeting, until it began to rain, when someone suggested they move to the Baptist Church. They arrived just as the pastor and leaders were leaving - from a special meeting where they had decided to send for Jock Troup! References to children in the reports are rare, and most of the accounts attest that the work was most successful among the fisher lads and lassies aged 18-25.[38] For example one lad declared that he would not 'swop the three weeks he had spent with

35. The Fraserburgh Herald and Northern Counties' Advertiser, December 27th 1921.
36. The Fraserburgh Herald, 20th December 1921.
37. The full account is recorded by Ritchie pp.28, 36 and 57.
38. In an article entitled 'The Revival in Scotland' T.C. of Thursday 22nd December 1921 states: 'The most devout and inspired of its followers are fishermen between the ages of 18 and 25.' A fortnight later it quotes from the report of the Home Mission Committee of the UFC of S: 'Those brought to decision in the revival are predominantly young men from 18 to 25 years of age.' The same issue (5th January 1922) quotes William Gilmour of Fraserburgh Baptist Church that 'scores upon scores of young men and women have professed faith in Christ.'

Christ for the eighteen years he had wasted with "the other fellow".'[39]
That younger people were converted may be inferred from Ritchie's
claim that whole families from Cullen, Portknockie and Findochty were
converted in Yarmouth, and that school age children normally accompanied their parents to the south.[40]

The Pilgrim Preachers were back in Wick in November 1921 and an
open-air on Sunday evening 25th attracted 1000 people. The principal
revival centres were the Salvation Army and the Baptists.[41] Later Rev
Duncan McNeil of Hermon Baptist church reported of the Wick meetings that 'in the beginning of the revival it was youth mostly who were
reached but later adults, many of them parents of the children who had
been converted.'[42]

Other fishing towns to experience revival at this time were Eyemouth,
Cellardyke, Whinnyfold, Peterhead, Hopeman and in 1933 Portsoy.
One story from Cullen deserves to be told. Reg Woods of the Salvation
Army:

> led some little girls to Jesus and told them to ask their mother to
> pray for them. Golden haired Anna Gardiner did so, and her war-
> widowed mother, sticken to the heart replied 'my quinie I canna'
> pray for masel' yet.' Said Anna, 'Mither, ye can be saved too!'
> *and she was the following day.*[43]

In February 1922 F B Meyer wrote from Scotland:

> There is everywhere a yearning for revival, but though this and
> that district seems to have been stirred, the fire has not caught to
> any wide extent and probably it will not until prayer and faith
> have been still further exercised.[44]

For most of 1921 the Christian ran a column entitled 'Days of
Revival', which indicated a much more widespread awakening than
that among the fishing communities. For example in April 1921 the

39. Fraserburgh Advertiser, 26th May 1922. This paper also carried favourable accounts
of the meetings and a description of Troup's preaching on 23rd and 30th December 1921.
40. Ritchie p.67. 41. Ritchie p.76.
42. T.C. 11th May 1922. 43. Ritchie p.98.
44. T.C. 9th February 1922

Evangelistic Association of Charlotte Chapel claimed a revival among the miners of Cockenzie.[45] Simultaneously the Methodist Recorder of 14th April speaks of 'The Great Revival in the North of Scotland Mission' which instances 100 conversions at Portessie 'many of them young men'. However, this movement definitely included children, for Mrs Katherine Young of Buckie clearly remembers being converted there as an eight year old, along with her sister who was eleven.

In Dundee at the Cherryfield Mission Hall, Blackness Road, 'many young people figure among the converts and the conversion of whole families is also a feature of the revival.'[46] Other statistics show a large response to the Gospel: Buckie 300[47], Dundee 6-700[48], Arbroath 100[49], Brora 200.[50]

When children's evangelist, John Stewart conducted meetings in the Hope Hall, Paisley, between three and five hundred attended per night. 'Many of them showed an intelligent interest in the gospel message.'[51] From there he went on to conduct 'a mission among Glasgow's newsboys'. At the end of the year he was responsible for a series of meetings in Maybole, Strathaven, Shawlands, St Andrews and Dunfermline: 'a large number of the older children who were asked to make confession of their faith in Christ, gave intelligent response, encouraging the hope that they had taken their stand on the Lord's side. At several of the places visited, a number of the young people testified to the blessing they had received on former visits by Mr Stewart.'[52]

Little historical research has been done on Scotland's Twentieth century revivals and it may well be that much more material has yet to be unearthed. For example Highland Church Historian, Donald Meek, asserts that his father, Hector (the last Gaelic Speaking Baptist pastor on Tiree) was converted in his mid-teens in an awakening on Tiree in 1920, but as yet I have located no written documentation of this. The only evidence of an awakening on the west side of the country is a report from Alexander Brown from Achnacloich in Lorne which speaks 'some young people who professed to have been impressed in our meetings

45. T.C. 21st April 1921. 46. T.C. 23rd February 1922.
47. T.C. 19th January 1922. 48. T.C. 9th February 1922.
49. T.C. 30th March 1922. 50. T.C. 20th April 1922.
51. T.C. 11th May 1922. 52. T.C. 14th December 1922.

and have begun to read their Bibles and pray in private.'[53] Likewise in
the Central Highlands Neil McLachlan reports from Tullymet of 'several young people having made decision for Christ and others quickened
to deep concern.'[54] Thus the move of the early 20's may have been of
much wider import than we now know.[55]

(c) The Hebridean Awakenings

No widespread revival has occurred in Scotland since the early 1920's.
However, there have been some local awakenings in several of the
Western Isles at different times and while young children do not appear
to feature as part of them, there are several instances of teenagers
touched and converted in them.

The first was an extensive movement across the Isle of Lewis in
1939. Murdo Macaulay, in one of the few written accounts of this work,
traces its origin to Carloway Free Church in 1934 under the ministry of
Rev John Maciver, when young people began to attend prayer meetings.
He quotes a Mrs Macleod who told him 'that when the first two young
lads came to the prayer meeting for the first time, Calum, her husband,
turned round in his seat and on seeing them behind him, he burst into
tears while her own reaction was a feeling of her heart being as hard as
flint.'[56] Macaulay concludes 'the revival did not touch the very young,
although some converts were in their mid-teens.'[57]

Mrs Catriona Bishop, now of Benbecula, remembers as a younger
teenager, being in a home meeting in Carloway when 'a dozen people
all passed out'. These were mainly mid-teens who had met for prayer,
singing and Bible reading. Macauley also mentions 'unusual prostrations',
and Rev John Murdo Smith, later to become minister of the Church of
Scotland in Lochmaddy, remembers as a teenager, house meetings in
Garyvard, during the 1939 Lochs Communion season, when 'there was
such power in the singing that people went out through the power of the
Spirit'. He says that children were certainly present in the kitchen

53. SBHM (1922) pp16-17. 54. SBHM (1923) p.13

55. The reports of the Faith Mission should also be studied. In 'Heritage of Revival' (The
Faith Mission, Edinburgh, 1986) Colin Peckham claims that Kinlochleven, Ardnamurchan,
and Balintore all experienced revival in 1922, with 230 converted in the last place (pp 53-
56).

56. 'The Burning Bush in Carloway', Murdo Macauley, Carloway Free Church, 1984.
p.32. 57. Macauley, p.34

meetings, but not in the church services. Many of the converts of 1939 were lost at sea during the War that immediately followed.[58]

The awakening that began at Barvas in the west of Lewis in December 1949 has been well documented by the Faith Mission.[59] Mary Morrison provides a graphic account of the effect of the revival on her as an unconverted 18 year old in her testimony 'Hearken, O Daughter' in which she describes 'hundreds of young people' being at the meetings[60] and of a kitchen meeting on Bernera where the preacher, Duncan Campbell, was drowned out by the noise of teenagers sobbing - 'weeping uncontrollably in the presence of God'.[61]

In a personal interview Mary (now Mrs Colin Peckham) stated that the majority of the conversions in the revival were among young people, but it was her own age group, the older teens. In retrospect forty years on, she says that some of the children were impressed, but they were not encouraged to come to the meetings. Had they been, she believes there would have been many more conversions. Apart from this absence of younger children there was no segregation on the basis of age within the church; everyone attended the activities together. The young people followed the old, looked up to them and listened to them.

Rev. Norrie Maciver, now parish minister of Newhills, Aberdeen,

---

58. Another collection of anecdotes from this revival, including the prediction of the War in visions given to Mary MacLean, is found in 'The Clash of Tongues, with Glimpses of Revival' by Hugh B. Black, New Dawn Books, Greenock, 1988 p.123-161. Mr. Black's particular interest has been to collect incidences of 'charismatic manifestations' during this movement, rather than provide an historic narrative.

There are also passing references to revival in the Diary of Kenneth MacRae (Banner of Truth, Edinburgh, 1980). Viz: 9.12.31 - his longing for it; 9.4.32 - a 'girl' from Back was awakened and had to be carried out of the church; 26.10.33 - One little girl of 13 seems to have been very much affected by a Gospel book for children. The poor little thing seemed so earnest and showed me the book. It was a lesson for me not to overlook children; 10.11.34 - reference to the Carloway awakening under John McIver; 22.2.36 - As for the movement in town among the school children inaugurated by the 'Pilgrim Preachers' I have no faith in it - *one suspects because the children still attend 'the pictures' rather than the prayer meetings!* Further comments are found on pp 363-370. Regrettably his diary for 1939, the most significant year, has been lost and he avoids references to the later awakening of 1949-52.

59. 'Channel of Revival' by A.A. Woolsey, Faith Mission, Edinburgh 1974, and 'Heritage of Revival' by Colin Peckham, Faith Mission, Edinburgh, 1986.

60. 'Hearken O Daughter', by Mary Morrison, Prairie Bible Institute, Canada, 1966, p.36.

61. Morrison, p.38

clearly recollects living on the Isle of Lewis between the ages of eight and eleven at the time of the awakening. In a personal interview he stated that the revival had a clear impact on him. Although he was not converted at the time, he nevertheless knew that he had a clear decision to make, and that he could have responded to the gospel. For him it confirmed the possibility of children being converted. He can also remember the impact upon the community: when people came under conviction of sin whilst working in the peat bogs or the potato fields, the whole community talked about it. He attended as a child some of the midweek revival meetings, but cannot remember if other children were there or not. On one occasion in his local church at Carloway he recalls people leaving the church, and it was as if an invisible glass wall dropped in front of them; they were unable to proceed and returned into the church building. The revival had a definite effect on him as a child: he knew that God was there and knew what he was up to - in fact his boyhood fear was that if his mother had a direct hot-line to God, then she would find out too! He also believes that it laid within him the basis of an evangelical faith, because after he returned to Glasgow at the age of eleven, he was never a member of an evangelical church, but retained his evangelical faith. He was questioned as to why children did not seem to be converted, and he felt the sociological background significant, especially the stress on worthiness before taking Communion. Also, the mark of conversion was to attend the prayer meeting, and for the men then to be called on to pray: this probably would militate against a response from children. It was as if childhood did not count as a time for conversion. Most of those converted in their late teens became ministers or missionaries. Another possible factor to be considered is the timing of this awakening: it was in the aftermath of the war, and the Western Isles had suffered severe losses of men folk at sea: every family he knew had lost some relation, and the whole community was in mourning. It was therefore not unrealistic to expect the mindset of the day to be focused on the needs of the adult population.

Donald Macphail as a schoolboy heard of an unusual minister who had arrived on the island and of lives being changed. He became aware of groups of children who began to meet together in school intervals, then stories circulated about the preacher who didn't dress in black, and of a pulpit ledge he had broken in preaching. Donald was not invited t any meeting: he went out of curiosity, but on the very first occasion things began to make sense to him. He found answers as to why there was a void in his life, why evil produced a tension within him, why trying to please his friends led to frustration and trouble. Something about the atmosphere of the meetings made him want to go back. Initially everyone went in isolation. Nobody wanted to talk about it, everyone wanted to be left alone. The religious people ignored him in the meetings until after about ten days he felt the need to get right with God. Then help was available. In two months in the spring of 1950 he estimates that 30 of the 200 pupils at the Junior Secondary school at Shawbost were converted. His own parents were converted the week after himself and their home became a centre of meetings. When he later transferred to the Nicolson Institute in Stornoway, he recollects the rector, Mr Addison, summoning him into his study to complain of his lack of homework and failure in exams due to attending so many meetings! but for a while at least, teachers were organising buses for pupils who wanted to attend the meetings, and providing Scripture Union notes for follow-up work.

The following is Andrew Woolsey's description of Donald's prayer life:

This lad became a 'front-line' prayer-warrior. Duncan called at his home one day and found him on his knees in the barn with the Bible open before him. When interrupted he quietly said: 'Excuse me a little, Mr Campbell, I'm having an audience with the King'. At school he was ridiculed; one young fellow taunted him with foul language and actually struck him, but with Scriptural meekness he simply turned his head and asked him to strike the other side.

Some of the most vivid outpourings of the Spirit during the revival came when he was asked to pray. In the police station in Barvas he stood up one night, simply clasped his hands together, and uttered one word - 'Father'. Everyone was melted to tears as the Presence of God invaded the house. In Callenish, with its ancient Standing Stones he prayed until the power of God laid hold on those who were dead in sins transforming them into living stones in the church of Jesus Christ. But the most outstanding example of God's anointing upon him was in Bernera, a small island off the coast of

Lewis. Duncan was assisting at a Communion season; the atmosphere was heavy and preaching difficult, so he sent to Barvas for some of the men to come and assist in prayer. They prayed, but the spiritual bondage persisted so much so that half way through his address Duncan stopped preaching. Just then he noticed this boy, visibly moved, under a deep burden for souls. He thought: 'That boy is in touch with God and living nearer to the Saviour than I am'. So leaning over the pulpit he said: 'Donald, will you lead us in prayer?'

The lad rose to his feet and in his prayer made reference to the fourth chapter of Revelation, which he had been reading that morning: 'O God, I seem to be gazing through the open door. I see the Lamb in the midst of the Throne, with the keys of death and of hell at his girdle.' He began to sob; then lifting his eyes toward heaven, cried: 'O God, there is power there, let it loose!' With the force of a hurricane the Spirit of God swept into the building and the floodgates of heaven opened. The church resembled a battlefield. On one side many were prostrated over the seats weeping and sighing; on the other side some were affected by throwing their arms in the air in a rigid posture. God had come.

The spiritual impact of this visitation was felt throughout the island; people hitherto indifferent were suddenly arrested and became deeply anxious. The contributor of an article to the local press, referring to the results of this movement, wrote: 'More are attending the weekly prayer-meetings than attended public worship on the Sabbath before the revival.'[62]

There is also a story of a sailor returning to Barvas on leave and when he shook hands with Donald on the bus, he felt something touch him: he was converted without a word being spoken.

Not all the ministers on the island supported the work, but Rev Murdo MacLennan of Carloway did and was burdened for the young people in his village. One morning he interrupted a dance at 3am by asking those present to sing part of a Gaelic psalm, then he prayed and shared what God was doing in Barvas. The gathering dispersed and the local schoolmaster, who had organised it, came under conviction with

62. Woolsey, pp 134-5. For further accounts of these incidents see also Morrison p.48 and Peckham p.176).

his wife and two children.[63] The youngest, Jack was at home in bed and awoke in the morning to find his parents searching for a Bible to conduct family worship. As far as can be ascertained, Jack Macarthur was the youngest convert of the revival at the age of eleven and has proved to be lasting fruit: he is currently minister at St. Columba's Glasgow, while his brother Allan is minister in Lochcarron and Applecross in Wester Ross.

In a personal interview given in 1992 Rev Jack Macarthur told the story of his own conversion. After his brothers were converted Duncan Campbell came to stay at their house. His father held the keys to the ATC hall which was where the meetings were held, next to the school. Jack went along to the meetings with his family and was also sent off to the village store three quarters of a mile away to fetch paraffin for the lamps. He remembers 'being conscious night after night that God was there in the meetings. There was a searching, an awareness, a knowledge that something had to be done. I had to respond. And yet also an amazing refusal to stay at the end of the evening. Knowing myself searched and judged and knowing the battle inside. Yet I was actually converted in 1950 during quiet evening worship in my own home through a Brethren man from Whitehaven speaking on the Second Coming. I was caught off guard because he wasn't preaching and I had to leave the room and go up to my bedroom. I knew there was no alternative, and he led me to the Lord in the morning.' One day this man, George Taylor, who with his wife Emily, worked from a caravan said to Jack, 'I hope I'll see the day when you come down these pulpit steps' when they were together in the parish church at Ness. That statement made a deep impression upon the boy, who recalls that Taylor was indeed there when he preached his first sermon after his induction to his first charge in Kinlochbervie.

When asked why he thought that children were not touched in this awakening, he replied that there was no expectation of it happening, and it was probably questioned theologically if children could understand. He did not recollect children going to church and he joined in the adult meetings with his family. 'The mark of conversion was to go to the prayer meeting regularly; that was a statement to the community as well as the church. There was nothing provided for the children, absolutely

63. Woolsey p.136.

nothing.' He also attempted an explanation of the paucity of accounts of the 1939 move: the revival had been so holy and precious that there was a great reticence to speak of it. 'People were not interested in talking about it. When someone did speak of it, you felt you were there. The '49 was spoilt by people going in too soon.'

Duncan Campbell visited Berneray for a week in May 1952 and an eye-witness claims that everyone on the island felt the Spirit of God.[64] However the youngest convert was probably 17 years old. There was another breath of revival when Faith Mission pilgrims Mary Morrison and Jean Wilson visited North Uist in 1956 and took meetings in a number of centres, including Lochmaddy, Sollas and Tigharry where there were 22 added to the church. They did include meetings specifically for the children, led by Daphne Parker. One twelve year old was clearly converted, but Mary does not recollect conversions among younger children.

Finally a localised awakening was reported in April 1980 in Kyleakin on Skye during the ministry there of Rev Jack Macarthur. Ian McPherson recalls a sense of the fragrance of God being felt in prayer meetings from about the time of the Broadford Communion and for a few months a small group of teenagers met together in a prayer group. The minister recollects that 'there was a healthy proportion of secondary school pupils among the converts of this period' and 'there was an awareness of God in the unconverted community'.

(d) Postscript: The Future?

Will we see another revival of religion similar to those of the past? Have we any right to expect such? These are questions that many people are asking today. While it is dangerous to write of contemporary events, because their significance and lasting impact can only be tested in retrospect, there have been signs over the last five years of a new surge of spiritual life among the older children of Scotland.

In the Spring of 1987 a number of preachers from outside of Scotland prophesied there would be a new awakening here. The fact that none were Scots ruled out any vested interest in the subject. Most prominent was Rev Jean Darnall who toured the country in May 1987, telling churches to 'watch for unusual manifestations of the Lord to boys and

---

64. See Woolsey pp139-141 for details

girls between the ages of 9 and 15. Jesus is going to appear to them. He is going to come to them in visions and dreams, He is going to make Himself known to boys and girls in non-Christian homes'. She believed the churches needed to prepare for a widespread move of God among this age group in particular. Very soon after this another American, Brad Thurston, working with YWAM in Germany and only on a weekend visit to Scotland, had a vision during a youth rally in Edinburgh. In it he saw hundreds of children aged 9-14 in a training camp, learning to paddle canoes. Suddenly the river split and these same children were going up the Congo, Amazon, Nile in their canoes: He believed that God was saying that these were the generation that would take the gospel to the ends of the earth. It is of significance to note that this age group was totally absent from the meeting he was addressing, and it was out of context in terms of the rest of that evening.

From the autumn of 1987 the author has been involved in many prayer gatherings at both local and national level, with children in this age range. He believes that there are early signs of a prayer move amongst them: children have travelled over a hundred miles to attend prayer celebrations, and weekends and week-long prayer camps have been booked out. In the summer of 1989 he camped with eight boys aged 12 and 13 who wished to join in the Torch Run down Scotland which fed into the March for Jesus from Edinburgh. After spending two days running in the relays down the A9 on the Inverness-Dalwhinnie section, it was suggested at bed-time that they ought pray that what they had been doing would not be merely symbolic (carrying a flaming torch across the country), but would achieve something in the spiritual realm. The boys then prayed non-stop for two hours interceding for the country with remarkable depth and concern: during that time a number had pictures or visions. One of them saw the group running down the A9, but leaving a trail of paraffin behind them. At a later date God lit the trail and the whole country went up in flames. At this, there was a gasp of astonishment, as the youngest in the group said he'd seen exactly the same thing at the same time. Another boy saw the St Andrew's cross as two sticks smouldering at one end: suddenly the whole flag was engulfed in flame.

In the summer of 1990 the first 'Kingdom Kids' prayer camp was held: it was very basic, on a bring-your-own-sleeping-bag and sleep-on-a-church-hall-floor for a week to pray for Scotland basis. There were 35 applicants aged 11-15 despite all the other Christian summer camps available offering decent accommodation and exciting adventure activities! God met with them in a very deep way and during a time of prayer in small groups one evening, all the youngsters were in tears. The following evening there was a time of exuberant praise during which many of the young people were clapping and some dancing and rattling tambourines, but in the middle of the group two were seen to be weeping bitterly. A boy of just 14 said that God was letting him feel His anger over the state of the church in Scotland and the girl slightly younger said she was feeling God's heart for the world. They were taken aside and encouraged to pray it through, while the rest of the meeting continued. We expected them to join in shortly after - in fact they each continued for over an hour. Personally I have never seen such a spirit of intercession in those so young as on that occasion.

The following week I witnessed a similar scene during a Christian Endeavour 'Inters' camp in Orkney. During a time of worship half way through the camp, as the children aged 11-13 were singing 'I give my life to You, I fall down on my knees...' an eleven year old boy did so quite literally: he crashed onto his knees on the floor and burst into tears. By the end of the following verse all except one of the 37 children present were in tears and unable to continue singing as the sense of the Presence of God swept through the room. There had been no preaching and it was unsought and unexpected, despite allegations of 'hypnotism' and other unfounded claims that appeared subsequently in a national newspaper. Many of the children believed they were truly converted that night and two years later some of them testified publicly as to the blessing received at that camp, indicating the lasting nature of their experience. The camp ended on the last night with two of the boys flat on their faces on the floor pleading with God to come and visit their schools in the way that they had just experienced. In summary I would have to say that in twenty years of Christian ministry I have never seen anything like the depth of prayer that I have witnessed among young people in the last two years. While prayer meetings are not revival, they do seem to be an indispensable pre-condition of it.

During the last school week before Easter 1991 in a Glasgow Primary School a parent was leading the weekly Christian lunchtime meeting in the absence of the regular teacher. She spoke on forgiveness, and afterwards asked the children to close their eyes and ask themselves if there was anyone they needed to forgive. She was aware of a sense of stillness in the room and the sound of gentle weeping. However, when she opened her eyes, she was amazed to see all twenty children flat on their faces on the floor. Nineteen of those children are said to have become Christians during that meeting - the one exception being a Muslim girl.

Finally, reference ought to be made to Billy Graham's visit to Scotland in Mission '91. In ten nights (Edinburgh, Aberdeen and Glasgow), over 250,000 attended and 18,611 went forward in response to the appeal. About half of these said they wanted to become Christians for the first time. The response among children was completely unexpected and although special provision had been made for children's counselling, the numbers were such that each adult was having to deal with six children on the first night at Murrayfield. The official statistics of those who went forward were:

Murrayfield (2 nights): 679 children under 12, and 986 youths aged 12-18.
Pittodrie (3 nights): 497 children under 12, and 813 youths aged 12-18.
Celtic Park (5 nights): 1631 children under 12 and 3108 youths aged 12-18.

While it has to be admitted that not all have lasted and not all were first time conversions, the fact that over 7,700 children and young people responded to the invitation surely indicates the existence of a new spiritual thirst in this generation of young Scots. Again it is not yet revival, but is a precursor of it. I believe that we are on the edge of a new spiritual breakthrough in our land. We may see similar manifestations to those which have occurred in the past - but we may not. We have a God who 'desires all men to be saved and come to a knowledge of the truth': He is committed to reaching the next generation and He knows how to do it, in such a way that 'every knee shall bow and every tongue confess that Jesus Christ is Lord to the glory of God the Father.' Let us join in praying that we each play our assigned part in it and don't miss it when it comes.

Appendix A

References prior to 1740

Couper[1] maintains that because of its isolation Scotland missed all the medieval revival movements of Europe, except for some penetration by Lollards into the south-west, so that 'The Reformation was Scotland's first great religious awakening'. Indeed, social historian, Janet R Glover[2] goes so far as to state that 'Hardly anywhere in Europe was the Church so degraded as in Scotland'. It is therefore not surprising that we can trace no parallel to the mass movements on the Continent that issued in the Children's Crusade of 1212 which may have mobilised as many as 60,000 children in France and Germany.

The first reference I have located to the religious experience of a Scottish child comes from the diary of James Melville, written in 1570, which is worth quoting in the original:

> In Montrose was Mr Thomas Anderson, minister, a man of mean gifts, but of singular guid lyff. God moved him to mark me, and call me often to his chalmer (room) to treat me when he saw anie guid in me, and to instruct and admonish me utherwayes. He desyrit me ever to rehearse a part of Calvin's Catechisme on the Sabothes at afternoone, because he hard the peiple lyked weill of the clearnes of my voice and pronouncing with some feiling; and thairby God moved a godly honest matron in the town to mak meikle of me thairfor, and called me her lytle sweit angle. The minister was able to teatche na ofter but annes in the ouk (week) but haid a godlie honest man reidar, wha read the Scripture distinctlie, and with a religius and devot feiling; whereby I fand my selff movit to giff guid eare, and lern the stories of Scripture, also to tak pleasure in the Psalmes, quhilk (which) he haid almost all by hart, in prose. The Lard of Dons (Erskine of Dun, one of the superintendents,) mentioned befor, dwelt oft in the town, and of his charitie interteined a blind man, wha haid a singular guid voice; him he causit the doctor (teacher) of our school teatche the whole Psalmes in miter, with the tones (tunes) thair of and sing them in the Kirk; he heiring of whom I was sa delyted, that I lernit many of the Psalmes and toones thairof in miter, quhilk I haiff thought ever sen syne a grait blessing and comfort. The exercise of the ministerie was keipit weekly then in Montrose, and thair assemblies ordinarlie; quhilk when I saw I was movit to lyk fellon weill (extremely well) of that calling, bot thought it a thing impossible that ever I could haiff

1. W.J. Couper 'Scottish Revivals' Dundee 1918, p.4
2. Janet R. Glover 'The Story of Scotland' Faber, London, 1960, p.105

the abilitie to stand upe and speak, when all helde thair toung and luiked, and to continow speaking abeen the space af an huire. Ther was also ther a post (carrier) that frequented Edinbruche, and brought hame Psalme buikes and ballates. He frequented our scholl, and of him also I lerned to understand the Calender, after the common use thair of.

And finalie I receavit the Comunion of the bodie and blud of the Lord Jesus Chryst first at Montrose, with a greater reverence and sense in my saull, than oft thairefter I could find, in the 13 year of my age; whar, coming from the table a guid honest man, ane eldar of the Kirk - Richart Anderson (brother of the minister) - gaiff me an admonition concerning lightnes, wantonnes, and nocht takin tent (not taking heed) to the preatching and word read, and prayers, quilk remeaned with me ever sen syne.[3]

The earliest revivals with classical manifestations were in 1625 under William Castlelaw at Stewarton and David Dickson at Irvine, and when John Livingston preached on Monday morning 21st June 1630 at Shotts, resulting in 500 conversions in one service. However, in the earliest account of these events[4] there is no reference to children either being present or affected - which is not to say that they were not! An outbreak of religious fervour swept the land after the signing of the National Covenant in 1638, and it is reported that 1000 people were in tears in Lanark.[5] It is hard to believe that there were no young people in that crowd, but again we can only speculate.

In a recent dissertation[6] Chang Won Shu has provided us with useful evidence of family religious life, including the provision of family worship, catechism and Bible reading, concluding that by 1660 most families had Bibles and the children were able to read them. It is to the end of the Covenanter period where we find the first evidence of a children's prayer group in existence. To quote Lumsden's description of the context in 1683:

> The last of the Covenants of Scotland... did not emanate like some others, from those in high stations in Church or in State, nor from devout men or pious women, but from the children. The home influence kept

3. Extract from James Melville's Diary in 1570, quoted in W.J. 5th January 1861.
4. Rbt. Fleming, 'The Fulfilling of Scripture' 1681, Edinburgh, p.347. See also GRT 4.
5. Couper pp8-9. 'The Covenant was signed, February 28th, 1638, and was the outward indication of perhaps the most extraordinary revival of religion that Scotland has ever seen. The whole country was moved by a religious fervour as even the Reformation had not moved it.'
6. Chang Won Shu 'Analysis of the Covenanting Family Religious Life in Seventeenth Century Scotland' MTh Dissertation, New College, Edinburgh, 1989 pp 65-67.

alive the faith and inspired the devotion of many a girl and boy. The evidence of such inspired the fifteen girls who subscribed what is known as the Children's Band or Covenant. The old men lamented the defections, the young men were restrained, the old and young women were feeble and powerless, but here the girls with child-like faith, put their trust in God, believing that he could bring to pass the accomplishment of His own wise purposes. The children of the village of Pentland had formed themselves into a society for prayer, and so, banded together, entered into a Covenant of which the following is a copy:

This is a Covenant made between the Lord and us, with our whole hearts, and to give up ourselves freely to Him, without reserve, soul and body, hearts and affections, to be His children, and Him to be our God and Father, if it please the Holy Lord to send His gospel to the land again; that we stand to this Covenant, which we have written, between the Lord and us, as we shall answer at the great day; that we shall never break this Covenant which we have made between the Lord and us; that we shall stand to this Covenant which we have made; and if not, it shall be witness against us in the great day when we shall stand before the Lord and His Holy Angels. O Lord, give us real grace in our hearts to mind Zion's breaches, that is in such a low case this day; and make us to mourn with her, for thou hast said 'them that mourn with her in the time of her trouble shall rejoice when she rejoiceth, when the Lord shall come and bring back the captivity of Zion'; when He shall deliver her out of her enemies' hands, when Kings can come and raise her from the dust, in spite of all her enemies that will oppose her, either devils or men. That thus they have banished her King, Christ, out of the land, yet He will arise and avenge His children's blood, at her enemies' hands, which cruel murderers have shed.

Them that will not stand to every article of this Covenant which we have made betwixt the Lord and us, that they shall not go to the Kirk to hear any of these soul murdering Curates, we will neither speak nor converse with them. Any that break this Covenant they shall never come into our Society. We shall declare before the Lord that we have bound ourselves in Covenant, to be covenanted to Him all the days of our life to be His children and Him our Covenanted Father.

We subscribe with our hands these presents... Beterick Uumpherston, Janet Brown, Helen Moutray, Marion Swan, Isobel Craig, Martha Logan, Agnes Aitken, Margaret Galloway, Helen Straiton, Helen Clark, Margaret Brown, Janet Brown, Marion M'Moren, Christian Laurie.

Whether any suffered for their adherence to it, or whether they all lived to see the return of their 'banished King, Christ', and the children's blood avenged which the cruel murderers had shed, one cannot say, yet their efforts at this critical juncture are worthy of our highest praise, and we gratefully remember them for what they have done.[7]

It is to be remembered that children at this time were not exempt from the penalties of the law: on 22/11/1684 the Privy Council passed at Act which allowed men and women over 14 to be instantly shot, and those over 12 to be transported for supporting the Covenanters.

References to children at the turn of the century are incidental, but provide snippets of information. For example, Fawcett[8] documents evidence of children able to read the Bible by the age of 6 - Jupiter Carlyle who stood on a tombstone outside his father's church at Prestonpans and read the Song of Solomon to twenty old ladies who could not get in; also Anne Wylie and Elizabeth Dykes (whose testimonies are recorded in the McCulloch Manuscripts). He also cites the story of Robert Riccaltoun, born 1691 who could read the Bible distinctly before he was five years of age. There are a few accounts too of childhood conversions. Fawcett informs us that William McCulloch, who was born in Whithorn in 1691 'began to be serious about religion' at the age of seven, and 'was brought into further concern about thirteen years of age under the preaching of Mr Ker, minister at Wigtown', when he became a communicant.[9]

The Wynd Journal of 3rd November 1860 publishes some details of the awakening of Andrew Lindsay in Cromarty, a remarkable story of spiritual hunger in a thirteen year old boy who was enduring extreme poverty at the time:

In its early days this family (the Lindsays of Cromarty) was one of the most affluent in the burgh, and had its friendships and marriages among the aristocracy of the country; but it gradually sank as it became older and, in the year 1729, its last scion was a little ragged boy of about ten years of age, who lived with his widow mother, in one of the rooms of a huge dilapidated house at the foot of the Chapel Hill. Dilapidated as it was, it formed the sole remnant of all the possessions of the Lindsays. Andrew, for so the boy was called, was a high-spirited, unlucky little fellow, too careless of the school and of his book to be much a favourite with the schoolmaster, but exceedingly popular among his play-fellows, and the projector of one-half the pieces of petty mischief with

7. J. Lumsden "The Covenants of Scotland" Alex Gardner, Paisley 1914 pp345-7
8. A. Fawcett "The Cambuslang Revival" Banner of Truth Trust, 1971, pp75-6
9. Fawcett p.38

which they annoyed the village. But, about the end of the year 1731, his character became the subject of a change, which, after unfixing almost all its old traits, and producing a temporary chaos, set, at length, much better ones in their places. He broke off from his old companions, grew thoughtful and melancholy and fond of solitude, read much in his Bible, took long journeys to hear the sermons of the more celebrated ministers of other parishes, and became the constant and attentive auditor of the clergyman of his own. He felt comfortless and unhappy...

Some time in the year 1732, a pious Scottish clergyman who resided in England - a Mr Davidson of Denham, in Essex - visited some of his friends who lived in Cromarty. He was crossing the frith at this time, on a Sabbath morning, to attend the celebration of the Supper in a neighbouring church, when a person pointed out to him a thoughtful looking little boy, who sat at the other end of the boat. 'It is Andrew Lindsay,' said the person; 'a poor young thing seeking anxiously after the truth.' 'I had no opportunity of conversing with him,' says Mr Davidson in his printed tract, 'but I could not observe without thankfulness a poor child, on a cold morning, crossing the sea to hear the Word, without shoe or stocking, or anything to cover his head from the inclemency of the weather.' He saw him again when in church, his eyes stedfastly fixed on the preacher and the expression of his countenance varying with the tone of the discourse. Feeling much interested in him, he had no sooner returned to Cromarty, than he waited upon him at his mother's and succeeded in engaging him in a long and interesting conversation, which he has recorded at considerable length.

'How did it happen, my little fellow,' said he, 'that you went so far from home last week to hear sermon, when the season was so cold and you had neither shoes nor stockings?' The boy replied, in a bashful, unassuming manner, that he was in that state of nature which is contrasted by our Saviour with that better state of grace, the denizens of which can alone inherit the kingdom of heaven. But though conscious that such was the case, he was quite unaffected, he said, by a sense of his danger. He was anxious, therefore, to pursue those means by which such a sense might be awakened in him; and the Word preached was one of these. 'For how,' he continued 'unless I be oppressed by the weight of the evil which rests upon me, and the woe and misery which it must necessarily entail on the future, how can I value or seek after the only Saviour?' 'But what,' said Mr Davidson, 'if God himself has engaged to work this affecting sense of sin in the heart?' 'Has he so promised?' eagerly inquired the boy. The clergyman took out his Bible and read to him the remarkable text in John, in which our Saviour intimates the coming of the Spirit to convince the world of sin, of righteousness, and of judgment. Andrew's countenance brightened as he listened, and, losing his timidity in the excitement of the moment, he took the book out of Mr Davidson's hand and for several minutes contemplated the passage in silence.

Sadly for us, the narrative ends with the words 'to be continued' and the next issue is missing from the bound volume in the Mitchell Library. Nevertheless the point has been made that even in the drier periods in the history of the Scottish Church there were children capable of serious religious thought and sentiment, and for all these that have been recorded, how many must have passed on unknown?

We also see evidences of spiritual hunger emerging among adults of this period. Hugh Watt contends that praying societies existed prior to 1723[10] and were therefore probably foundational to both the formation of the Secession church and the revival of 1741-3.

Appendix B

Dr Alexander's Visit to Musselburgh

What I am about to state has been found interesting to Christian people in other places, and I have no doubt it will be interesting to every Christian present this evening. I will give expression to one or two feelings that have been excited in my mind with regard to the Musselburgh Meeting.

The first thing that struck me in going out was the increased number of attendants. I went out upon a week evening, and preached in a place where I hardly ever saw a full house upon the Sabbath, and found myself called on to address a congregation that crowded the place from wall to wall, and even filled up the steps leading to the pulpit. That struck me as very remarkable, and it immediately satisfied my mind that some very great work was going on there.

Another thing that struck me very much was the multitude of young persons, of children, who were in the meeting, and who seemed interested in the work. I confess I had something of an unbelieving state of mind on that subject. Having never come in contact myself with anything of the kind, I frankly confess I had not just the same cordial belief in the conversion of Children as I have now. I happened to leave my great coat in one of the small vestries. When I went to the door for it, I found it bolted. I was going to retire, when the door opened, and a very little girl appeared. I asked if there was anybody in. She said,

10. Original Secession Magazine, Feb 1934, pp49-53 "The Praying Societies of the early eighteenth century."

'Yes, sir'. Whispering, I said, 'I was going in for my great-coat, but I will not disturb you; but who is here'? She said, 'A wheen o' us lassies'. I said 'I will not go in then; could you get me my coat'? She said 'it's here, sir; but I canna get up to 't'. I was going away, when she said 'You might come in.' So I went in, and there I found (I forget exactly how many) little girls upon their knees, and one of them was engaged in prayer. Whether she had overheard us talking at the door, or supposed that some person had come in, I do not know; but her voice faltered, and she concluded very quickly, so that I hardly heard her. But directly she had concluded, another little girl began to pray and a very simple, very childlike, but very beautiful prayer it was. I stood listening to that child's prayer and the tears started in my eyes as I listened. I could not help it. I felt that I was reproved; that I had doubted the work of God in that particular and now He had brought me face to face with the work itself. When she had concluded her little, simple prayer, they all rose up, and very abashed the poor little things looked when they saw I was standing in the midst of them.[1]

I began to talk to this little girl who had been engaged in prayer, and I said to her, after I had reassured her a little, 'Well now, I heard you thanking God for pardoning your sins, and for the peace of mind you have; I suppose you feel that you have been converted.' And she said 'yes, sir', with great quietness, and great assurance of mind. I said, 'Now, how did that come to pass? You did not always think of these things'. 'Oh no!' she said, 'I never cared about them at all'. 'Well', I said, 'just tell me how it came to pass that you did come to care about them'. She said, 'I came to the Meetings, and attended them for a while; but I did not care much about what was going on. One night I went, with some others into a room. There were a good many women there and some of them were greetin' about their sins. A lady was present who spoke to them; told them about their sins, and told them how they were to get pardon; and', she added in her simple sort of way, 'the thought just came into my mind that I was a sinner too'. I said 'And did you go away with that thought?' 'Yes', she replied. I said, 'Did that grieve you?' Looking up in my face with a most earnest and striking expression, she said, 'Eh, sir, I was in an awfu' way!' In this state she continued, she said, for a good while. I asked, 'how did you find peace of mind?' 'Oh, sir', she replied, 'it was something that Mr Hammond said when he was preaching'. I asked 'what gave you peace of mind?' Turning on me again the same intense and earnest look, she exclaimed, 'Oh, there is nothing *can* give peace of mind to the sinner but the blood that was shed on Calvary.' Now, I just put it to any experienced minister, if such a statement does not show that this child knows the way of salvation, and if it does not afford evidence that she has experienced

---

1. This incident is wrongly attributed to Hammond by Orr in 'The Second Evangelical Awakening' on p232

the grace of God in truth. For my own part, all my doubts and unbelieving suspicions were gone.

I may just mention, that as this talk was going on, there was a little boy in the corner of the room, so little a fellow that he had just emerged from the condition of petticoats, and had not reached the dignity of a jacket; his whole costume being in one piece from his neck to the heels. He was standing in the corner of the room, and sobbing very hard. The only idea that came into my mind was that the little fellow was sleepy, and that he wanted to go home, as it was now about ten o'clock. I said to one of the girls that he was wearied, and that someone had better take him home. She said 'Oh no, sir; he is not wearied, he is greetin' about his sins'. I went to the little fellow and I spoke to him; however, he was really past speaking to. He was in a state of great distress, whatever was the cause. I said to one of the girls, 'perhaps you could speak to him better than I could;' and she replied, 'well, yes sir; I will speak to him, but he does not belong to this place'. I said, 'Indeed!' 'No puir fellow; he has walked all the way frae Prestonpans tonight'. Now this was a dark, wintry night, and yet this little creature had walked, by himself, about four miles, to get to the Meeting. I asked about him the last time I was out. This little girl told me that she believed he was going on in the right way.

This was a very striking instance to me: and I was struck, also, with the manifestation of a kindly interest in him on the part of his juvenile companions. I said, 'this poor little fellow cannot go home at this time of night'. 'Oh', said one of the little ones, 'I'll no let him gang hame; I'll tak' him hame with me'. This seemed to me as like the time of the beginning of the Gospel at Jerusalem, when they had all things in common, and every man received into his house those from a distance who were converted to the truth.

Several persons went down to Musselburgh from Edinburgh. Among them was a female servant. She entered into conversation with one of the little girls, who immediately began to preach Christ to her as the Saviour, to the utter amazement and astonishment of this woman. She said to her, 'Lassie, where did you learn this?' After a little while, the little girl, to her still further astonishment, said, 'If you kneel down, I will pray with you'. And to use the woman's own words, 'she just drappit down on her knees and I couldna but gang down too!' And the little girl prayed; and the woman, strongly moved, when they rose up, exclaimed, 'lassie, wha ever learned you to pray?' The child's answer was, 'naebody learned me; I think the Lord just pits't into me'. That was the means of that woman's conversion; and she is now one who gives evidence of being really converted.[2]

---

2. From E.P. Hammond, 'The Conversion of Children' pp6-10.

Appendix C

Descriptions of children's meetings in Glasgow

BRIDGEGATE SABBATH SCHOOL - *The teachers ask that all dear friends of the Bridgegate would pray the Lord for a great blessing on Sabbath first.* Such was the request last week. It is difficult to give account of the answer. We were like them that dream. O give thanks unto the Lord, for He is good; for his mercy endureth for ever. An unusual stillness was over the classes at the opening. This was made more evident by the levity of two Roman Catholic girls who came in to mock. Prayer was asked for them privately in a class of young girls. A little girl melted into tears and was greatly distressed. She could not bear to hear of her Saviour despised. In another part of the church a whole class was awakened. As the teacher could only deal with one of her boys, volunteers were asked from an adult class, who pressed to help in the blessed work of pointing the others to the Lamb of God, who took away their sins. In the boys' class referred to in our last were some who had come for a night from another school, with the permission of their teacher, earnestly seeking a blessing, having heard that Jesus was in the place. Three of these had their hearts' wish granted. They pledged themselves to become missionaries on returning. At various points over the school, souls were awakened and at the close about forty remained in distress, who were removed to the session-house. For about two hours the place seemed like a battlefield; every part was strewn with the wounded; the wails of tender children, stifling sobs and groans from harder hearts, piercing cries for mercy, mingled and rent the air. The teachers were unable to deal with all at once, from the number. Some children who had been converted followed their example, and taking their distressed companions in their arms, pled promises, warned, urged, and entreated them to yield their hearts to the Lord. By degrees a change came, as one by one obtained peace.

> The storm is changed into a calm,
> At his command and will;
> So that the waves, which rag'd before,
> Now quiet are and still.
> Then are they glad, because at rest
> And quiet now they be:
> So to the haven he them brings,
> Which they desir'd to see.

The reaction of peace and joy from forgiveness, was equal to the former distress. Beaming countenances were raised in singing the sweet songs of Zion. 'What will you do now?' 'Oh, I will tell father and mother, and ask them to come to Jesus.' Some boys have obtained a room where they meet during the week for reading and prayer, and invite their companions of the district to seek the Saviour. During the distress of the children, a woman came into the room. A sad gloom which was over her, was deepened at the sight. 'Can you give no help here?' 'Ah, I've been a Sabbath school teacher for seventeen years, and thought I had done much for Christ, but I have no comfort from that now, though I used to have. I have lost even hope. I have been in great distress for days together and had to leave my employment in my trouble: a heavy cloud is over me, and I don't know what to do.' 'Wait on the Lord, he has a good purpose in all this; he does not afflict needlessly, nor grieve his children.' 'Oh, if I thought I were a child, I could endure it but I'm just in despair.' 'Don't despair; had you no love, you would have no jealousy. When the parent hides his fare, strange children do not care, though a son will break his heart.' Her drooping faith caught at the thought of being really a child of God in her distress, and by a master stroke struggled up from sinking. Her distress abated; quick, burning sighs followed, and she exclaimed - 'I see him now! I see Jesus! I see him as Stephen saw him! Heaven is opened! Oh, bear with me!' Kneeling, she poured out her heart in prayer and thanksgiving, in language that could only be uttered by a soul sustained in the presence of the Majesty of heaven. *The Teachers ask that friends would pray the Lord for a greater blessing on Sabbath next.*[1]

We are glad to know that arrangements are being made by the churches, to reap the fruit of the present spiritual awakening in the city. The Presbyteries of both the Free and the UP Churches have taken up the matter, and in all parts of the city nightly union meetings are to be held in addition to those which have been already established. Special conferences of ministers and office-bearers have also been held on the subject, and the movement spreads.

On Saturday a children's meeting was held in the Wynd Church at 3 o'clock. The church was crowded to the very door with the children and their parents and friends. The meeting was opened by Mr Howie, who, after having engaged in prayer, spoke of sin and the Saviour, founding his remarks on some expressions in the hymns, 'Happy Day' and 'Just as I am', which were sung by the children with as much sweetness and delight as if they had been long familiar with them. Although the singing of hymns was a novelty among the children of the Wynds, their delight was very great. It will gladden the heart of every lover of the Lord Jesus Christ, if through such meetings as these, we could even succeed in supplanting the profane songs so commonly sung in our Wynds by those sweet and simple hymns which contain in themselves so many of the precious germs

---

1. W.J. 29th September 1860.

of God's eternal truth. When the children have begun to relish the milk, they will by-and-bye be able to digest the strong meat. The meeting was thereafter shortly addressed by Mr Hammond in his usually felicitous manner - by Mr Henderson, who gave an account of the way in which the Lord had brought him out of the spiritual Egypt - by W Laurie, a lad of 17 or 18 years, who gave an account of his conversion about 17 months ago in the Wynd Church, and with great tenderness and earnestness urged his youthful audience to close at once with Jesus. The effect of his striking appeal was very great - many seemed to be deeply impressed. Mr Hogg in a few feeling and appropriate remarks, confirmed the impressions already made; while Mr Ross, with his wonted tact, addressed very solemn words to both old and young. At the close of the first meeting, the area of the church was full of inquirers of all age; and it was truly refreshing to see so many of the district people in their working clothes earnestly putting the question 'What must I do to be saved?' Several of these rejoiced before leaving in having found the pearl of great price. The Lord's arm was outstretched. By a perfect forest of upraised hands the children indicated their earnest desire for the continuation of these Saturday meetings, and it was intimated that by postponing the usual Church services until five o'clock, the children's meeting could be held on Saturday next at three o'clock, and would be continued thereafter. Such a meeting is well worthy of the countenance and prayers of all who take an interest in the spiritual reclamation of the Arabs of the more destitute parts of our city. It was very cheering to notice the interest manifested by many of the West-end children in this meeting, many of whom were present directing the anxious to Jesus, and some of whom sent contributions for the purchase of hymn books, to be gratuitously circulated. What a fine illustration of the truth, that we are all 'one in Christ Jesus'.

A meeting of the most interesting kind also took place on Saturday morning last, in the Hall of the College. There have been of late so many services exclusively for children, and the benefits have been so very conspicuous, that it became desirable to secure the same advantages for the children of the better classes resident in the West End. So cordial was the response to the invitations given, that the hall was entirely full, mothers bringing their dear little children, some of them not much more than five years of age, and all of them seeming glad to be present. It was a fine sight. Dr Hetherington presided, the Rev Mr Arnot and Mr Hammond on either side. On the platform there were also Rev Messrs Muir and Alexander; Robert McCowan Esq; Mr Gall from Edinburgh and others. After singing Psalm 23rd, which may justly be regarded as the child's psalm and a short prayer by Dr Hetherington, Mr Arnot made some interesting remarks, clustering them round the lovely idea of 'Ministering children'. Religion had first pointed her finger to them that she might draw attention to their importance, their influence, and their value. One case had come under his own notice the other day. An elderly man had called on him in great distress of mind. He had been at the revival meeting in St Peter's on Thursday last and had left it unmoved, but sauntering along the street, a group of very young children were singing,

> I love Jesus, Hallelujah,
> I love Jesus, yes I do;
> I love Jesus, He's my Saviour;
> Jesus smiles and loves me too.

The man of fifty summers found that he had no song wherewith he could glorify his Lord and Saviour. He had made a discovery of his poverty, and that the lisping child was richer than him. The melody of these young voices had done what the stirring sermon of the preacher had failed to do - melted the frozen heart. The services were drawn to a close by a quaint anecdote from Mr Hammond, who made a kind promise that were he in the neighbourhood, he would come to be present at the next meeting - LAUDIO.[2]

Appendix D

The death of a Portessie boy

After this, my little boy Johnny used to go in my hand to James Turner's meetin'. One time that he went alone, he stoppit owre lang - the whole night indeed, for he didna come hame till mornin'. Then I questioned him about bidin' sae lang, a' the answer he gae me was - 'O, mither! it was sic a fine meetin' I couldna leave 't; an' O, if I could only pray like John Smith-body.'

'Ye'll seen be able to pray like him, my dear,' said I, 'Jesus is wantin' yer young hairt, and if he gie Him 't, He'll seen enable ye to pray.'

'But I would be ashamed to pray afore the fouk, for the fear of man is on me, mither. I'm feart that I would say onything that they would pick up and speak aboot it,' &c.

This fear of man remained the child's snare up to within nine days of his death, but from this time, he lived a quiet obedient life, and communed much with God, but could not lisp a word about his spiritual state, not even to his father. But his Bible was his constant companion, and often he shut himself up in his closet, or 'up the stairs' for prayer, and he was often heard with great earnestness and simplicity, pouring out his soul to God.

About six months before his death he took a cold, and grew worse and worse.

---

2. From the Wynd Journal, April 13th 1861.

As he grew weaker in body, he seemed to grow stronger in spirit, and greatly regretted his past shamefacedness; and one day when Mr G—, UP Minister, had prayed for him as one perfectly ready to go home, he said at the close, 'Mr G— , I'm not in the state you think me in - I'm in darkness, and I do not want to deceive myself nor others.'

From that time, his uncle, a godly man, never left his bedside and was the means of leading him into the light. About nine days before his death, he got great liberty and told his father that he could now rejoice as one of God's children. After this, he regretted still more deeply his past reticence on soul matters. 'O, mither', he would say, 'if my strength were to be given back again, I *would* speak for the Lord'. He was very anxious that his death might be made a blessing to his brothers and sisters, and charged them earnestly to meet him in heaven.

One day a young man asked him if he was happy - 'Yes, Bob, praise the Lord, I'm happy', and when the lad turned away, he said very earnestly, 'come back and tell me if yer happy yersel'.'

'You're going to leave us, John,' said an ungodly neighbour.

'Yes, J—, an' isn't comin' time for to you to think that you have to *leave us*, as well as me? You know you've got a changed son, and you need to be a changed father; and you know that its his desire to have a changed father'. The man sat dumb. The deein' lad sat gazin' steadily at him as if he would, through his e'e, affect his hairt. Then he speer't, 'what o' clock is it?'

'A quarter past nine'.

'Weel, mither,' he said turnin' to me, 'I'm yours till a quarter past five'.

That night - it was the last - his twa uncles were in the room. 'Tell my uncle James to pray and Peter tee,' he whispered. I was sittin' on the bed aside him and he raised himself up and throwin' his arms - his thin wasted arms, roon' my neck, he kissed me wi' sic a lang yernin' kin' o' kiss - it was the last.

'Yer feet are in the river noo, Johnny, my dear.'

'Yes, mither, gie me up to the Lord - I'm yours nae langer - you've had your time o' me; an' ye've others left ye to care for. Good-bye,' he said, and shook hands wi' them a' roon' the room. Just afore he deed, he lookit roon' as if seekin' for somebody; then a gleam o' licht, that I canna describe, shot across his face. 'Jesus is come,' he said, griping his father by the breast. 'Father,' he said, an' held out his hand, then gripit the hand hard - smiled - closed his eyes - raised his hand and as he waved it backwards - died.[1]

---

1. From James Turner, pp144-6.

Appendix E

The Elgin Courant: 30th March 1860 'Revivals in Elgin'
The wisest and best men in our community have this week been so astonished at revival manifestations that they have been at a loss what to think or say regarding them. The subject is a delicate and difficult one, when it is asked whether there is reason to believe that we are in reality witnessing an extraordinary outpouring of the Spirit of God in the conversion of sinners. Some think such is the case, others are doubtful of it; but whether it be the work of the Holy Spirit or not - regarding which a public journalist may be excused from giving any opinion - we are at liberty to describe the public conduct of those who, under some influence or another, are acting in a most extraordinary manner. In the end of last week a party of revivalists from Lossiemouth, including a number of boys and girls, held a meeting in the Rev Mr Watt's church at which none of our clergymen were present except the minister of the Baptist church. The church was well filled, many attending, no doubt, from sincere motives; but as all novelties draw crowds, curiosity had no doubt something to do in bringing together so large an assemblage. This meeting was comparatively orderly. Hymns were sung apparently with extatic joy and three boys prayed with great fervour, producing excitement, especially among the juvenile part of the audience, and not a few of the old seemed deeply affected. The extraordinary sight of mere children rising up and praying in a full church, as best they could, astonished all and their fervour, by sympathy, appeared to pervade the congregation. About ten o'clock those who had the management of the meeting thought it was time to disperse, but after notice was given to this effect the singing of hymns, certainly far inferior to the Paraphrases, continued for some time and the lively tunes increased the excitement. When this meeting dispersed, the more affected resolved to adjourn to the Baptist chapel and as they sung all the way on the street between the two places of worship, a crowd followed and the new place of meeting was at once crowded to excess, the audience being composed chiefly of boys and girls.

We shall not attempt to describe this midnight meeting, which continued till about four o'clock on Sabbath morning. Girls as well as boys spoke, some crying one thing and some another; and praying singing, sighing, weeping, and incoherent exclamations, accompanied by strong emotion characterised the meeting. The service was extravagant, and occasionally approaching to rediculous; but when laughing was seen the cry was 'pray for the scoffers'. The leading juvenile revivalists seemed delirious, and much was said and prayed so surprising and so extravagant as to confound and astonish every calm onlooker that was present. Far be it from us to hold up such a scene to derision - it is too serious for that; but what an apostle calls 'decency and order' were grossly violated by mere children, who for the time, seemed to think the more noise they made and the more impertinent they were, that they were the more religious.

On Sabbath evening there was another meeting in the same place, when the chapel was again crowded to suffocation and a similar scene took place. Hundreds, drawn together by curiosity, could not obtain admission to hear the children praying and lamenting over the great sinfulness of our city. After this meeting had dispersed, a number of them retired to a private house, where boys and girls joined in singing hymns and praying till midnight, but we may state that the same features characterised this meeting as those already mentioned. On Monday another meeting would have been held in the Baptist chapel, but some members of the congregation, acting the part of rational men as well as Christians, kept the church shut, resolving to put a stop to such unseemly proceedings in a place dedicated to the worship of that Almighty Being who has declared that he is the God of order and not of confusion. Monday night came, and hundreds of children were to be seen going up and down the street seeking for places of meeting. To one house (there were more meetings than one in private houses) the police were sent for, and had to interfere. A room was crowded to suffocation, and in the midst of children praying and singing and saying extraordinary things, but such as excited children might say at any times, two girls, we are told, fainted. The sensation was great; they were supposed to be 'struck', but a few minutes and a little water restored them to consciousness.

This is a summary of the revival scenes that have occurred here during the past week; the particulars will be found in another column. What, as rational men, are we to think of the matter. The fruits of the spirit are love, joy, peace, long suffering, gentleness, goodness, faith, meekness, and temperance; but the cardinal virtues and Christian graces are neither manifested nor inculcated in such meetings as we have been describing. Instead of these, there is nothing seen but disorderly joy, and the Deity addressed in prayer in a no less disorderly manner. To be a Christian it is not necessary to make a noise in the streets, nor to make long prayers, for which the Pharisees were condemned. They thought they would be heard 'for their much speaking', but they were not, and had to learn that their words ought to be few and well chosen. Christian zeal has in all ages of the Church been admired, and will continue to be so; but, the very best things in the world may be carried to excess and commendable zeal in religion may be carried to the wildest fanaticism. Thousands of examples of this could be given, as every reader of history knows; but surely the age is nearly past when the common order and decencies of society must be set aside, that children may be thought to be under the influence of the Holy Spirit.

There may be sudden conversions of great numbers as well as of individuals, and young as well as old may be brought to see the errors of their ways; but such scenes as have occurred here during the past week have no necessary connection with such outpourings of the Spirit in our day, any more than they had in the days of the Apostles when those who believed went their way rejoicing to search the Scriptures at home to see 'if these things were so'. It is not by sudden impulses or nervous excitement that men are known to be Christians, but by their works - by their 'working out their own salvation with fear and trembling' and being ready for every good work, performing it with meekness and quietness and, like the Apostles, not only speaking forth the words of truth, but speaking them with soberness and worshipping God with decency and order. Upon order in worship the apostle laid great stress, and reprimanded a body of Christians sharply for not observing it. He ordained that a woman should not be allowed to speak in the church; but here we have mere boys and girls taking the place of the elders in worship, and giving vent to excited feelings in incoherent language. If this be the work of the Spirit the Apostle Paul condemned it; and we therefore think the clergy in Elgin perfectly right in standing aloof from such scenes as have been witnessed this week among us. Much stress is laid upon the opinions of some ministers regarding revivals, but the Bible should be consulted on the matter. No man can penetrate into the workings of the Spirit more than another; and as such manifestations as have occurred here are patent to common observation, the reason that has been vouchsafed to us all ought to be employed in judging, as well as our feelings. We have had union prayer meetings in our city for a considerable time past, no doubt productive of much good, but they have been conducted by rational and Christian men, not by thoughtless boys and girls, encouraged to acts of extravagance by a few whose zeal has blinded their judgement, and made them forget that common sense and the good order of society will not tolerate midnight meetings of the young of both sexes in any church in our city. A few nights such as that of Saturday last would be followed by some losing their reason, and being sent to lunatic asylums. This would become a common occurrence, for want of sleep and food, and long-continued nervous excitement soon unhinge the mind, and then strange visions are seen in the disordered imagination. Some never think of this; but they should remember that God did not give us reason to destroy it, and that when we do so by whatever means, we sin against our Maker. In one word, the revivals, such as we have seen them in Elgin, should be curbed by the sensible part of the community for they are becoming a disgrace to that pure and peaceable religion which is gentle, retiring, contemplative, and rendered more engaging when accompanied with superior intellect, and observed in accordance with the rules of well ordered society.

Bibliography

Where a book is cited only once, full details appear in the respective footnotes.

Hugh B. Black, THE CLASH OF TONGUES WITH GLIMPSES OF RE-VIVAL, New Dawn Books, Greenock, 1988.

Marjory Bonar, ANDREW BONAR - DIARY AND LIFE, Banner of Truth Trust, Edinburgh, 1960.

W.J. Couper, SCOTTISH REVIVALS, Mathew & Co., Dundee, 1918.

Arthur Fawcett, THE CAMBUSLANG REVIVAL, Banner of Truth Trust, 1971.

Robert Fleming, THE FULFILLING OF THE SCRIPTURE, First Edition, 1669.

John Gillies, HISTORICAL COLLECTIONS, Edited by J. Bonar, Kelso, 1845.

GLASGOW REVIVAL TRACTS, or Narratives of Revivals of Religion, Collins, Glasgow 1839. Reprinted as RESTORATION IN THE CHURCH, Christian Focus Publications, Tain, 1989.

Mrs. Gordon, HAY MACDOWALL GRANT OF ARNDILLY, Seeley, London, 1876.

E. Payson Hammond, THE CONVERSION OF CHILDREN, Revell, Chicago, 1901.

Mrs. Kemp, JOSEPH W. KEMP, BY HIS WIFE, Marshall, Morgan & Scott, London c.1935.

D. Maccoll, AMONG THE MASSES or WORK IN THE WYNDS, Nelson, London, 1867.

Duncan MacFarlan, THE REVIVALS OF THE EIGHTEENTH CENTURY, particularly at Cambuslang. John Johnstone, London, 1847.

E. MacHardie, JAMES TURNER, or How to reach the Masses, Brown, Aberdeen, 1875.

John MacInnes, THE EVANGELICAL MOVEMENT IN THE HIGHLANDS OF SCOTLAND, Aberdeen University Press, 1951.

John MacPherson, LIFE AND LABOURS OF DUNCAN MATHESON, Morgan & Scott, London, 1871.

John MacPherson, REVIVAL AND REVIVAL WORK, Morgan & Scott, London, 1875.

Alexander MacRae, REVIVALS IN THE HIGHLANDS AND ISLANDS, In the Nineteenth Century, MacKay, Stirling, 1905.

Edwin Orr, THE SECOND EVANGELICAL AWAKENING, Marshall, Morgan & Scott, 1949.

Mrs. R. Peddie, A CONSECUTIVE NARRATIVE OF THE REMARK-
ABLE AWAKENING IN EDINBURGH, Religious Tract Society, Edinburgh,
1874.

Mrs. Radcliffe, RECOLLECTIONS OF REGINALD RADCLIFFE, Morgan
& Scott, London.

REMINISCENCES OF THE REVIVAL OF FIFTY-NINE AND THE SIX-
TIES (Anon), Aberdeen University Press, 1910.

William Reid, AUTHENTIC RECORDS OF REVIVAL, Nisbet, London,
1860.

James Robe, NARRATIVE OF THE REVIVAL OF RELIGION AT KILSYTH,
Cambuslang and other places in 1742. Page numbers refer to Collins edition,
Glasgow, 1840. Recently re-edited as WHEN THE WIND BLOWS, Ambas-
sador Publications, Belfast, 1985.

Jackie Ritchie, FLOODS UPON THE DRY GROUND, Peterhead Offset,
1983.

R.M. Roberston, WILLIAM ROBERTSON OF CARRUBBER'S CLOSE
MISSION, Oliphant, Edinburgh, 1914.

THESE FIFTY YEARS, The story of Carrubber's Close Mission, Edinburgh.
The Tract and Colportage Society of Scotland, Edinburgh, 1909.

A WAVE OF BLESSING IN BLACK ISLE AND EASTER ROSS (Editor
Unknown), Scottish Bible & Book Society, Glasgow, 1906.

On Northern Ireland see:

John Carson, GOD'S RIVER IN SPATE, Publications Board, Presbyterian
Church in Ireland, Belfast, 1958.

William Gibson, THE YEAR OF GRACE, Oliphants, 1909.

Henry Montgomery, THE CHILDREN IN '59, Sabbath School Society for
Ireland, 1909, Reprinted 1936.

On Wales see:

Mabel Bickersteth, SOMETHING WONDERFUL HAPPENED, Committee
of the 1904-5 Memorial Fund, 1954.

Eifion Evans, REVIVAL COMES TO WALES, Evangelical Press of Wales,
1979.

Eifion Evans, REVIVALS, THEIR RISE, PROGRESS AND ACHIEVE-
MENTS, Evangelical Press of Wales, 1960.

Index

Harry Sprange has been a Baptist minister in Scotland since 1974. Since 1987 he has been Director of Kingdom Kids (Scotland), a network of children and young people praying for revival, which is part of the Prayer For Revival Network (Scotland). He runs prayer conferences for children, and is concerned to see them playing their full part in the life of the local church. He is also a keen amateur historian and lectures occasionally in Church History. He is a graduate of London Bible College with BD Hons (Lond).